Cooking with Columbo

Jenny Hammerton

ISBN-10: 978-1981417421
ISBN-13: 978-1981417421

Jenny Hammerton © 2018

All rights reserved. No part of this book may be reproduced or transmitted in any form or by any means without the written permission of the author.

Jenny Hammerton asserts the moral right to be identified as the author of this work.

Cover photograph of Peter Falk's Pumpkin Lasagna by Joan Ransley - joanransley.co.uk

Cover design by Greg Swenson of Recipes for Rebels - recipes4rebels.com

OTHER BOOKS BY THIS AUTHOR

Cooking With Joan Crawford is a coffee table collection of over 30 of Joan's favorite recipes. It was published in 2014 and is available via blurb.com or blurb.co.uk

For Ladies Only? Eve's Film Review: Pathe Cinemagazine 1921-33 is based on Jenny's film archiving post-graduate dissertation. It was published in 2001 by The Projection Box.

www.silverscreensuppers.com

DEDICATION

This book is dedicated to my parents Dottie and Stan
and to my soulmate Mr. Rathbone. Luckily, he loves Columbo too.

Cooking With Columbo
Suppers With The Shambling Sleuth
Episode Guides

FOREWORD	1
INTRODUCTION	5
PRESCRIPTION: MURDER - 1968	10
RANSOM FOR A DEAD MAN - 1971	11
MURDER BY THE BOOK - 1971	15
DEATH LENDS A HAND - 1971	17
DEAD WEIGHT - 1971	20
SUITABLE FOR FRAMING - 1971	22
LADY IN WAITING - 1971	24
SHORT FUSE - 1972	26
BLUEPRINT FOR MURDER - 1972	29
ÉTUDE IN BLACK - 1972	35
THE GREENHOUSE JUNGLE - 1972	37
THE MOST CRUCIAL GAME - 1972	39
DAGGER OF THE MIND - 1972	42
REQUIEM FOR A FALLING STAR - 1973	44
A STITCH IN CRIME - 1973	46
THE MOST DANGEROUS MATCH - 1973	49
DOUBLE SHOCK - 1973	52
LOVELY BUT LETHAL - 1973	54
ANY OLD PORT IN A STORM - 1973	61

CANDIDATE FOR CRIME - 1973	63
DOUBLE EXPOSURE - 1973	66
PUBLISH OR PERISH - 1974	68
MIND OVER MAYHEM - 1974	71
SWAN SONG - 1974	73
A FRIEND IN DEED - 1974	76
AN EXERCISE IN FATALITY - 1974	81
NEGATIVE REACTION - 1974	82
BY DAWN'S EARLY LIGHT - 1974	85
TROUBLED WATERS - 1975	88
PLAYBACK - 1975	91
A DEADLY STATE OF MIND - 1975	93
FORGOTTEN LADY - 1975	97
A CASE OF IMMUNITY - 1975	99
IDENTITY CRISIS - 1975	101
A MATTER OF HONOR - 1976	102
NOW YOU SEE HIM - 1976	105
LAST SALUTE TO THE COMMODORE - 1976	107
FADE IN TO MURDER - 1976	113
OLD FASHIONED MURDER - 1976	115
THE BYE-BYE SKY HIGH I.Q. MURDER CASE - 1977	117
TRY AND CATCH ME - 1977	123
MURDER UNDER GLASS - 1978	125
MAKE ME A PERFECT MURDER - 1978	128
HOW TO DIAL A MURDER - 1978	131
THE CONSPIRATORS - 1978	133
COLUMBO GOES TO THE GUILLOTINE - 1989	139
MURDER, SMOKE AND SHADOWS - 1989	141
SEX AND THE MARRIED DETECTIVE - 1989	143
GRAND DECEPTIONS - 1989	145
MURDER: A SELF PORTRAIT - 1989	149
COLUMBO CRIES WOLF - 1980	151
AGENDA FOR MURDER - 1990	153
REST IN PEACE, MRS. COLUMBO - 1990	155
UNEASY LIES THE CROWN - 1990	158
MURDER IN MALIBU - 1990	159

COLUMBO GOES TO COLLEGE - 1990	165
CAUTION: MURDER CAN BE HAZARDOUS TO YOUR HEALTH - 1991	167
COLUMBO AND THE MURDER OF A ROCK STAR - 1991	169
DEATH HITS THE JACKPOT - 1991	171
NO TIME TO DIE - 1992	173
A BIRD IN THE HAND... - 1992	175
IT'S ALL IN THE GAME - 1993	177
BUTTERFLY IN SHADES OF GREY - 1994	179
UNDERCOVER - 1994	182
STRANGE BEDFELLOWS - 1995	184
A TRACE OF MURDER - 1997	186
ASHES TO ASHES - 1998	189
MURDER WITH TOO MANY NOTES - 2001	191
COLUMBO LIKES THE NIGHTLIFE - 2003	193
COLUMBO'S CHILI AND OTHER DELIGHTS	199
RECIPE SOURCES	223
ACKNOWLEDGMENTS	229
TEST COOKS	230
ABOUT THE AUTHOR	231
AUTHOR NOTE	232

Cooking With Columbo
Suppers With The Shambling Sleuth
Recipes

Gene Barry's Kibbee 11
Lee Grant's Chicken Malibu 13
Jack Cassidy's Rainbow Trout in a Pouch 16
Ray Milland's Chicken Chow Mein 19
Eddie Albert's Butterfly Lamb 21
Ross Martin's Beef in Anchovy Cream 23
Susan Clark's Shrimp Curry 26
Roddy McDowall's Poached Pears 28
Patrick O'Neal's Ragout de Boeuf Bourguignon (Beef Stew in Red Wine) 30
John Cassavetes' Youvarlakia (Minted Beef) 36
Ray Milland's Lobster Salad 39
Valerie Harper's Summer Squash 41
Richard Basehart's Beans and Frankfurters 43
Anne Baxter's Genuine Swiss Quiche 45
Leonard Nimoy's Potatoes La Jolla Chez Jay 48
Laurence Harvey's Chicken Pie 51
Martin Landau's Jerk Beef Steak 54
Vera Miles' Mexican Casserole 56
Donald Pleasence's No-name Curry 62
Jackie Cooper's Curried Eggs and Macaroni 64
Jack Cassidy's Quickie Green Bean Casserole 70
Jose Ferrer's Eggs Ferrer with Fried Potatoes 72
Johnny Cash's Chili 74
Ben Gazzara's Leg of Lamb, Sicilian Style 77
Robert Conrad's Infamous Hangover Eggs 82
Dick Van Dyke's Breast of Chicken Florentine 84
Peter Falk's Pumpkin Lasagna 87

Robert Vaughn's Mushroom Stuffed Zucchini	90
Oskar Werner's Wiener Schnitzel	92
George Hamilton's Ginger Snap Dandy	94
Janet Leigh's Cheese Soufflé	98
Hector Elizondo's Famous Pasta Pomodoro	100
Peter Falk's Avocado	102
Ricardo Montalban's Cream of Asparagus Soup	104
Jack Cassidy's City Chicken	106
Robert Vaughn's Special Fettuccine Alfredo	108
William Shatner's Steak Picado	114
Celeste Holm's Celestial Chicken	116
Theodore Bikel's Glorified Meatloaf	119
Ruth Gordon's Zucchini Omelet	124
Lieutenant Columbo's Veal Scallopini (aka Escalopes de Veau aux Cèpes)	127
Trish Van Devere's All Day Chili In The Pot	129
Nicol Williamson's Steak Mince and Stovie Potatoes	132
Jeanette Nolan's Sizzling Livers and Walnuts	135
Anthony Andrews' Spicy Yogurt Chicken Cooked in a Brick	139
Columbo's Black and White Ice-Cream Soda	142
Bavarian Chocolate Cream Pie	144
Peter Falk's Veal Scallopini and White Wine	146
Vincent Price's Cioppino	150
Playboy's Stewed Pheasant in Champagne with Dumplings	152
Olympia Dukakis' Greek Meatballs	154
Ian McShane's Salmon Steaks with Watercress Sauce	156
Nancy Walker's Chicken a la Nancy	159
Brenda Vaccaro's T-E-R-R-I-F-I-C Italian Sausages	160
Peter Falk's Barbecued Spare Ribs, Chinatown Style	166
George Hamilton's Smoky Chicken	168
New York Steak Dabney Coleman	170
Rip Torn's Omelet Mexicali	172
Juliet Mills' Chive-Sausage Hoppin' John	174
Tyne Daly's Key Lime Pie	176
The Faye Dunaway Cocktail	178
William Shatner's Lime-Garlic Broiled Chicken	180
Ed Begley's Citrus Dressed Asparagus	183
Rod Steiger's Baked Chicken Grand Marnier	185
Shera Danese's Italian Stuffed Peppers	188
Rue McClanahan's Wonder Women	189
Billy Connolly's Stuffed Trout	192
Peter Falk's Pork Chops With Vinegar Peppers	194
Chasen's Chili	200
William Shatner's Deluxe Hamburgers	201
Myrna Loy's Senegalese Soup	201
George Hamilton's Candied Fruit Parfait	202
Ross Martin's Chocolate Mousse	202
Martin Landau's Vodka Martini Straight Up	202
Donald Pleasence's Sole Bonne Femme	203
Susan Clark's Peach Salad	204

Roddy McDowall's Red Cabbage	204
Gena Rowlands and John Cassavetes' Cherry Torte	205
Mariette Hartley's - Chicken Wonderful	205
Vincent Price's Quenelles Ambassador	206
Vincent Price's Hollandaise Sauce	207
Janis Paige's Feijoada	208
Diane Baker's Scampi	209
Mexican Calves' Brain Soup, House of Ricardo Montalban	210
Suzanne Pleshette's Bread Pudding	211
Ida Lupino's Hot Pot Casserole	212
Anne Francis' Gazpacho Soup	212
Honor Blackman's Golden Sponge Pudding	213
Edith Head's Chicken Casa Ladera	214
Vincent Price's Saffron Rice	214
Steve Forrest's Honey Cake	215
Steven Bochco / Barbara Bosson's Brie en Croute (Brie in Pastry)	215
Julie Harris' Curried Zucchini Soup	216
Shirley Temple Cocktail	217
Peter's Vanilla Pudding	217
Helen's Veggie Chili for Johnny Cash	218
Neil's Slow Cooker Version of Ross Martin's Beef in Anchovy Cream	220
Susan and Kent's Baked Chicken Grand Marnier a la Rod Steiger	220
Battenburgbelle's Pastry and Crumb Crust Recipes	221

FOREWORD
By Lieutenant Columbo (aka the Columbophile)

When I first heard word of this *Columbo* cookery book, I was skeptical, to say the least. A book featuring recipes for chili, hard-boiled eggs, and black coffee was bound to be a pretty thin volume, surely?

But then I had a think about the role food played in *Columbo*. And I realized it's a pretty important one. From the Lieutenant cooking an omelet for Joanna Ferris in *Murder by the Book* to him whipping up scaloppini for Paul Gerard in *Murder Under Glass*; from him gulping Dr. Keppel's caviar in *Double Exposure* to assisting Dexter Paris on a live cookery show in *Double Shock*, food is an ever-present and enjoyable ingredient of the show.

Beyond the confines of the show itself, I had also never considered that the favorite recipes of *Columbo* stars might have been immortalized in magazines and books of a by-gone era. The 70s really were special times.

Having had the opportunity to have a sneak preview of this book prior to its publication, I can only commend author Jenny for her passion for the subject matter and her devotion to the *Columbo* cause. What you have here, is a fantastic collection of recipes suitable for every occasion, from a light dinner for one to opulent banquets for a house full of friends.

And that got me thinking again. If we were to host a magnificent, 70s-style feast using the recipes found here, which *Columbo* stars would be top of the guest list? Here's my list. And naturally, you're very welcome to join us. Lieutenant Columbo and Mrs. Columbo were invited, of course, but they had a bowling league dinner dance to attend, so can't make it. Those tickets cost $17.50 a couple, you know...

#1 Adrian Carsini (*Any Old Port in a Storm*)

Top of the list, in no small measure due to his magnificent turn of phrase and impeccable manners. More importantly, because an exciting meal can easily be ruined by the presence of liquid filth, having a man of such discerning wine-matching skills has to be an advantage at a high-caliber *soirée*.

#2 Nora Chandler (*Requiem for a Falling Star*)

Even if her star is waning, Nora Chandler remains a household name, a *fashionista extraordinaire* and cracking company, well accustomed to the sort of shallow small-talk of the showbiz world that would make her a smash hit at any social gathering. She'd be the center of attention without a doubt.

#3 Ken Franklin (*Murder by the Book*)

You want charm, wit and winning conversation? You got it with Ken Franklin, who would be *impossible* to beat for entertainment value. Watching ladies' man Ken repeatedly trying to have his wicked way with *every* female guest would be quite riveting.

#4 Viveca Scott (*Lovely but Lethal*)

The beauty industry Empress knows how to turn on the charm, and as long as arch-rival David Lang isn't in attendance, one couldn't wish for a more genial and stylish dinner guest than Viveca. We can only hope and pray that on this night of all nights she'll dust down the legendary fashion turban she saves for special occasions.

#5 Dr. Ray Flemming (*Prescription: Murder*)

The human personification of 'highbrow', Dr. Flemming is as much at home at upper-crust shindigs as Lieutenant Columbo is at Barney's Beanery. The good doctor's presence would not only guarantee some stimulating hypothetical conversations around the table but would also ensure that the pre-dinner parlor games kicked things off with a bang.

#6 Goldie Williamson (*Blueprint for Murder*)

Every opulent 70s' dinner party needs a dame of sass and personality to drive conversation and keep fellow guests on their toes. Goldie delivers both in spades, and would ensure there were no dull moments. Her end of the table would be where you'd secretly want to be sitting.

#7 Dale Kingston (*Suitable for Framing*)

He may be a vile toad, but give Dale Kingston a couple of glasses of Champagne and an excuse to exhibit his superior knowledge of art and just watch him go! In an audience of intellects and *bon viveurs* like this, he'd be in his element. And even if no one else understood his high-culture gags he'd fill any silence by yelling with laughter at his own jokes. Plus he rocks the crushed velvet tuxedo look…

#8 Leslie Williams (*Ransom for a Dead Man*)

A woman succeeding in a typically male-dominated profession, elegant legal eagle Leslie Williams is razor sharp, supremely confident and mildly flirtatious to boot. She'd be the mental equal of anyone around the dining table and could go toe-to-toe with any leering gents (yes, *you*, Ken Franklin) and knock 'em for six.

The entertainment

During the starter and main, we'll be serenaded by **Tommy Brown**, who will play some gentle acoustic covers of his greatest biblical hits at a volume sensible enough to not interrupt conversations. He'll be followed by the **Great Santini**, whose jaw-dropping magical feats will be the perfect accompaniment to dessert, coffee, and liqueurs.

The chef

With French *gourmet* Paul Gerard regrettably unavailable due to filming some silly commercial for 'Bon Snax' crackers (how *thoroughly* low brow), laugh-a-minute TV chef **Dexter Paris** heroically steps into the breach. He'll prove there's more to him than just being a housewife's favorite by whipping up a dazzling array of dishes, before dashing off in his Ferrari 330 DTS, electric mixers safely in tow.

**

Do give your ultimate *Columbo* dinner party guest list some thought as you work your way through this marvelous book. And if you do find yourself thoroughly enjoying some of the delectable delights tucked within the pages, please raise a glass to the good Lieutenant himself, and the man who made it all possible, Peter Falk.

I hope you enjoy the book.

LC

Columbophile is a *Columbo* expert, blogger, and influencer based in Sydney, Australia. One of the world's leading authorities on the show, his mission is to keep the memory of Lieutenant Columbo alive and close to the hearts of fans everywhere.

Blog: columbophile.wordpress.com
Twitter: @columbophile
Facebook: www.facebook.com/columbophile/
Instagram: @columbophile

INTRODUCTION
Pop On Your Raincoat and Party!

I've been a fan of *Columbo* for as long as I can remember, but my real obsession kicked in around 1997. At that time, I often worked from home and *Columbo* always seemed to be on TV in the afternoons. I was working very hard you understand, but also watching *Columbo* with my one good eye. I printed out a list of the episodes and used a blue highlighter to mark each one off as it aired, just like a kid with my tongue sticking out. I still have that list and have watched all 69 episodes of *Columbo,* many times over.

I have become quite evangelical about the Lieutenant over the years. I screech when someone reveals that they love *Columbo*. I grab them, give them a big bear hug, and yell: "I KNEW you were the kind of person who would love *Columbo*." Thankfully, this type of person is everywhere I turn.

Until recently, watching *Columbo* has always been a self-indulgent treat. It reminds me of lost afternoons skiving off school, or of days when I've felt a bit under the weather and in need of some comfort TV. Recently though, I've been sharing my guilty pleasure with others. Introducing or re-introducing friends to the wonders of *Columbo* is such a fun thing to do. I haven't met anyone yet who doesn't enjoy watching the detective. Have you? Rustling up an episode-specific dish to share with family and friends is a great way of making a *Columbo* session even more of an event. Grab a cigar, pop on your raincoat, and make a night of it!

If you can't be bothered to cook, don't worry. Here's a crib sheet for quick-fix *Columbo* related goodies.

Chili - Lieutenant Columbo loves this - with or without beans, he's not fussy. There are four recipes for chili in this book but you know what? If you bought a few cans of ready-made chili and bunged them in a fancy casserole dish and heated them up, I wouldn't tell anyone…

Hard-boiled eggs - Food on the run for the Lieutenant. He often produces one from his raincoat pocket, when called out to a crime scene early in the morning. Why not have a bowlful of them on the coffee table when friends come over and tell them that's dinner?

Canapés - Columbo is always picking away at canapés from parties that he hasn't been invited to, parties that are already over, or parties that haven't even started yet. If you scrabble around in your local supermarket you can usually find little amuse-bouche-type-things to stick in the oven. It doesn't really matter what they are. Just spread them out on a shiny, metal platter with some serviettes. It will impress your guests I am sure. Sometimes *Columbo* folk call these little nibbles "hors d'oeuvres". Up to you!

However, if you do fancy donning your apron and rustling up a delicious dinner, herein are loads of *Columbo* related recipes to tickle your fancy. They are all genuine favorites of the actors and actresses appearing in the show and all the episode-specific dishes have been kitchen-tested at Silver Screen Suppers Towers and by many willing friends, family, and total strangers! You'll find photographs of the finished dishes and many additional recipes on the Silver Screen Suppers website. I have standardized recipes, whilst staying as close as possible to the original. I have also translated American cup measurements to metric, for those who are more used to weighing ingredients rather than measuring by volume. It's best to stick to one or the other. If you wish to track down the original recipes, I have included my sources in the back of the book.

I tried not to give away too much of the plot in my episode summaries. It's almost always obvious whodunnit in *Columbo*, but the fun is in finding out *how* our shambling sleuth finds out whodunnit…

Oh, just one more thing… I love getting emails, so do let me know how your *Columbo* related dishes turned out, just drop me a line via the Silver Screen Suppers website contact page. Happy eating, and happy viewing my fellow Lieutenant lovers!

NEW TO COLUMBO?

Here's a primer.

The wife - Lieutenant Columbo is married, to Mrs. Columbo - she is mentioned umpteen times but never seen. Does she really exist? I think so. We hear him talking fondly to her on the telephone many times. Why would he make her up? She likes Bette Davis films, Italian food, paint-by-numbers kits, and marmalade. She's not a great cook and she definitely doesn't have a green thumb. Her African Violets always snuff it.

The extended family - Columbo's many nephews, nieces, and in-laws are often mentioned in conversation. He appears to have a very large family with many unusual interests. One of his nephews, for example, enjoys weightlifting as well as needlepoint.

Animals - Columbo has a beautiful Basset Hound that he adores. The dog's name is simply, "Dog". The Lieutenant is definitely an animal lover, a real softy when it comes to pooches, kitties and even chimps. He calls his dog "darling" and "sweetheart".

Chili - As mentioned in the introduction, chili is Columbo's favorite food, without a doubt. His favorite chili emporium is Barney's Beanery - this is a real eatery in Los Angeles. Columbo is often to be found at the Beanery, eating chili, chatting to "Barney." Once, he even wined and dined a female suspect there at a gingham-clothed table.

Hard-boiled eggs - Columbo's favorite snack, especially early in the morning when he is called out to a murder scene. He'll crack these open on anything that's handy, including the murder weapon.

Coffee - He drinks a lot of this, sometimes from a thermos he brings from home, sometimes from styrofoam cups. He needs a lot of caffeine - he works very odd hours.

The raincoat - It's his trademark. Peter Falk said, "It was quite smart in the first episode, and just gets grubbier and grubbier."

Cigars - These get Columbo into trouble sometimes, especially with housekeepers like the legendary Mrs. Peck, and with office-proud secretaries or chicks who work in fancy hair salons. Not everyone likes the smell of cigars or the ash that falls off them. It sends Mrs. Peck berserk.

Domestic staff - Usually they love Columbo. There are lots of great scenes involving cleaners, housekeepers, and maids scattered throughout the series. He also has a way with "working girls."

Columbo likes Westerns.

He has sweaty feet.

He can play the tuba.

He can't swim. He says he "doesn't even like a deep tub."

THE FIRST SEASON
(1971-1972)

PRESCRIPTION: MURDER - 1968

Are you married? Have you had your 10th wedding anniversary yet? If it's coming up, why not plan a *Columbo* night and watch this movie with your loved one? Or throw a glamorous party? You can wheel in an enormous, three-tiered cake, fired up with multicolored sparklers, and have a huge bucket of iced Champagne on the side as the couple in this fabulous pilot episode does.

Gene Barry and Nina Foch play the unhappily married duo. Actually, it's probably only a good *Columbo* to watch if you *are* happily married; because as you can imagine, one of them does the other one in. I'm not giving away which way around it is, but as with all episodes of *Columbo*, you'll guess who has murder on their mind quite soon after you've tuned in.

This was the very first *Columbo* to air. It is beautifully shot, the colors are muted, the decors super-chic, the coiffures perfect, and the clothes drool-worthy. Everyone looks so groomed and beautiful. I really want to live in this world (without the possibility of being bumped off, of course).

If you are used to seeing Columbo turn up in a crumpled raincoat with a grubby collar, you may be surprised by how dapper he looks in this episode. He's positively handsome and tidy! If you've seen many, many *Columbos*, it's great fun to see which elements of his character were already in place from day one. You can almost tick them off.

Compared with many of the villains that follow, psychologist Dr. Ray Flemming is fairly civil towards Columbo. The two of them are very polite with each other until it dawns on Ray that Columbo is much more intelligent than he seems.

"Has anyone ever told you, you're droll?" asks the Doctor, "You're a sly little elf and you should be sitting under your own private little toadstool." How very rude! He tells the Lieutenant that he is irritated by him, but that he respects his tenacity; then he offers him a drink. The two of them enjoy a bourbon together. So if you have a drinks cabinet secreted behind a bookcase, as Dr. Ray does, you could offer bourbon to your dinner guests and serve it on the rocks.

So to kick off our trip into dining like the stars of *Columbo*, here is a great recipe from Gene Barry for really tasty lamb meatballs. You will probably have a fair amount of the filling left over, but you could use this to add to rice, or to stuff some peppers. Two dinners in one, brilliant! There is something meditative about making these meatballs, you can reminisce about when you were a kid and made pinch pots in pottery class as you make them. Small ones are nice as canapés.

Gene Barry's Kibbee

¾ cup / 170g fine cracked wheat/bulgur wheat
1½ lbs / 675g ground/minced lamb (divided use)
Salt and pepper
¼ cup / 35g minced/finely chopped onion
3 tablespoons butter or margarine
¼ cup / 35g pine nuts
½ teaspoon cinnamon

Rinse wheat and drain thoroughly. Combine half the lamb with wheat, onion, ½ teaspoon salt, ¼ teaspoon pepper and cold water. Mix well and set aside. Heat butter in a frying pan. Add pine nuts, remaining lamb, ½ teaspoon salt, ½ teaspoon pepper and the cinnamon. Cook meat, breaking up with a fork until meat is browned. Divide reserved meat mixture into 24 appetizer balls, using approximately 2 tablespoons of meat mixture for each meatball. For large meatballs use ¼ cup (about 50g) for each. Press a finger into each ball and fill indentation with pine nut filling. Press meat over filling and shape with hands into an oval or round shape. Fry in hot oil until golden on all sides.

Makes 12 large or 24 small kibbee.

Just one more thing... Test cook Sarah Bailey of Sarah's Cooker-ebook enjoyed these, (as did her husband). She writes that she usually soaks bulgur wheat for a while before rinsing and cooking, but her hubby liked this crunchier version. Sarah added a top tip: wet your hands when you are shaping the meatballs. That's a really good idea!

RANSOM FOR A DEAD MAN - 1971

Lee Grant is Columbo's first female adversary, and she sets the pattern for many to follow. Smart, sexy, sassy, and slightly sinister, Lee's character, Leslie Williams is steely when she needs to be and flirty with the Lieutenant when she thinks it will help her get away with murder.

Leslie is an attorney, so we know she is super-intelligent. She's fierce in the courtroom and sweet outside of it, but we know what she did, so she's not to be trusted. We can tell that she thinks Columbo is a bumbling fool when she gives him instructions to her "powder room." Later she revises her opinion of him saying, "You know Columbo, you are almost likable in a shabby sort of way." Leslie has definitely got his number, seeing through his fumbling and stumbling along. She accuses him of having a "shopworn bag of tricks" including fake humility, seemingly absent-mindedness, and the homey anecdotes about his family. Of course, these are all techniques that will serve Columbo well throughout the series. I love it that they are flagged up to viewers, so early on.

When Leslie offers to cook dinner for a group of police officers gathered at her home, Columbo volunteers to help, by peeling potatoes. It's good to know that the Lieutenant is happy to help out in the kitchen! He's not convinced by Leslie's seemingly calm demeanor though, calling her "a unique person." Knowing Columbo as we do, this means he's extremely suspicious of her conduct. Like many female villains, Leslie soon becomes intrigued by the Lieutenant and will begin to get closer to him as events unfold.

Columbo makes easy friendships with his suspects. He takes an interest in them; what they do for a living; how they behave; what their passions are. Leslie has a pilot's license and loves to fly. Even though it's an understatement when the Lieutenant says that flying is not one of his favorite pastimes, he accepts an offer to get airborne. During the flight, Leslie hands him the controls and tells him that he has to treat a plane like a woman; very gently. This scene offered the first hint of comedy elements that became a staple part of the *Columbo* series. The Lieutenant continues to be a nervous flyer throughout.

Lee Grant and Peter Falk were friends in real life. This episode first aired in March 1971. Later that year, they began a two year run on Broadway, playing the main roles in a Neil Simon play, *The Prisoner of Second Avenue*. In Falk's memoirs *Just One More Thing,* published in 2006, he said of his co-star, "She's a joy onstage and off it. I love Lee."

Lee wrote her own memoirs, and they are equally as engrossing as Falk's. She writes of her time blacklisted during the MacArthur era in Hollywood and of her slow resurgence on the stage and screen. Thank goodness she made a comeback. As Falk himself observed, she's one of Columbo's most formidable adversaries.

The Lieutenant's chili obsession is also firmly established in this pilot episode. He visits the legendary Barney's Beanery, and after a game of pool, orders a bowl of chili. So if you don't fancy Lee's chicken, you could definitely have a bowl of chili with crackers. In fact, you could have chili with any episode of *Columbo*, it's the Lieutenant's signature dish!

When Leslie offers him a drink at the end of this episode, Columbo waits to see what she orders. She asks for a sherry, he orders a root beer. This tickles Leslie and she tells him that he always has a way of making her feel decadent. So if you are feeling sensible, drink root beer. If you are feeling decadent, get amongst the sherry!

Lee's recipe is a big, colorful crowd pleaser. We can tell from her autobiography that she loved to cook for a multitude. There's a great story in the book about her hosting a cast party, cooking hundreds of chicken legs and wings, wearing a paper bag over her head with the eyeholes cut out because of the splattering fat. You won't need a paper bag for this one though.

I don't have a cooking vessel big enough for Lee's whole recipe so I make ½ her recipe. I usually serve this on the day I make it, but you can make it a day ahead. Do take note of Lee's advice about removing the fat though if you do this.

Lee Grant's Chicken Malibu

2 chickens, each cut into 8 pieces
8 chicken wings
½ cup / 120ml olive oil
2 onions, peeled and chopped
2 large green peppers, chopped
1 large clove garlic, crushed
2 carrots, peeled and grated
½ lb / 225g mushrooms, sliced
4 tablespoons of butter
Salt
¼ teaspoon white pepper
2 or 3 teaspoons curry powder
2 or 3 tablespoons chopped parsley
2 bay leaves
Pinch of thyme leaves
2 cans chicken broth or stock (about 28 oz or 800ml in total)
4 tablespoons flour
Hot cooked rice

Preheat oven to 350 degrees F / 175 degrees C / gas mark 4.

Heat oil in a large frying pan that has a lid or a Dutch oven/casserole dish. Brown the chicken pieces quickly on both sides, remove to drain on paper towels to absorb excessive fat. Add the onion, green pepper, garlic and carrot to pan drippings. Sauté vegetables, stirring over low heat, until limp. Cook mushrooms slowly in butter in another frying pan, adding 2 teaspoons of salt, the white pepper, and curry powder. Cook until mushrooms are browned and seasonings are well blended. Add mushroom curry mixture to large Dutch oven / ovenproof casserole dish along with the chicken. Add parsley, bay leaves, and thyme. Pour in chicken broth, enough to cover vegetables and chicken pieces, adding water if necessary. Cover the dish and bake for about 40 minutes until chicken is tender. Remove from oven and cool to room temperature. Refrigerate until fat congeals on top. Skim off chicken fat with a large spoon. Make gravy, using flour blended with a little chicken broth, forming a smooth paste. Add gravy back into the main dish. Reheat the chicken, stirring to blend and thicken the gravy. Taste for correct seasonings. Serve over hot cooked rice.

Serves 12

Just one more thing... Jessica Maitland of the Colmworth Micro Bakery emailed, "We LOVED this dish, and I know it will feature regularly on our dinner table. Both toddlers gobbled it up and my husband and I thoroughly enjoyed it." Pointing out that this is a great meal for making ahead of time and then heating up when ready, she adds, "It is amazing that this dish also delivers with huge taste and has a few veggies in, making it a real one pot wonder. Nom, nom!"

Writer and illustrator Jodie Botha had never disjointed a chicken before, so took to YouTube to find out how. She felt a great sense of accomplishment and proclaimed the chicken to be lovely and juicy when cooked to Lee's recipe. Leftovers were good with rice. Shortly after making this dish, Jodie turned vegan. She told me this chicken recipe is the only thing she misses.

Vintage Gramophone DJ, Ms. Chameleon, and her beau enjoyed this dish, but she had a few suggestions for the modern chef. Firstly, she would halve the amount of oil, secondly, use a little less broth, and thirdly, use a strongly flavored curry powder. She'd never cooked with curry powder before, so plumped for a mild one. This recipe can take a fuller-flavored curry powder for sure. I loved her comment, "Man, it did create a lot of dishes to wash." Indeed it does, but it's worth it!

MURDER BY THE BOOK - 1971

Writers love writing about writing. There are several *Columbo* episodes that feature writers as central characters. This, the first of them, sets the bar very high. It's a superb episode put together by the *Columbo* dream team. The script was written by the legendary Steven Bochco, it was produced by the series' creators Richard Levinson and William Link, and directed by Steven Spielberg. The cherry on the cake is Jack Cassidy, widely thought of as the best *Columbo* co-star, playing a cold-blooded killer with real panache.

Jack plays the first Columbo adversary who is downright rude to him. Prickly from the moment they meet, his character Ken Franklin constantly challenges Columbo's skills of detection. Famous for co-writing a crime series that features a female sleuth, Ken says with a condescending air: "See, if Mrs. Melville were on this case - oh she'd be leaps and bounds ahead of you by now." Columbo pretends to be pleased when Ken forces ten Mrs. Melville mysteries on him to read. "Maybe I could pick up a few pointers," observes our detective. He looks at the weighty tomes, playing along with the idea that Mrs. Melville and by extension Ken, *are* possibly smarter than him.

Later in the episode when Columbo returns the books, they seem to have multiplied. He has trouble carrying them all. He interrupts a flirty magazine interview Ken is giving to an attractive female reporter. Our shabby sleuth raves about the Mrs. Melville books, his voice rising to a screech, "the lady detective, what a character, what a brain, and what logic! The way she figures it out!" Ken looks exasperated. In a classic example of the fake humility mentioned by Lee Grant's character in the previous episode, Columbo apologizes: "I'm sorry. I'm making a pest of myself.... It's because I keep asking these questions, but I'll tell ya, I can't help myself, it's a habit!" As with most *Columbo* villains, the more questions Ken is asked, the more rattled he gets.

When Columbo announces that he's going to arrest him for the murder of his writing partner and begins to read him his rights, Ken snaps, "Will you cut that drivel, I've written that stuff so many times, I know it by heart." He then concedes with a sarcastic tone, "All right Lieutenant, you got me, I'm your prisoner, clamp the irons on me." Ken still thinks he's got away with it, but as Columbo explains, at some length, how he worked out how to catch him, Ken's confidence begins to fade. Irritated, he interjects: "Come on, get to the climax Lieutenant, you're talking to a writer!" As Columbo continues to explain his theories, Ken scowls, "Go ahead I'm fascinated, as boring as it may be." Our hero finally clinches it with a piece of written proof. Ken laughs, with a wry grin looks up at the Lieutenant and says: "You've gotta admit I had you going for a while there, didn't I?"

Champagne would be the most suitable beverage for this episode if you can afford it, as it flows freely throughout. If you prefer something stronger, you could always drink bourbon. When Ken offers Columbo a drink, he requests bourbon and it's served on the rocks, just like in *Prescription: Murder*.

If you are making the trout exactly to Jack's recipe you'll need some Chablis. Chilling the rest of the bottle to have with your fish would be appropriate too. The recipe serves six, but it's easily adaptable for as many folks as you like. Personally, I think this is a really nice thing to make as a supper for one. As you only need a few drops of Chablis for each fish, if you are dining solo, you'll have almost a whole bottle to enjoy with your Columbo!

If you don't feel like making trout in a pouch, you could rustle up a cheese and onion omelet. Columbo makes one in this episode. Instructions for the Lieutenant's exact methodology for making this classic brunch or supper dish can be found in the entry for the *Double Exposure* episode. Columbo claims that an omelet is the only thing he can cook, but as we'll see in *Murder Under Glass,* this is simply not true!

You could serve hot dogs rather than Jack's trout if you prefer, as they also feature in this episode. When trying to glean some information pertinent to his case, Columbo treats an insurance agent to lunch at the legendary food stand, "Tail of the Pup," which is shaped like a giant hot dog. Hot dogs are a perennial favorite of the Lieutenant's. They are good fodder for eating on the run as he often has to do.

For dessert, you could have masses of strawberries served on an enormous bed of ice. Eat these with your fingers, as the magnificent character Lilly La Sanka does in this episode, with great relish!

Jack Cassidy's Rainbow Trout in a Pouch

6 rainbow trout, each weighing about 1 lb / 450g
Salt and pepper
½ lemon
1½ tablespoons fresh parsley, finely chopped
2-3 tablespoons melted sweet/unsalted butter
¼ cup / 60ml Chablis (approximately)

6 tablespoons flour
6 tablespoons butter

Preheat oven to 375 degrees F / 190 degrees C / gas mark 5.

Rub cleaned fish inside and out with salt and pepper. Place each fish on a sheet of aluminum foil, large enough to completely encase the fish. Sprinkle lemon juice over them and top with parsley and melted butter. Then sprinkle few drops of Chablis over each fish.

To close the pouch, loosely overlap the long end of foil over other side about one inch; close ends of the pouch by squeezing ends together in an upward direction.

Place packets in a baking dish. Bake for about 5 minutes.

Open pouches, forming a drip tray for each fish. Mix flour and butter together until it is a spreadable consistency and spread about two tablespoons of this mixture onto the surface of each fish. Cook under broiler/grill until crisp and brown.

Serves 6

Just one more thing... My archivist chums Dylan and Arike, had a lot of fun making this dish. They watched the episode as they ate their trout and were pleased to have an excuse to visit their local fishmongers. I'm a big believer in fishmongers, and even better when possible, buying from the real-life fisherman that made the catch.

I know screenwriter, Trix Worrell loves this too, as he lives on the coast in Hastings and one of the local fishermen is a character in one of his forthcoming projects, *Sea Dogs*. Trix said of this dish, "It was fab!" despite the fact that his missus, Lady Jane, attempting to help out, dropped the butter in the washing-up water. Lady Jane doesn't frequent the kitchen very often…

DEATH LENDS A HAND - 1971

Some people consider Robert Culp, rather than Jack Cassidy, to be the quintessential *Columbo* villain. He's in four episodes and is certainly brilliant in all of them. In this one, he is steely, condescending, and egotistical; all good qualities for a foe to the Lieutenant.

Robert's character, Investigator Brimmer, runs a very successful private detective agency. In an interesting twist, the murder victim's husband (played by Ray Milland) asks the murderer to assist Columbo in an investigation into his wife's death. Columbo doesn't object to this too much, it's a good way for him to observe Brimmer at close quarters. As they discuss the crime together, Columbo observes that whoever committed the murder, must be a man with a terrible temper. Thus Brimmer really gives himself away, when he bawls out an employee within the Lieutenant's earshot. His face is a picture.

From the start, Brimmer obviously thinks Columbo is a fool. At their first meeting, the Lieutenant tries to leave the room via a cupboard, after confiding that he's a superstitious man and believes in palmistry and astrology. Brimmer looks amused, rolling his eyes and saying to Ray Milland's character: "I think police techniques have changed a little over the years." Later, Brimmer attempts to get into our man's good books, by flattering him and offering him a job, promising three times the money a cop could make. "Lieutenant, you have a marvelously convoluted mind," smarms Brimmer, "I like it!" When Columbo turns up at Brimmer's house to discuss the job offer, he gets sidetracked, admiring a thick, soft pile rug. "Bet you could lose a shoe in here for a week, you wouldn't find it," jokes the Lieutenant. Perhaps he guesses that his suspect has just been scouring it with a flashlight, hunting for a piece of incriminating evidence? Brimmer soon gets impatient with Columbo's rambling conversation and wants to know if he'll take the job. The Lieutenant eventually explains that he wouldn't be happy making a change. Although Mrs. Columbo is always telling him that he doesn't have enough ambition, he likes it where he is, noting: "it's not a bad life."

It strikes me that in real life, Robert Culp may have been a little bit like his character in this episode; self-contained, not very expansive or friendly, and not the kind of man you could imagine regularly putting on an apron and cooking up something delicious to share with company. I may be wrong of course, but search as I might, I can find no reported trace of anything that Robert Culp liked to cook (or even anything he particularly liked to eat).

Luckily, legendary Welsh actor, Ray Milland shares screen-time with Robert Culp here, and he offered quite a few recipes to journalists and cookbook compilers of the day. So it is his Chow Mein that I propose making as an accompaniment to this episode. It is an easy peasy recipe and surprisingly delicious.

If Chow Mein is not to your taste, why not prepare some Quenelles de Sole with a tomato sauce? The Lieutenant and his adversary share a working lunch and this is on the menu. Brimmer asks, "do you like Quenelles de Sole?" Columbo's response: "Well, if it's fish. I like fish. Love fish." In the middle of Brimmer's office, there is a big round table laid out with china plates, shiny cutlery and both wine and water glasses. A waiter stands by until he is dismissed, then Brimmer grabs a bottle of wine from the ice bucket beside the table and serves Columbo and himself a glass. He is obviously not the kind of man to grab a quick sandwich at his desk, like most of us do. Columbo is very taken with the Quenelles de Sole, and asks, "how do you make this stuff?" Amused, Brimmer promises to send the recipe over.

If you do choose to have Quenelles rather than the Chow Mein, there is a Vincent Price recipe for these in the "Columbo's Chili and Other Delights" section. But don't be like Columbo and accidentally dip your tie in the tomatoes.

Ray Milland's Chicken Chow Mein

1 green pepper, finely chopped
1 large onion, sliced
1 cup / 120g sliced celery
2½ cups / 600ml chicken bouillon (or chicken stock)
Salt
3 teaspoons soy sauce
1 cup / 75g whole or sliced mushrooms
2½ cups / 375g diced cooked chicken
1½ teaspoons cornstarch/cornflour
Chinese noodles - enough for 2
Cooked, sliced chicken, white meat, paper thin to serve

Cook green pepper, onion and celery in bouillon or stock for 20 minutes. Add 2 teaspoon salt [but see note below], soy sauce, mushrooms, and diced chicken. In another pan, combine cornstarch with 2 tablespoons of water. Add to rest of ingredients and cook mixture for 15 minutes, stirring frequently. Serve on heated noodles. Top with sliced chicken.

Serves 2

Just one more thing... I was thrilled when Ray Milland's second cousin, Rosie Jones, offered to test this recipe, how cool is that? Rosie used low-salt soy sauce in her version (which I think is a very good idea as the salt content is quite high). I would actually recommend halving the amount in this recipe, knowing what we know now, that we didn't back then... Rosie also added some 5-spice and celery salt to her version of the dish, which I think is a top idea. She declared the finished result to be, "Light and delicious, not as salty as my usual cooking – now there's a lesson!"

DEAD WEIGHT - 1971

Are you single? Have you been single for a while? When someone suddenly pays you a lot of attention, it's often difficult to know whether you should be interested in them or not, isn't it? Suzanne Pleshette's character, Helen Stewart, has her head turned by Maj. Gen. Martin J. Hollister, and who can blame her? He's a war hero. He's on television. He takes her to fancy places for dinner. He has a YACHT! I have been in her shoes, I understand all of this.

It's worth pointing out, that at the time this episode was made, Suzanne was around 34 years old and Eddie Albert was about 65. Let's face it though, if you are spending every evening drinking pre-dinner cocktails in a kaftan with your mother, it's easy to be swept off your feet by a military man who tells you he's been fascinated by you since the very first moment he met you. The fact that General Hollister is very wealthy obviously helps. As Helen's mother puts it, "You play your cards right, bourbon today, Champagne tomorrow!"

The General's pursuit of Helen has an ulterior motive of course; she spotted him committing a crime, and he has to find a way of convincing her that she was mistaken. Eddie plays this role with great charm and sophistication. The General is not afraid of the Lieutenant at all, and unlike most of the bad guys in *Columbo*, seems to treat him more or less, as an equal. Perhaps it is something to do with the Lieutenant's rank. As an ex-military man, the General would be a stickler for rank.

When the General comes home after a suspicious early morning trip in his boat, he finds Columbo waiting for him on his dock, fishing. Realising that Columbo suspects him, he implies that the Lieutenant is looking in the wrong place, "I don't think you'll catch anything big around here Lieutenant, you are too close in." As Columbo asks some tricky questions about the General's trademark, pearl handled, single action Colt 45, he's told, "Just a piece of advice. Find a different spot, or use a different bait, otherwise, you're not going to catch anything Lieutenant."

But of course, the Lieutenant will catch something, and it will be the General. A conversation with Bert, one of the Lieutenants favorite chilidishers gives him the lead he needs. As Columbo is about to tuck into a bowl of chili and crackers, it suddenly dawns on him where he will find the proof of the General's guilt. All thanks to Bert's WWII memorabilia.

It seems as though Eddie Albert liked to cook. I have a few of his favorite recipes in my collection, and all of them are good. His Butterfly Lamb is really delicious. If you aren't handy with a boning knife, ask the butcher to butterfly the leg for you, this makes the dish quick to cook and makes more surface area for the marinade to permeate. I like to serve this with the traditional British accompaniment to a big chunk of lamb; crispy roast potatoes and some plain boiled or steamed vegetables.

Red wine, "before-dinner cocktails," and martinis all feature in this episode. The General takes Helen to a swanky cocktail bar, to try and persuade her that the murder that she thought she saw, was just a trick of the light. When she concedes it's possible she made a mistake, he claps his hands and exclaims, "The Defence rests. For today," she smiles demurely. Then he announces, "Now, I think we ought to prosecute these martinis before their statutes of limitations expire," (which is a great phrase to practice if you fancy serving martinis before Eddie's Butterfly Lamb).

Eddie's recipe is vague about quantities, but it's the kind of marinade you can make by using your spider sense! It would be difficult to mess this up. Go freestyle! Check with your butcher about how long to cook your leg of lamb and at what temperature. This is all dependent on the size of your leg.

Eddie Albert's Butterfly Lamb

Ask your butcher to butterfly a leg of lamb.

Make a marinade of:

Your favorite oil
Little bit of cumin
Chopped, small green/spring onions, use both green and white parts
Basil
Lots of freshly chopped parsley
Drop of white tarragon vinegar
Light sprinkle of salt and cracked pepper

To serve:

Onions
Avocado

Rub leg of lamb lightly with a cut garlic clove. Marinate lamb in the marinade mixture for several hours, turning it for taste. Barbecue lamb or broil/grill it, like steak, in the oven.

Serve with thin slices of onion and avocado on the side. Eddie says that he likes to put the slices of onion over the meat and the avocado over that. He says: "The sizzling meat melts the avocado slightly and it's a delicious combination."

Serves 6-8

Just one more thing... Prize-winning baker, Gaye Fisher of Sticky Mitts, enjoyed this dish with her husband, Peter. She wrote, "Didn't like the idea initially, of avocado with roast lamb but it worked surprisingly well made into a salsa. No accompaniments were mentioned in the original recipe, we definitely felt the roast potatoes were necessary." Ooh, yes, I agree, definitely roast potatoes!

SUITABLE FOR FRAMING - 1971

Can you tell a Degas from a Goya?

The central character in this episode, Dale Kingston, wears a crushed-velvet jacket, oversized bow-tie and a white shirt with frills on the chest and cuffs. He looks like he could be a cabaret performer in a sleazy, 1970s club, but this kind of get-up was probably normal for a famous art critic of the time. He has gained fame by appearing on television explaining art in simple terms, to the hoi polloi. But what he really wants is his uncle's priceless art collection. A will has recently been changed, and not in his favor.

This episode contains the first concrete example of a recurring theme within *Columbo*. When finding himself close to an expert in something, whether it's fine wine, fine dining or fine art, the Lieutenant zeros in on the specialized subject of his adversary. When Dale returns home late and finds Columbo there, asleep in one of his armchairs, he is understandably alarmed. Columbo has, of course, been browsing amongst the art books, reading them to glean a little knowledge about the new world he finds himself in. He expresses an appreciation of Matisse.

Dale thinks Columbo is a "very haphazard character" and accuses him of being a "compulsively suspicious bureaucrat." It's quite obvious that he is irritated by the Lieutenant and he takes great pleasure in proving Columbo's theory about him murdering his uncle to profit from his will, is completely wrong. He snarls, "You are so transparent, Columbo… will you please do me a favor and stop pestering me?" Of course, he underestimates the Lieutenant's intellect and believes he can outwit him by planting evidence to incriminate his scatty Aunt Edna in the murder. Naturally, he's not as smart as he thinks he is.

I don't want to give away the ending, but if you are planning a full-on *Columbo* experience, it might be worth watching this episode beforehand. You'll then know what item of clothing to have in your pocket to surprise and delight your guests with, at the very end of your screening.

The Champagne flows freely in this episode, and it's wall to wall lurex and polyester at a gallery event Dale attends. You could throw a little party with fizz for this one, and have everyone stand around in long dresses and frilly shirts talking about art. It would be good to have some grapes around the place, as Columbo eats these at Aunt Edna's place. But for the main course, this dish cannot be beaten. Your guests will feel like they have been to the most glamorous dinner party ever if you serve this up.

This Beef in Anchovy Cream is my favorite film star recipe of all time and is utterly delicious. There is much debate about whether the term Chateaubriand refers to a specific cut of beef, or rather a particular method of preparing it. Either way, I recommend that you buy the best quality beef you can afford, for best results. I'm sure that Ross would. I use sweet paprika rather than hot paprika, but if you like your food spicy, it's worth trying with hot. If you fancy making a whole meal to accompany this episode, Ross's excellent recipe for chocolate mousse is in the "Columbo's Chili and Other Delights" section. I can't think of a nicer combination. Cream and then more cream!

Ross Martin's Beef in Anchovy Cream

3 lbs / 1350g of tender beef (Chateaubriand) sliced ⅛ inch thick
¾ cup / 180ml heavy cream
½ cup / 120ml beef stock
¼ cup / 5g parsley
¼ cup / 25g chopped shallots
Dozen anchovy fillets

2 tablespoons brandy
Paprika to taste

Put the beef in a casserole dish with the cream, beef stock, parsley, shallots and anchovy fillets. Simmer uncovered, over a low heat for one and a half hours, adding extra cream and stock, if needed to keep meat covered. Add the brandy and paprika during the last hour of cooking.

Serves 4-6

Just one more thing... My fabulous friend and superb short story writer, Sanja Adamovic, thought this dish was "fantastic" and admitted that she and her brother found it so good, that they ate a little bit more of it than they should, and ended up "huffing and puffing on the sofa." She wondered about the instruction to slice the beef into ⅛ inch slices. I agree, that's very thin. I think I would just say to cut it as thin as you can. No need to get the tape measure out. Sanja used sirloin steak and felt it needed an extra half an hour of cooking.

Another test cook, work colleague and baker extraordinaire Neil Owens, made a version of this dish in his slow cooker/crockpot with beef short ribs. It is so good, I've included it in the "Columbo's Chili and Other Delights" section.

LADY IN WAITING - 1971

Has power ever gone to your head? Have you ever worn an oversized, pink, broad-brimmed cap and a floral suit with huge lapels to a board meeting? Have you suddenly gotten a radical, racy haircut and bought a snazzy sports car soon after a family tragedy? These things say something about you to a certain canny detective you know.

I love Susan Clark in this episode. Following the fabulous Lee Grant, she's an equally strong female lead, with complex motivations and violent mood swings. Her character, Beth Chadwick has got crazy eyes. She binges on chocolate. She buys inappropriate clothing. She loses her rag a bit when things don't go quite as she planned…

When Columbo is called in to investigate what seems like an accidental shooting, he's suspicious of Beth's story. He continues to ask lots of questions, long after she's been cleared of any wrongdoing. But Beth is confident that she has got away with murder and gets annoyed when Columbo visits her at home, telling him, "All right Lieutenant, I think you have finally overstayed your welcome. The official verdict is death by accidental means, and that should satisfy you."

Beth flirts with Columbo a little when he says that his wife tells him that he's "compulsive." She laughs, "Are you really?" But eventually, she firmly puts her foot down, warning, "Whatever your little compulsions may be, I'm afraid I must insist you leave me alone." I get the feeling, that unlike most of his female antagonists for whom he usually has a little affection, Columbo doesn't like Beth Chadwick at all.

After the murder of her brother, Beth takes over the family firm and suddenly becomes very businesslike indeed. She's the classic example of power going to someone's head. Columbo persists with his inquiries and visits her in her boardroom, asking questions about a suspicious lightbulb. Beth gets very dictatorial, "I want you to listen to this very carefully. I don't ever want to see you again. You'll be refused admittance to my house, and to this office. I have a great deal of work to do and I no longer can indulge your suspicions." The Lieutenant gives her the lightbulb and leaves. After the door closes behind him, she smashes the bulb, screeching, "What can we do about him?!" Despite her calm and collected demeanor, she is very rattled indeed.

Of course, the seemingly insignificant lightbulb is just one of the things that point Columbo to the solving of the crime. Mrs. Columbo has a little hand in it too.

We also learn a little more about what the Lieutenant likes to eat and drink. At a drive-in, fast food joint, he has a burger with a malted milk, but asks the go-go booted waitress to "hold the whipped cream." He likes onion rings too and is a little disappointed when he is told that they are off the menu. He can't think of anything he'd like to replace them with (and I certainly know that feeling). When you want something, in particular, you want it, right? Burgers, onion rings, and malted milks would be fun to have with this episode.

This is a strange looking recipe from Susan but bear with me. It's really tasty! If you don't fancy a curry, her peach salad is in the "Columbo's Chili and Other Delights" section, so you could try that instead. Alternatively, you could just do a Beth Chadwick, and watch Columbo all on your own, eating a great big box of chocolates in bed. All good options!

I am guessing that Susan used condensed tomato soup for her recipe, she didn't specify. As this isn't readily available in the UK, I have suggested using a whole 400g tin of tomato soup rather than half tomato soup and half water. I would suggest doubling this recipe so you are not left with half a can of condensed milk that will sit around in your fridge for ages until you decide to throw it away. This curry freezes fine so if you aren't going to eat it all in one go, freeze some!

Susan Clark's Shrimp Curry

2 strips/rashers of bacon, finely chopped
2 tablespoons finely chopped onion (about half a small sized onion)
½ can / 200ml condensed milk
½ can condensed tomato soup and ½ can water OR for Brits, 400g can ordinary tomato soup
½ tablespoon flour
½ teaspoon curry powder
Salt and pepper
6 large shrimp, raw and peeled (prawns if you are in the UK)
Rice to serve

Fry bacon with onions, mix with milk, add soup, water, flour, curry powder and salt and pepper to taste. Cook until thick. Add shrimp/prawns and cook through. Serve with rice.

Serves 2 (or one if you are very hungry)

Just one more thing... Several people volunteered to test cook this for me, looked at the ingredients, then declined! The lovely Peter Fuller, curator of the Vincent Price Legacy UK website is made of stronger stuff though, and made it TWICE! He proclaimed it to be, "Strangely tasty." Result! Peter notes (and I agree) that you can use a good hot curry powder for this, it can definitely take it! He also added a couple of dried, red chilies to his second batch of this dish, to boost the flavor. I do recommend this curry, even though it does sound weird, as it is really quick to make on a work night. If you put the rice on to cook first, the curry will probably be ready by the time your rice is.

SHORT FUSE - 1972

How do you feel about practical jokes? Do you make them? Please don't. On the other hand, when a prank is played on you, do you take it on the chin and laugh about it or does it make your blood absolutely boil?

The Roddy McDowall character in this episode is known as Junior, and although a fully grown adult, he behaves like a spoiled, precocious child.

Early on, he skulks around a secretarial pool, checking out the lovely, young things who wear pristinely pressed clothes with freshly coiffed hairdos. He suddenly springs into action, spraying them all with silly string. I'd be absolutely fuming, wouldn't you?

When Junior's uncle is killed in a suspicious car crash, the Lieutenant is sent to investigate. Junior (like Roddy in real life) is a keen photographer and has his own darkroom where he performs scientific experiments. When he finds the Lieutenant mucking around in there, accidentally covered in silly string, it cracks him up. Columbo (with silly string in his hair) admires Junior's National Science Fraternity medal, proudly displayed on his blouson-style shirt, like a medallion. Flattered, Junior reels off all his many academic qualifications, proving that although he behaves like a fool, he certainly isn't one. He giggles like a kid when Columbo tells him, "My problem with chemistry, that started way back in high school...I said, to heck with this chemistry stuff, I'll take another year of wood shop. You know, you just build a birdhouse, you paint it red, you get an A."

But of course, the Lieutenant is being disingenuous. When he suggests to Junior that his uncle's car accident could have been murder, he's already thinking about how an explosion could have been remotely set with some kind of trigger device. The young pretender has come up with a very clever method of murder, but will Columbo be able to unpick it? Of course he will.

Junior takes on some airs and graces at the family firm once his uncle is out of the way. He has obviously informed the staff that they are no longer to call him Junior, but Mr. Stanford. He wears a smart suit instead of his hippy-ish large-collared shirts, and takes over his uncle's office, swinging himself around in the plush leather chair and putting his feet on the table. All of this is an echo of Beth Chadwick's behavior in the previous episode. But Columbo is on his tail, and when he turns up at Junior's new posh office, the young upstart gets exasperated with him, exclaiming, "Lieutenant you take an inordinate length of time to come to the point." Columbo uses clever psychology to persuade Junior to accompany him on a trip to the location of his uncle's car crash. Even though the Lieutenant is afraid of heights, he takes a precarious cable car ride with the murderer that will end with Junior revealing his culpability.

If you are having friends over to watch this episode, you may wish to have a box of Cuban cigars on the coffee table for reasons that will become clear. For a party atmosphere, you could get ahold of a little 1960s go-go music to recreate the action in the Narcisse nightclub, frequented by Junior and his squeeze. And if you really can't resist a practical joke, silly string can be purchased on the internet.

Cooking these pears will make your kitchen smell divine. This is a very elegant, but very easy dinner party dessert which you can make ahead of time. Assemble them when it's time to serve, and bring them to the table with a flourish, as I'm sure Roddy would have done.

Roddy McDowall's Poached Pears

4 ripe pears
3 cups / 700ml red wine
½ cup / 100g sugar
1 stick of cinnamon
½ lemon
1 package (4 serving size) vanilla pudding mix (cooking type) or for Brits, enough custard for 4 people
2⅓ cups / 560ml half and half/single cream [you won't need this if you are using custard]
2 tablespoon sherry
1 pint / 340g fresh blueberries

Peel pears leaving stem end intact. Cut a thin slice from the large end so pears will stand upright.

Place wine, sugar, and stick of cinnamon in a large saucepan over medium-high heat. Heat to boiling. Add pears. Squeeze lemon over pears. Add the squeezed lemon half to wine mixture. Cover. Reduce heat to low and simmer 15 to 20 minutes or until pears are just fork tender. Let cool. Refrigerate in wine mixture 2 hours or overnight.

Prepare vanilla pudding sauce according to package directions using half and half in place of milk. Cool slightly. Stir in sherry. Refrigerate 2 hours or overnight.

To serve, drain pears. Pat dry. Place on dessert plates. Spoon vanilla pudding sauce over pears. Arrange blueberries around pears.

Serves 4

Just one more thing... Dedicated test cook Peter Fuller of the Vincent Price Legacy UK, made this and kindly sent me the method he used to make his own vanilla pudding. (We don't get vanilla pudding mix here in the UK so this is a wonderful idea.) You can find it in the "Columbo's

Chili and Other Delights" section. Peter suggests a lovely additional step to this recipe: when he made this for dinner party guests, he reduced some of the left-over wine mixture to a syrupy consistency and dribbled it over the pears. Genius!

BLUEPRINT FOR MURDER - 1972

There is a lot of shouting in this *Columbo*, partly because much of the action takes place on a noisy building site. The laconic Patrick O'Neal character, Elliot Markham barks orders at his staff and there is no please or thank-you in evidence when he talks to his secretary, except for the moment when she makes a telephone call on his behalf and he hatches a dastardly plan. "Thanks, Miss Sherman," he mutters without a smile, "I think I love you." We know by the way he says it, that it's a flippant remark. She replies in a plaintive Miss Lonelyhearts manner, "Thanks, I needed that."

Elliot is a high powered architect who has a way with the ladies. He has a millionaire's wife wrapped around his little finger, persuading her to bankroll his current project while her husband is away on business. But he has bargained without the sugar-daddy's ex-wife, Goldie. She has Elliot's number and is immune to his charms. As is Columbo too, of course.

If I had Goldie's money I would dress just like her, and whoever got to work on Janis Paige's wardrobe in this episode, hit pay dirt. As Goldie, herself swaggers, "If gold lamé was legal tender, I'd rule the world." Goldie's got "solid gold instincts" and she smells a rat when her ex-husband goes missing. Finding an instant rapport with the Lieutenant, she flirts with him and calls him "lover." She's a thoroughly likable character, in complete contrast with the villain of the piece.

Elliot has no time at all for Columbo. A man of a different type would have invited our detective to dine with him (as many of Columbo's adversaries do when they are both hungry). Instead, he rudely refuses the Lieutenant's generous offer of some of his raisins, and later, half a candy bar produced from his raincoat pocket. Our villain doesn't seem to be interested in food at all, unlike the actor who played him.

In 1969 when this recipe was published, Patrick O'Neal was the proprietor of a very successful restaurant in New York called, The Ginger Man. The restaurant was named after a play Patrick starred in on Broadway. The restaurant specialized in French cuisine, and Patrick's favorite dish on the menu was this beef ragout, made to his wife

Cynthia's recipe. It takes some time to prepare, but it's well worth it! You will need a MASSIVE ovenproof casserole dish if you make the whole recipe. It's easy to halve the quantities though if you are not feeding the five thousand, and this freezes well.

Patrick O'Neal's Ragout de Boeuf Bourguignon (Beef Stew in Red Wine)

5 lbs / 2250g lean boneless rump pot roast cut into 1-inch cubes
Seasoned flour
2 tablespoons vegetable oil (or butter)
1 lb / 450g piece lean bacon, cut into strips, ¼ inch thick by 1 inch [I use pancetta]
4 leeks, chopped (white part only)
4 onions peeled and coarsely chopped
2 cloves garlic, crushed
3 carrots, peeled and coarsely chopped
Large handful of parsley, washed and coarsely chopped
3 stalks celery, coarsely chopped
Bouquet garni, tied in a cheesecloth bag (large bay leaf, large pinch thyme, 7 bruised peppercorns)
Salt and pepper
1 bottle Beaujolais (or high quality dry red wine)
2 dozen pearl onions, peeled
1 lb / 450g fresh, button mushrooms, stemmed and cleaned
1½ teaspoons sweet/unsalted butter

Preheat oven to 375 degrees F / 190 degrees C / gas mark 5.

Dredge meat cubes in seasoned flour; brown meat on all sides in vegetable oil (or butter); set aside. Half fry bacon strips over medium heat in Dutch oven / ovenproof casserole dish; pour off excess fat. Add chopped vegetables (leeks, onions, garlic, carrots, parsley, and celery); cook over medium heat until vegetables are transparent. Add bouquet garni, 1½ teaspoons salt, black pepper to taste and wine. Bring to simmer; correct seasonings. Cover, place in oven, cook for one hour.

Add pearl onions, re-cover, cook about 1½ hours longer (or until meat is fork tender). Meanwhile, slowly brown mushrooms in sweet butter, and add these to stew during last few minutes of cooking. Remove cover to allow moisture to evaporate and sauce to thicken during last half an hour of cooking. Baste meat and vegetables several times. To serve, remove remove bouquet garni, adjust seasonings, and reduce the sauce if necessary by cooking rapidly over high heat. Serve the stew in its cooking dish (or arrange the meat and vegetables on a heated platter) with parsley-buttered new potatoes (or noodles) and pass the sauce.

Serves 12 - 16

Just one more thing... Gaye Fisher of Sticky Mitts, tested this for me and proclaimed it to be, "Delish!" Indeed it is. Gaye used rump skirt (as it's her favorite cut of beef for a slow-cooked dish). Gaye says, "I shared the meal with my husband and we both enjoyed it. There was some leftover gravy which we gave to our dog Brody, but he turned his nose up at it. Clearly, no gourmet!" Gaye shared a tip for peeling the pearl onions: cover them with hot water for a few minutes to loosen the skins.

Fellow Bread Angel, DiCooks of the Aston Parish Bakery made this for a dinner party of 6, using shin of beef and braising it for longer than the recipe suggested. Her verdict was, "Unanimous opinion - very tasty and would love to eat again." I'm afraid her guests did not feel quite the same way about the Leonard Nimoy Potatoes La Jolla Chez Jay (see entry for *A Stitch in Crime*).

THE SECOND SEASON (1972-1973)

ÉTUDE IN BLACK - 1972

If everyone you work with calls you "maestro," it would tend to inflate your ego, right? Even if you are a musical genius, it's still going to puff you up when everyone, including Columbo, keeps telling you how fabulous you are. I'm guessing that you would start to believe your own hype and consider yourself pretty invincible. Which is why nothing can be allowed to stain the reputation of the virtuoso conductor, Alex Benedict, played by virtuoso actor, John Cassavetes.

For a while, I wondered if Alex was wearing sunglasses indoors for sartorial reasons, but there is a brilliant "blink and you'll miss it" moment in this episode where something is reflected in them, which is absolutely crucial to the plot. In this excellent *Columbo*, with a screenplay written by the brilliant Stephen Bochco, nothing is superfluous to requirements, absolutely everything counts.

When Columbo visits the maestro's extremely grand house, he is obviously very impressed with the architecture and décor. He thinks it's a "Terrific place, terrific." Later the Lieutenant announces, "This is a dream house!" He questions Alex about how much he pays in taxes on the place and does some sums in his head about how much the house is worth. Alex wonders if he's ever going to get to the point. As Columbo continues to ask questions about money, how much Alex's furniture cost, how much he earns from touring and concerts, Alex looks increasingly annoyed. "What's the point, huh?" he asks Columbo. "I guess the point got delayed because I got so wrapped up in the house," interjects the Lieutenant, who continues to ramble away, asks for an autograph for his wife and then leaves. If I was Alex, I would be very, very worried indeed.

The maestro plays along with Columbo's bumbling routine, and calls him an "audacious fellow" and a "cocky fellow." When the Lieutenant eventually reveals that he believes the conductor has committed the murder, Alex pretends to be amused by his hunch. He laughs, "I'm having a little difficulty imagining this hypothetical court case, I mean, there's no real proof... I don't think your theory holds up too well Lieutenant." But he is rattled of course. In fact, of all the villains in the 69 episodes of Columbo, I think John Cassavetes plays it the most rattled of all.

When Columbo reveals his key piece of evidence at the end of the episode, Alex knows he's been rumbled and says: "You're a great detective. You knew from the very beginning, didn't you?" Columbo doesn't respond. As Alex is about to be taken away by the cops, he shakes Columbo's hand, "goodbye genius!" It's great when the villain finally acknowledges the superior intellect of the Lieutenant!

There is great chemistry between the two leads in this episode, as they were very close friends in real life. It's a great *Columbo* to watch with friends of your own. I would buy an appropriate amount of pink carnations and give one to each of your guests. If you've got enough sunglasses around the place, you could each wear these too and have classical music playing before and after your screening. If you are not a bunch of boozers, you could drink great big glasses of iced tea, or if you like a drink, maybe some chilled white wine as both are featured in this episode.

A note before we begin, I think that these meatballs need twice the amount of sauce this recipe makes - this makes a LOT of meatballs! I would personally make the sauce x 2 - or halve the meatball mix. But here is the recipe with quantities as provided by John, with due credit to his wife Gena Rowlands.

John's recipe specifies putting meat through a grinder with one of the chopped onions, but if you don't have a grinder, you could either ask the butcher to do this for you or buy ready ground / minced beef then mix this thoroughly with the chopped onion. John's recipe for meatballs doesn't call for frying up the balls first, which I sometimes do. In John's recipe, they just poach in the sauce. This is a great dish for a crowd (in my opinion this amount of meatballs would serve more than 4), you could get chums to lend a hand making the meatballs. You might have to cook them in a couple of batches though unless you have enormous pans!

John Cassavetes' Youvarlakia (Minted Beef)

2 large onions, very finely chopped, divided use
2 tablespoons butter
1 x 16 oz / 400g can chopped tomatoes
1 can water (use the can the tomatoes were in, to measure the water)
½ teaspoon sugar
Salt and pepper
1½ lbs / 675g top round steak/rump steak, ground/minced
2 teaspoons fresh mint, chopped
2 eggs, beaten
1 cup / 190g rice, uncooked

Sauté one of the onions in butter until golden. Add tomatoes, water, sugar, plus salt and pepper to taste. Simmer for about 30 minutes, or until volume has reduced by about ⅓, stirring often. Mix meat with the other onion. Add mint, eggs, and rice. With hands, form meat mixture into 1½ inch balls. Drop meatballs into boiling sauce. Cook 10-15 minutes, or until rice is cooked. John advises adding some water so that the meatballs won't stick to the pot.

Serves 4

Just one more thing... Bread guru, Liz Wilson, aka Ma Baker, enjoyed this dish with her daughter and a glass of red. She agreed with me about the ratio of sauce to meatballs and exclaimed, "What a lot of meatballs! Couldn't fit them all in the pan!" Liz added a lot of water to the sauce and threw in some tomato paste to give it a richer taste. I agree with Liz that you can't taste the mint much in the finished dish, so you could always sprinkle a little chopped mint on top to increase the minty flavor.

Lynne Barnsley who lives in the Staffordshire Moorlands, and has a wonderful blog called Moorlands Eater, also felt that the dish needed a lot more mint. Lynne cooked her meatballs for twice as long as the recipe states, so that her rice was fully cooked. She made double the sauce (as we all agree that there is something screwy with the recipe ratio). For her doubled up sauce, Lynne also upped the ratio of mint to 4 tablespoons, (admitting that mint is her favorite herb). Lynne pointed out, "Individual appetites naturally vary, and it depends what you accompany it with, but I think for most people it would serve more than 4. We're pretty greedy, but it still made 5-6 portions for us." Yes, this makes a LOT of meatballs - get a gang of chums over!

THE GREENHOUSE JUNGLE - 1972

Ray Milland appears in two episodes of *Columbo*. He's the only co-star to play a baddie and a goodie. I think he's better at the baddie.

As a Brit, I always love it when one of Columbo's adversaries is super-British. Ray (although he was born in Wales), plays a very upright English ex-pat called Jarvis Goodland, with more than a little of the Cary Grant about him. Nobody could intone: "Why do you insist upon being in love with a wife who spends all your cash on some skiing instructor?" with more venom than Jarvis does, I'm sure. He's pompous, opinionated, and therefore, a great foil for the Lieutenant. Anyone who believes that they are infinitely superior to Columbo, as Jarvis obviously does, will be in for a rude awakening.

There are some excellent comedy moments in this episode, not the least of which, is Columbo hurtling down a hillside and falling over. It makes me laugh every time I see it (and I've seen it many, many times). As an expert on expensive, rare orchids, Jarvis' face is a picture when Columbo turns up with a ropey African violet belonging to his wife, hoping for some advice on how to perk it up. Jarvis remarks, "That is the most miserable specimen I have ever seen. My only advice to you Columbo is to throw it in the trash can."

I love it when Jarvis admits, "Frankly, I'm a little unraveled," after delivering some ransom money to a kidnapper. When Columbo wishes him a pleasant night, he scowls, "I suppose that's gallows humor," and drives off. He is quite rude to the Lieutenant, but then, he does have a body in the trunk of his car. When Columbo beats around the bush a bit, asking Jarvis some questions about a gun, Jarvis seems amused, "Columbo, you are marvelous. Transparent, but marvelous." But when the Lieutenant turns up at 3 o'clock in the morning, skulking around in the villain's greenhouse, our orchid expert loses his temper. He barks, "Lieutenant, it's been a trying evening, and I'm quite distressed. Now, will you please take your African violet and get out of here?" But Columbo is waiting for "some things from headquarters" and when he reveals how he has mastered a modern new method of detection, to find the crucial evidence, it's an absolutely brilliant gotcha!

A character in this episode mentions they have met a strange policeman. Jarvis asks, "Rumpled raincoat? Rumpled face?" which is a great way of identifying the Lieutenant. He may be rumpled, but he's also a deep thinker. When the case is going cold, he goes to a roadside chili stand, to get some sustenance and thinking time. The cook asks Columbo if he wants his chili with or without beans, and he asks, "Last night I had it with beans?" The cook answers in the affirmative. The Lieutenant replies, "I'll have it without beans. Variety."

Like Columbo, I could probably eat chili night after night. But here's something that, these days, unless you live close to a lobster pot, is a bit of a fancy dish to have once in a while as a treat. It does make you feel like a million dollars if you can afford to buy fresh lobster, especially if you live somewhere landlocked.

Martinis get a mention in this episode when Jarvis states, "Blood is thicker than martinis," which I think is as good an excuse as any to rustle some up! Martin Landau's specifications for the perfect martini can be found in the "Columbo's Chili and Other Delights" section.

Martinis and lobster? Living the life, Ray Milland style!

Ray Milland's Lobster Salad

1 cooked lobster (1-1½ lb / 450g-675g)
French dressing
1 cup / 325g cooked potatoes, diced
Mayonnaise
Salt and pepper
Lettuce or other salad greens
½ cucumber, thinly sliced
5 firm tomatoes, peeled and sliced
2 hard-boiled eggs, cooled and sliced
1 cup / 120g celery, finely sliced
1 teaspoon chopped parsley
Watercress or another cress

Remove lobster shell and cut lobster meat into pieces. Soak lobster meat in French dressing, and chill. Marinate potatoes in mayonnaise, adding salt and pepper to taste. Ingredients can be placed on the salad greens in separate "lines" (overlapping slices of cucumber down one line, tomato down the next, egg slices down the next and so on, with the potatoes sprinkled with chopped parsley dividing each "line") Allow lobster meat to drain before serving, and place at base of "lines". Garnish with watercress or another cress.

Serve with French dressing and salt and pepper to taste.

Serves 6

Just one more thing... I made this with my wonderful and much-loved friend, Cathy (aka Battenburgbelle), and it was such a fun thing to rustle up together. Neither of us had ever eaten lobster before (such sheltered lives) and we loved it. We wondered whether our enthusiasm for it was due to the fact that lobster is very expensive in the UK, and therefore a super-treat. Cathy didn't think so and said something that really made me guffaw, "I don't like things just because they are expensive, unless they are clothes!"

THE MOST CRUCIAL GAME - 1972

It does not do, to lose your temper in front of the Lieutenant. Robert Culp does this in two of the episodes he appears in, and when someone is "excitable," Columbo gets suspicious. You can see why the Lieutenant would annoy someone like Paul Hanlon. He thinks he's planned the perfect murder, but of course, he's left some loose ends. Columbo loves to grab hold of a loose end and worry away at it until he can tie it up.

Paul, the manager of a football team, gets exasperated by Columbo very soon after he turns up at his office. Their interactions are full of suppressed anger, and Robert Culp depicts someone gripped by a simmering furiousness, absolutely brilliantly. Rare amongst Columbo's adversaries, Paul actually shouts at the Lieutenant. When he finally loses it with the Lieutenant's persistent questioning, he turns down his radio and bellows, "Columbo, I'm trying to watch this game, what IS it?!" This gives the Lieutenant an important clue. Tantrums always interest Columbo. They don't bother him, but they interest him.

Paul doesn't mince his words and says a couple of things I am sure many have thought, but not articulated. "Your wife has my sympathy," he proclaims when Columbo is chattering on about how his wife is always talking when he's trying to watch football and he only has half an ear on what she is saying. Paul also pleads: "will you please find someone else to pester?" But pestering is what Columbo does best, and the manager eventually yells, "Columbo, I'm gonna throw you out of here on your ear!" little knowing that the Lieutenant's ear, is the very thing that has found the clue that will break his alibi.

As mentioned before, I can't find a recipe for Robert Culp, so here's one from another great Columbo co-star who appears in this episode, Valerie Harper. Valerie plays a call-girl, the kind of chick who loves to be taken to dinner at Chasen's, a legendary Hollywood eatery where movie stars liked to hang out. If her "special friend" isn't hungry though, she'll accept being taken to a Hawaiian luau for drinks instead. A bit more down to earth in real life, Valerie offered this simple but tasty vegetarian recipe for Summer Squash.

If you are having your *Columbo* screening in the summer, it would be marvelous if you could coordinate your meal around the time the ice-cream truck comes to your neighborhood. When the music sounds, you can proclaim "Ding-a-Ling ice-cream!" and run out and get some for your guests. If you don't feel like making the Summer Squash, how about having the traditional food served at an American football game, hot dogs?

You could, of course, have the Lieutenant's favorite dish, chili, with this episode. He has an untouched bowl in front of him at a seaside cafe at one point. He's listening some taped telephone conversations, and is so distracted he doesn't eat a forkful. Chasen's, mentioned by Valerie, was famous for its chili and we see the Lieutenant having a bowl there in *Publish or Perish,* so I've provided the recipe for Chasen's chili in the "Columbo's Chili and Other Delights" section of this book.

Valerie Harper's Summer Squash

3 tablespoons butter
1 onion, finely chopped
1 clove garlic, finely chopped or crushed
1 green pepper, chopped
4 medium tomatoes, peeled and chopped
Salt and pepper
1½ lbs / 675g summer squash or for those in the UK, courgettes
1 cup / 90g grated Parmesan cheese

Preheat oven to 350 degrees F / 175 degrees C / gas mark 4.

Sauté onions, garlic and green pepper in butter until tender and light brown. Add tomatoes, ½ teaspoon salt, and pepper to taste; cook, stirring occasionally while you prepare the squash. Peel squash if the skin is not tender. Cut into slices or cubes. Add ½ cup boiling water, cover tightly and cook until squash is just tender; drain.

Turn half of the squash into a deep pie pan or casserole dish. Cover with half of the tomato sauce and half of the cheese; repeat layers. Bake until cheese topping is bubbly and beginning to brown (about 10 minutes).

Serves 2

Just one more thing... My own personal Bread Angel and bread making guru, Juli Farkas of the Our Bread East Sheen Microbakery tested this recipe for me and shared it with her son. She left out the garlic (as he was eating just before a shift as an anesthetist and he didn't want to breathe garlic over people). They enjoyed the dish, but Juli suggested the following tweak: "I would have extracted some water from the courgettes, by shrinking with salt and leaving to drip for about 20 min and then rinsing it and roasting in the oven with a little olive oil." Yes, I think that is a very good idea. The verdict from East Sheen? "My son thought it was nice even without the garlic - 'it is the Parmesan that makes this dish' he said before he went off to put people to sleep."

Fellow film archivist, Margie Compton in Athens, Georgia, enjoyed Valerie's dish with some pasta. She went a bit off-piste on the recipe and added matchstick carrots (which is a good modification in my book). Margie sent me a photo of her dish and I was jealous of the fact she had access to a yellow summer squash (rare as hen's teeth here in the UK).

DAGGER OF THE MIND - 1972

Columbo in London? Blimey! What larks.

There is, of course, much fun to be had with the Lieutenant being out of his familiar milieu of sunny Los Angeles, stumbling around in rainy old England. The Brits are amused by his accent, his misunderstandings of English customs and manners, and his manic tourist routine with a camera borrowed from his brother-in-law.

Honor Blackman and Richard Basehart play stage actors Lillian Stanhope and Nicholas Frame, just about to launch a new Shakespeare play in London's West End. If you have ever been around Shakespearian actors, you'll know that overacting is the norm, both onstage and off. It's certainly the case with these two.

I was shocked at first when Lillian said the name of the play out loud in her dressing room; *Macbeth*. Were the writers of this episode not aware that British actors believe that uttering this name inside a theatre will surely cause disaster? Thespians always refer to *Macbeth* reverentially as *The Scottish Play*. Mind you, disaster does ensue, so perhaps this is a deliberate ploy by the writers, an in-joke for those in the know.

When the Lieutenant starts asking the two leads probing questions, Nicholas leaps up and accuses him of having "some vulgar American notion of a love triangle" between himself, Lillian, and the murder victim. He pretends to believe that Columbo has been influenced by the theatrical setting they are in, proclaiming, "The play is rather suggestive of murder I suppose, to impressionable minds." The Lieutenant confesses he's never seen anything like this theatrical couple. He knows that they are giving a performance for his behalf, but he can see through their playacting.

Columbo's host in London, Detective Chief Superintendent Durk wears a Macintosh (British term for raincoat) too, but it's much cleaner and smarter than Columbo's. It appears to have a detachable fur collar, I wonder if Columbo is envious of this? I think he would be! Durk takes Columbo to his gentleman's club and the Lieutenant is thrilled to see the "tea" on offer; lots of cold meats, Stilton cheese, chops and a massive trolley laden down with cakes and other goodies. He'd been expecting,

"...nothing but those tiny sandwiches," so he thinks this spread is, "... terrific." Unfortunately, the pathologist arrives and puts Columbo right off his grub, describing the victim's injuries and flashing gory photos of them around. The poor Lieutenant! He can't eat a single mouthful.

I have a feeling that Columbo would have really enjoyed Richard's signature dish. We know for sure that the Lieutenant likes frankfurters, as we see him eat them in several episodes. These wieners are hot dogs with a twist. If you want to make a meal of it, Honor's recipe for Golden Sponge Pudding is in the "Columbo's Chili and Other Delights" section.

If you are watching this episode before luncheon, you might take the very English and very proper butler's advice to Columbo, that a glass of sherry, a nice Amontillado would be appropriate. Otherwise, there's plenty of good old British beer quaffed in this episode too, which might seem more appropriate for this down to earth dish. If you are in the mood for celebrating, you could make a day of it; have breakfast in bed with Champagne and croissants like Lillian and Nicholas do. Even better if you can arrange for an English butler to serve them to you.

Finally, there is a classic Columbo scene involving fish and chips. The Lieutenant eats some out of paper, as he walks along the Embankment, wiping his mush with a handkerchief after observing, "Those fish and chips are greasy, but they're sure good." So if all else fails, get yourself down to the chippy and get takeaway cod and chips with a wally (an oversized gherkin or pickle to those outside London or Essex).

Richard is very vague with his ingredients, so it's up to you how much brown sugar you use, depends on how sweet your tooth. Ditto the parsley, just sprinkle over however much you fancy. Richard specified lean bacon for this recipe, but I prefer this made with what we here in the UK call streaky bacon. You'll need thin cut bacon so you can wrap it easily around your franks. Delicious! I also heat up the beans first to ensure they are piping hot when served.

Richard Basehart's Beans and Frankfurters

2 medium cans baked beans
Brown sugar
Chopped parsley
12 wieners/frankfurter sausages
Mustard
Dill pickles/gherkins
12 or more rashers of bacon

In the baking pan of the broiler/grill, empty the cans of baked beans. Sprinkle with brown sugar and chopped parsley. On the wire rack place twelve stuffed wieners/frankfurters prepared as follows: Cut wiener in half lengthwise and spread with prepared mustard. Add a slice of dill pickle. Put together and wrap with lean bacon, fastening the ends with toothpicks. Place in broiler / under the grill and cook on a low heat until wieners are nicely browned on all sides, by which time the beans will be thoroughly heated.

Serve together.

Serves 6

Just one more thing... Silver Screen Suppers blog reader, Bethany B. in Michigan, tried this with her mom. They enjoyed the flavor but felt that too much of the bacon fat made its way into their beans. I think that British bacon tends to be leaner than American bacon, so you might wish to bear this in mind when cooking this dish. Bethany recommends 2 x 28 oz cans of Bush's Original Baked Beans, drained, 1-2 tablespoons of brown sugar, and 1 tablespoon of chopped parsley. For Brits, I would suggest 4 x 400g cans of beans for 6 people (or more if they are bean lovers). I loved Bethany's comment about the parsley in this recipe, "it's really not there for taste, it's really just there for presentation and to give the illusion of healthy eating." Yes!

REQUIEM FOR A FALLING STAR - 1973

I adore Anne Baxter, and Columbo does too. We know he does, because when he meets her he exclaims, "I've been in love with you all my life!" She plays actress Nora Chandler, and he tells her that Mrs. Columbo and himself have been fans of hers since high school. Nora takes Columbo's declaration of his love in her stride, "I know!" she states, "You never expected to meet a legend!" holding out her arms in a dramatic pose. But of course, being a homicide detective in the vicinity of Hollywood, Columbo meets many legends, most of them murderers.

Our man is a little star-struck, or at least pretends to be, but it isn't long before he's cottoned on to the fact that Nora is a great actress in real life, as well as onscreen. Like many of Columbo's female suspects, Nora flirts a little with the Lieutenant, deciding that she can find a much nicer tie for him to wear. She asks legendary costume designer Edith Head if she can find him one. In these days where fewer men are wearing ties, it's not as easy for us girls to charm a man by replacing his tie with one we prefer. This scenario, however, appears in a couple of *Columbo* episodes, and he seems to like it. Or at least pretends to like it. The Lieutenant is a good actor too.

Nora behaves like the great star she is throughout, and is polite and gracious to the Lieutenant, almost until the very end of the episode. When he begins revealing to her how he's worked out what really happened, she gets a little nervous. "You know, you're priceless!" she announces. As he is closing in and her perfect movie star facade is beginning to crumble, her irritation with him reaches a peak. With wild hair and wild eyes, she rages, "I find you amusing up to a point Lieutenant, but you've passed that." When he reveals that he has worked out her big secret, she looks suitably broken. Columbo accepts her offer of a drink and she confides in him, confessing everything. Downing her drink and regaining her composure, she returns to being the consummate professional, proclaiming, "Well, I'll get a coat, and we'll go."

Anne's is the best quiche recipe ever. I have won prizes for this in my local horticultural society show several times! Her spicing with nutmeg, cinnamon, cayenne, and mustard is perfect. It also makes a pretty big quiche, so you'll need a large quiche dish. I always have too much filling for my quiche tin, so I make a few small individual ones too, adjusting the cooking time. I usually pop the unfilled pie crust back into the oven for a minute or two after taking out the baking beans. This avoids having a quiche with a soggy bottom. You don't want that, do you?!

It's great to see legendary costume designer Edith Head in this episode, though it's easy to see she's not an actress! If you don't fancy Anne's quiche, why not try Edith's recipe for Chicken Casa Ladera which you will find in the "Columbo's Chili and Other Delights" section.

Anne Baxter's Genuine Swiss Quiche

Shortcrust pastry for a 9-inch quiche tin
3 slices bacon, chopped into small pieces or cubes
1 cup / 150g sliced onions
4 eggs
1 cup / 240ml milk
½ cup / 120ml light or heavy cream/single or double cream
¼ teaspoon salt
1 tablespoon flour
¼ teaspoon dry mustard
¼ teaspoon nutmeg
¼ teaspoon cayenne pepper
¼ teaspoon cinnamon

8 oz / 225g Swiss cheese such as Gruyere thinly sliced or grated

Preheat oven to 400 degrees F / 205 degrees C / gas mark 6.

Line a quiche dish with the pastry. Use a fork to make holes in the pastry. Cover the pastry with waxed paper or foil, weighed down with dried beans. Place in oven and bake for 15-20 minutes. Remove crust from the oven and discard the paper liner.

Fry the bacon until crisp, remove the bacon, leaving the fat in the pan, and allow to drain on paper toweling. Sauté the onions in the bacon fat until transparent, do not brown. Pour the contents of the pan on top of the pastry, spreading the onions around.

Beat the eggs well. Add the milk and cream, and beat. Add salt, the flour, and all the seasonings. Beat until well blended. Distribute the cheese evenly over the onions and then pour in the beaten mixture. Crumble the bacon and distribute over the top.

Put back into the oven and bake for 25 to 30 minutes. Test by inserting knife, if it comes out clean, the pie is finished.

Delicious with a nice green salad.

Serves 6

Just one more thing... Prolific test cook Peter Fuller of the Vincent Price Legacy UK, sent me a hilarious photograph of the results of using a flan dish with a removable bottom for this quiche. A stream of creamy deliciousness escaping all over his kitchen counter, down his kitchen cupboards, and onto the floor - oops! It's best to use a solid receptacle unless you can be very sure your pastry will have no holes in it... Despite his misadventures with the tin, Peter's feedback was, "Nice golden texture and really tasty, especially the cinnamon and nutmeg. And even though rather flat, the cheese and onion gave it some body. Will certainly attempt again... but with a different quiche tin."

A STITCH IN CRIME - 1973

Columbo rarely loses his temper, but he does so in this episode. I wonder if it is because his foe is so totally, steely cool. Leonard Nimoy plays surgeon, Dr. Barry Mayfield. Very well respected, he is suitably inscrutable, super-controlled, and self-contained. But someone is standing in the way of his career advancement and he plans to do something about that.

The doctor is standoffish with the Lieutenant when they first meet. Columbo has had a sleepless night and is desperate for his morning java. At the hospital, he asks Mayfield, "Is there a coffee machine on this floor?" The curt response is: "No," with no polite follow up to advise the detective where he might find some caffeine. As Mayfield strides away, Columbo collars him to ask something in confidence. He confesses that hospitals make him queasy and he sometimes faints, asking if there is anything he can do about that. Doctor's advice? "There's only one, surefire cure Lieutenant, stay out of hospitals as much as possible."

There's a great scene that perfectly illustrates how Columbo often seems out of place at the grand homes of his rich or famous suspects. The Lieutenant arrives at Mayfield's house whilst a glamorous party is underway. Unshaven, disheveled and hungry, he sticks out like a sore thumb amongst the beautiful people milling around the pool. When he arrives, Columbo is offered an hors-d'oeuvre. He studiously examines the tray and asks the maid what a particular canapé is. She explains, "Salmon on toast with caviar and sour cream, it's delicious!" He hesitates and asks, "You don't have anything with just plain cheese?" He's shown to a buffet table heaving with food, and he piles up a plate. When the party host spots this uninvited guest, the Lieutenant explains to him, at great length, why he's so hungry. While Columbo munches his way through an enormous plateful of nibbles, his perfectly poised adversary barely sips his martini.

The doctor's bedside manner, such as it is, starts to get a little shaky when he realizes that the Lieutenant is not as dumb as he seems. When Columbo is closing in, Mayfield laughs in his face and asks, "You don't really believe all those foolish things you say, do you?" Columbo bangs a coffee pot on his desk and flat out accuses him of murder. The doctor's responds, "Lieutenant Columbo, you're remarkable. You have intelligence, you have perception, you have great tenacity. You have everything except proof."

But as always, the Lieutenant's powers of detection will find him the proof. Although the perfectly presented and mega-intelligent surgeon appears to be on a higher plane, he's ultimately brought right back down to earth by an unshaven man in a grubby raincoat.

I think that this is the first time we see Columbo produce one of his staple dietary items from his raincoat pocket, a hard-boiled egg. So if you decide to throw a Dr. Mayfield-style party with a buffet, make sure you have some of these on hand for your guests.

This dish was invented by Leonard Nimoy, and Jay Fiondella, founder of legendary restaurant Chez Jay. They were flat-mates at some point. It's a bit odd, but it's good! If this is not your kind of thing, there's a recipe for Gazpacho from the kitchen of Ann Francis in the "Columbo's Chili and Other Delights" section which would be good with this episode too.

Leonard Nimoy's Potatoes La Jolla Chez Jay

½ medium onion
4 cold baked potatoes
3 bananas
6 tablespoons butter
2 tablespoons melted chicken fat (or butter)
Light / single cream
2 teaspoons meat extract / Bovril for the Brits
½ teaspoon salt
Grated parmesan cheese
Paprika

Chop the onion, peel and cut the potatoes into ½ inch cubes, peel and slice the bananas. Melt the butter in a frying pan or saucepan that has a lid and fry the onion in it until it is soft. Add the potatoes, bananas, chicken fat, meat extract, salt and enough light cream to cover the mixture. Mix well. Cook covered over very low heat for about 45 minutes, stirring occasionally, until the bananas disappear into the sauce. Do not let it boil. While the mixture is cooking, preheat the oven to 400 degrees F / 205 degrees C / gas mark 6.

Place mixture into a baking dish spread it out evenly, and sprinkle with Parmesan cheese and a little paprika. Bake uncovered for about 10 minutes until the cheese is lightly browned.

Serves 2

Just one more thing... I invited my cherished friend, Lucy Brookes, to try this recipe for me. Her response was: "Potato, onion, and banana - yowzer! No, I'll not be test cooking that bad boy, Hammertoes." Cult film-maker, Jan Manthey, emailed that he regretted that he wouldn't have time to cook the "Spock Potatoes" by my publishing deadline. Ben Reed reported that his girlfriend Laura, "... has ruled out the Nimoy potatoes with bananas - she's not brave enough." There has been tumbleweed from several other test cooks who have volunteered for this recipe, then disappeared. Is it really that weird? Why not try it and see for yourself. "It's potatoes Jim, but not as we know them."

Stop the presses! Ace chef and fellow Bread Angel, DiCooks made these to accompany Patrick O'Neal's Ragout de Boeuf Bourguignon. I loved Di's very Spock-like, "damning with faint praise" comment, "Interesting but would not try again." She reported that her dinner guests were craving anchovies in this dish and loved everything about the meal, "… except those bloody bananas!"

THE MOST DANGEROUS MATCH - 1973

Laurence Harvey plays chess champion, Emmett Clayton, in this episode, and very suave he is about it too. He's got a stiff upper lip and is very, very uptight.

Some chess fans feel that the only reason Emmett holds the chess Grandmaster title is because Tomlin Dudek, "the greatest master of chess that ever lived," had to retire due to ill health. But unfortunately for Emmett, Dudek has just about recovered enough, to challenge him to a match.

The year before this episode was aired, American chess legend Bobby Fischer won the World Chess Championship by beating Boris Spassky of the USSR. This match attracted worldwide interest, as it was pitched by the press as a Cold War battle. It's very likely that viewers of this episode's first airing would have linked the main protagonists, in their minds, with Spassky and Fischer.

As always when the Lieutenant is thrust into a world of experts, he's keen to bone up on their specialized subject. Columbo suspects Emmett of murdering his opponent. When he begins the pursuit, our detective claims that he was only hoping to learn some chess moves from him. When he says that he'd "love to learn the game," Emmett's curt response is, "If you'd love to learn the game, I suggest a correspondence course." He can't brush Columbo off that easily though, and the Lieutenant continues to badger him.

Columbo observes, "From what I know about chess players, that is, the important ones, they are like geniuses, unpredictable, erratic…" This is certainly true of Emmett, and like many geniuses, he can't resist showing off his intellect to his pursuer. Key to the chess player's skill is the possession of a photographic memory, and when Emmett reveals he can remember the very first thing the Lieutenant said to him by saying it backward, Columbo seems genuinely impressed. Emmett's memory is finely tuned, but it isn't this sense that fails him in the end, it's his hearing.

In a scene where Emmett is attempting to play multiple games of chess with an audience watching his every move, Columbo is leaning over the boards, asking increasingly difficult questions. Emmett begins to get very angry, accusing the Lieutenant of using: "innuendo, insinuation, circumstantial trivia" to try and trap him. Looking fiercely across the chessboard at Columbo he growls: "Do you really think the finest chess player in the world would make even half the mistakes you have ascribed to me?" When his partner stealthily moves a chess piece and announces, "Mr. Clayton, sir, I'm afraid that's check, and mate, sir", Emmett looks mortified. Columbo rubs salt into the wound by saying: "Just a foolish blunder, could have happened to anybody."

If you know how to play chess, you will almost certainly be itching for a game after this. Get yourself a chequered tablecloth, then grab yourself salt and pepper pots, bits of cheese, bottles of Tabasco and olives for your pawns, rooks, and bishops. Just as the great rivals do in a classic scene in a French restaurant, you can have a game without leaving the dinner table.

For health reasons, Emmett's opponent Dudek is on a strict diet. As he puts it "Sugar substitutes, everything low calorie. Bleaugh!" But he's a gourmand, so the night before his big match, he sneaks away from his entourage to grab something more toothsome. He revels in his chosen dinner, snails with butter and garlic, french bread and good wine. If you like escargots, this would be an ideal dish to serve alongside a screening of this episode. Make them good and garlicky, you'll see why. You could practice saying, in a Russian accent: "Garlic? Of course garlic is all right, why NOT garlic?" for the benefit of your guests.

Alternatively, when asked how he will relax the evening before a big chess match, Emmett replies, "A small martini perhaps, a large steak definitely." But if you are not a fan of steak or snails, here's Laurence's recipe for Chicken Pie. As he put it himself in the recipe book this appeared in, it is, "Yummy for the tummy."

Laurence Harvey's Chicken Pie

1 cooked chicken
3½ cups / 820ml chicken stock
½ lb / 225g bacon
Salt and pepper
1 onion, sliced
½ lb / 225g mushrooms, sliced
Parsley
3 leaves gelatin, divided use
2 hard-boiled eggs, cooled and sliced
Flaky pastry/puff pastry

Bone and cut the chicken into convenient sized pieces. Make a good strong stock with the carcass and 3½ cups / 850ml water. Strain off and allow to cool before making the pie.*

Preheat oven to 425 degrees F / 220 degrees C / gas mark 7.

Line the pie dish with the slices of bacon. Season the pieces of chicken well with salt and pepper. Mix the onion, mushrooms, and parsley together and add a little chicken stock with 1 gelatin leaf to help set.

Put the ingredients in the pie dish in layers of chicken, onion and mushroom mix, hard-boiled egg, etc… Then fill the dish with stock, reserving a little for the aspic. Cover with pastry and decorate.

Bake for approximately 35 minutes, with a piece of greaseproof paper wrapped around the pie. Decrease the heat of the oven, and continue cooking for about 1 hour.**

Leave to stand, but while still warm, coat the pastry with some chicken aspic made from the remaining chicken stock, boiled with the remaining leaves of gelatin. Allow to cool slightly before brushing onto the pastry.

* If you are in a hurry (or lazy like me) just use a good quality, pre-made chicken stock.

** I'm not sure why Laurence wrapped his pie in greaseproof paper - perhaps to avoid any filling spilling out? I didn't bother. He also didn't say how much to decrease the oven temperature by. I turned mine down to about 375 degrees F / 190 degrees C / gas mark 5.

Serves 4-6

Just one more thing... Raconteur, bon-viveur, bread-connoisseur Mike Nicholson was a pie making virgin, and so approached Laurence's recipe with the due mixture of reverence, fear, and excitement. He was pleased with the results, "I had always thought of pie making as a great skill, but this is a pie for novitiates, simple, an easy way in." Mike switched some veggies for the mushrooms (which made for a rather soggy pie), however, it was much enjoyed by himself and his lovely assistant Tracey. With some mash and greens to mop up the "jus," he proclaimed it would be, "Perfect Saturday night in front of the log-burner food." (With an episode of Columbo of course!)

Sarah Bailey of Sarah's Cooker-ebook, also made Laurence's pie and was a little puzzled by his use of gelatin. She wrote, "The recipe worked, but to be honest in its use of gelatin, it was a little odd. I'm quite at home using gelatin, and as per the recipe, I added some to the mushroom and onion mix, and it set. However, pouring stock over the whole filling in the pie dish and heating it during cooking of the whole pie, diluted the mushroom/onion/gelatin mix and reversed the gel effect. Once the pie cooled, it gelled again, but the bacon lining isn't one that creates an enclosed pie, so it can't be used as a picnic dish. I was a bit puzzled by the function of the gelatin in the filling." Me too Sarah! Laurence was very good looking, but I'm not sure he really knew what he was doing in the kitchen...

DOUBLE SHOCK - 1973

In the very first shot of this episode, we see an electric whisk. A clue that food is going to be important in this storyline. Our main character, played by Martin Landau, is a celebrity chef called Dexter Paris. His daytime TV show is called, *The Pleasures of Paris* and he's very much a hit with the ladies.

He charms his uncle's housekeeper, Mrs. Peck, by making some fancy strawberry cakes for her to take over to her sister's place. Getting her out of the way, so he can get up to mischief.

Dexter takes a facetious tone with the Lieutenant. When they first meet, Columbo is carrying a bath towel belonging to the murder victim. The Lieutenant explains that he has thrown some water on his face in the upstairs bathroom to clear his head, and Dexter inquires, "What were you planning to do? Dry your face on the way down the stairs? Was that your plan?" When the Lieutenant stages a re-enactment of the murder scene, lying in a bathtub fully clothed, Dexter seems to be amused. "Columbo, you're marvelous, you're absolutely bizarre," but he underestimates the Lieutenant, of course.

Dexter prepares asparagus with hollandaise sauce for his cooking show, so you could make some of this for a fun side dish to Martin Landau's steak. Dexter proclaims hollandaise sauce to be "an inexpensive magic, which transforms your lowly mundane vegetables into a gourmet delight". He tells the mostly female studio audience, that the dish he's going to demonstrate is so simple, that even their husbands could prepare it. Asking for a volunteer to help him demonstrate the recipe, he deliberately picks the Lieutenant, calling him an "everyday, average, typical downtrodden American husband." Some comedy cooking ensues. Peter Falk, quoted in Mark Dawidziak's, *The Columbo Phile*, explained that this scene was almost totally improvised on the day of filming.

The quantities in Dexter's hollandaise look a little screwy. Although he specifies four eggs, we clearly see him and the Lieutenant put eight into the blender, which makes the ½ cup of butter he specifies, seem far too little. He's a bit heavy-handed with the lemon juice too. So I'm proposing a recipe from a Columbo co-star we can trust, Vincent Price, who wrote several cookbooks and was a gourmet chef. His recipe for hollandaise sauce made in a blender is in the "Columbo's Chili and Other Delights" section. Vincent appears in the very next episode of Columbo, *Lovely but Lethal,* so you could serve something with hollandaise sauce alongside that episode too.

Jeanette Nolan plays my absolute favorite *Columbo* character, Mrs. Peck, a housekeeper who flies into a frenzy at the Lieutenant's terrible manners and clumsiness. Their burgeoning love/hate relationship is a lovely thing to behold. If the idea of making the steak doesn't appeal, you could make Jeanette's Sizzling Livers and Walnuts instead, the recipe for which you'll find in the entry for *The Conspirators.* Jeanette is almost unrecognizable in the later episode after you've gotten to know her as Mrs. Peck. If you don't fancy making a whole meal, how about making some "health cookies," which is what Mrs. Peck offers Columbo as a peace offering. I think Rue McClanahan's Wonder Women would classify as health cookies, you'll find her recipe in the entry for *Ashes to Ashes.*

So many food choices, for a very foodie episode… Oh, there's a Martin Landau Martini recipe in the "Columbo's Chili and Other Delights" section too!

Martin Landau's Jerk Beef Steak

¾ cup / 180ml Italian salad dressing
1 tablespoon Worcestershire sauce
1 tablespoon firmly packed brown sugar
1 large jalapeño pepper, seeded and finely chopped
1 teaspoon ground allspice
1 teaspoon ground ginger
1 beef top round/rump steak, 1-inch thick (about 1½ lbs / 675g)

For marinade, combine all ingredients except steak. Place steak in large, shallow, non-aluminum baking dish or plastic bag. Pour ½ cup / 120ml marinade over steak; turn to coat. Cover, or close bag, and marinate in refrigerator, turning occasionally for 6 to 24 hours. Refrigerate remaining marinade separately.

Remove steak from marinade, discarding the marinade remaining in the dish or bag.

Grill steak, turning occasionally and brushing frequently with the marinade that was reserved in the refrigerator. Grill for 16 to 18 minutes, or until steak is medium-rare to medium doneness.

Slice and serve.

Serves 4

Just one more thing... Silver Screen Suppers blog reader and Vincent Price fan, Kelli Cline of Seattle, made this dish at a BBQ dinner for her husband and some friends. Everyone really enjoyed it and said that they would definitely like to have it again. I loved the fact that Kelli wanted to be true to Martin's recipe and looked for the kind of salad dressing that he might have used himself. She decided upon Paul Newman's "Newman's Own," which she felt was appropriate given Paul's own star status. Absolutely perfect. Kelli rented the DVD of this episode and everyone settled down to watch it as they had dessert. This made for excellent entertainment and Kelli added, "I enjoyed the dual sides of Martin. He was quite a looker too!" I agree, Kelli!

LOVELY BUT LETHAL - 1973

Anyone who wears an entirely white outfit topped by a pristine white turban is fine by me. The wardrobe department for this episode pulled out all the stops, and Vera Miles looks absolutely sensational in every single outfit. Vera plays Viveca Scott, Queen of Cosmetics, who is ruthless in her quest for the ultimate anti-wrinkle cream. Her business rival is played, with great panache, by screen legend Vincent Price, and the two of them take great relish in throwing insults at each other.

It's an early morning murder-callout for Columbo, but luckily he has a hard-boiled egg in the pocket of his raincoat to snack on for breakfast. In the kitchen of the murder victim, he searches in vain for salt to sprinkle on his egg. Usually, he says, he carries a shaker in his pocket, but alas, not so on this occasion. Luckily for Columbo, while he is on his condiment hunt, he spots a clue he might otherwise have missed...

Beauty Mark is the name of Viveca's cosmetics business. For British readers, a beauty mark is what Americans call a beauty spot. This might seem irrelevant, but nothing is lost on Columbo of course, and there is a clue bound up with Viveca's beauty spot. Also worth pointing out to those not in North America, and too young to remember the popular 1960s song, poison ivy is a plant that causes a violent reaction when touched. Remember this refrain: "Poison ivy, Lord'll make you itch!"

Viveca gets annoyed with the Lieutenant when he questions her about a romantic relationship she once had with the murder victim. She screeches, "I like young men Lieutenant, lots of them, and if that shocks your masculine double-standard, I'm sorry." She thinks he belongs "in a museum," but Columbo is not a judgmental man when it comes to the love-lives of his suspects. We know this from many other episodes.

When Columbo comes to search for evidence at Viveca's health farm, he is suffering from poison ivy. She condescendingly asks him, "Poor thing, still worried about your itch?" But Viveca should be worried about hers. It's the itch that will send her to the Clink.

In the newspaper article from which this recipe of Vera's is taken, published in 1974, she is quoted as saying that she felt that there weren't many good acting roles for women. "It's a man's world, and so many of the writers are men who write for men." She must have been happy with this role in 1973 though, striding around her health farm in a bright, white jumpsuit, Viveca is the epitome of someone who "owns it." Vera is a fabulous actress and one of my very favorite *Columbo* adversaries.

Viveca's favorite tipple is apparently a tequila cocktail with organic cactus juice, so if you can get your hands on such a juice, that would be a fun thing to serve. It would fit with Vera's Mexican inspired dish too. A super-cheesy treat with chilies.

Vera Miles' Mexican Casserole

1 lb / 450g of Jack/Gouda cheese
1 lb / 450g of Cheddar cheese
6 eggs, separated
Salt
1½ tablespoons flour
Two small cans of green chili peppers
One fresh tomato, sliced
Dash of oregano

Preheat oven to 375 degrees F / 190 degrees C / gas mark 5.

Grate the two kinds of cheeses and mix together. Beat egg whites until stiff, adding about 1½ tablespoons flour for added body. Beat the egg yolks until fluffy and gently fold into the egg white mixture. Add a dash of salt to taste.

Chop the chili peppers. Vera says: "If you desire less of a hot taste, remove some of the chile seeds, as they contain the hot flavor." Grease a large casserole dish that would serve about five people and layer a portion of the egg mixture into the dish. Next layer part of the chopped chili pepper, ending with a portion of the cheese. Repeat until ingredients are used up. Arrange the fresh tomato over the top, and sprinkle with oregano.

Bake for 30 minutes or until mixture is set.

Serves 6 (or more according to test cooks!)

Just one more thing... Stalwart test cook Peter Fuller, curator of the Vincent Price Legacy UK, made a rather deluxe version of Vera's casserole, searing fresh chilies over a naked flame and scraping off the charred flesh before adding them to the dish. His feedback was as follows, "My tasters called it a glorified cheese toastie (grilled cheese sandwich), minus the bread. And I have to agree. It certainly should not be viewed as a main, rather as a side dish. I would suggest after baking, to cut it into small bite size pieces as a warm side dish, hors-d'oeuvre, canapé, or amuse bouche depending in what country you're celebrating. As for reheating leftovers, this doesn't work in a microwave as it turns into a slab of hot cheese. Best to reheat under a grill."

I think it is fair to say that this is a super cheesy dish that might be TOO cheesy for some. Test cook Samantha Ellis' husband, put it like this when he sampled a slice, "just tastes of cheese," so you might need a big salad with a sharp dressing or a ton of vegetables alongside this dish to cut through the cheesiness.

THE THIRD SEASON
(1973-1974)

ANY OLD PORT IN A STORM - 1973

There is no snob quite like a wine snob, and Donald Pleasence plays a superior wine snob in this episode. Adrian Carsini runs a vineyard in California but spends most of the profit on exceedingly expensive bottles of rare European wine. He thinks Columbo is an uneducated peasant who can't appreciate the finer things in life, but the Lieutenant proves him wrong of course. We know that Columbo enjoys his Bourbon, but he also has the capacity to enjoy a good Californian vintage too. He gets to drink a fair number of glasses of the good stuff in this episode.

Adrian finds Columbo very amusing. When the Lieutenant reveals he knows nothing about wine, Adrian asks, "You're an Italian aren't you?" Columbo replies that he is, on both sides. "Well, you should know about good wine, it goes with the heritage," laughs Adrian. Columbo admits that he messed up in that department. Later, he decides to go on a crash course in wine appreciation. Naturally, it doesn't take him long to learn. When he does exceedingly well in a "guess the wine" situation, the wine snob is astounded. After explaining his clever method of working it out, Adrian calls him "a sly one." He is indeed.

Donald Pleasence must have liked his curry. Two of the three recipes I have from him in the Silver Screen Suppers collection are for curry. The recipe is almost exactly the same in both recipe books, except that one features prawns, the other features canned salmon. I prefer the latter, purely because of its name Donald gave this dish. If you feel like a fancier din dins, Donald's recipe for Sole Bonne Femme can be found in the "Columbo's Chili and Other Delights" section.

In the episode's opening scene, Adrian is serving a superb claret to fellow wine experts. Produced in his own vineyard, he never sells any of this particular wine. He announces: "I'd rather serve it to my friends and watch their faces than sell it to some Texan bumpkin who'll stick it in the freezer and bring it out with a homemade chili." So if you don't fancy the curry, you could always serve Columbo's favorite - a nice bowl of chili - with a fine wine, just to poke a snook at Adrian Carsini. Serve the chili Columbo-style with saltines crumbled over. Beans or no beans in the chili? Columbo tends to alternate…

There is a brilliant phrase in *Any Old Port in a Storm* which is worth learning by heart if you plan to drink wine with guests. Hold up a glass and yell, "An exciting meal has been ruined by the presence of this liquid filth!" It's a classic *Columbo* catchphrase!

Donald Pleasence's No-name Curry

1 teaspoon ground coriander
2 teaspoons ground turmeric
½ teaspoon chili powder
1 tablespoon butter
½ teaspoon ginger
Ground garlic/garlic powder to taste
½ pint / 285ml milk*
2 tablespoons heavy/double cream
Large can of drained salmon
Shredded/desiccated coconut
Rice to serve

Preheat oven to 425 degrees F / 220 degrees C / gas mark 7.

Put coriander, turmeric and chili powder into a saucepan, add the butter, ginger, garlic and salt and pepper to taste. When the butter has melted, add the milk and cream, stirring until yellow. Add the can of drained salmon, cooking gently for a few minutes. Pour into a casserole dish, and cook for another 15 minutes in the oven. Just before serving, sprinkle shredded coconut over it and grill until lightly brown. Serve with a bowl of rice.

Serves 2

* This recipe appeared in a British cookbook, therefore Donald's pint would have been an imperial pint - 20% larger than an American pint so please add the amount of milk appropriate to the pint measurement in your neck of the woods. I use 2 x 213g cans of salmon for this recipe, that's around 15 oz.

Just one more thing... This dish is a bit of an acquired taste. I like it (but then I like weird food). Helen Coniam of the fabulous Dinner With Zelda Manners tried this with tofu instead of salmon and made me laugh by saying, "This isn't a recipe I would really recommend. I don't know (obviously) what it is like with the salmon, but I have better things to do with tofu than this." Indeed! She added, "I like curries which are either spicier or more packed with flavor. You could rustle this up in a hurry, though." This is very true Helen! It's a good thing to make in a rush when you have everything in the recipe on hand, but perhaps not something to scale up to make for a special dinner party! For Dave, Helen's other half, it was far too mild. In fact, Helen reports him saying, "If it was the only port in a storm, I might consider heading for it." Helen adds, "But we do need to remember that this is the opinion of a man who likes his curry so hot that it makes him sweat (and, on occasions, cry)."

CANDIDATE FOR CRIME - 1973

Politicians have to have a certain amount of bravado to get to the top, and Nelson Hayward has confidence in spades. But his super-cool exterior has been partly created by his campaign manager, Harry Stone, who acts as his spin doctor and scriptwriter. Nelson is running for a place in the United States Senate and appears to be a sure bet to win. But when puppet master Harry begins meddling in the puppet's private affairs, something's got to give and there's only one way Nelson can wrestle back control. Murder, of course.

Nelson believes that he should be able to have his cake and eat it too. As he puts it himself, he "likes to win." Selfishly, he wants his wife by his side as a campaigning companion, plus he wants to keep his mistress close by too. He tells his campaign manager, "Harry, I need her!" Nelson, like many politicians, believes he is above the law and will do whatever needs to be done so that he can have what he wants. It doesn't seem to cross his mind that he might be found out. Especially by a shambling sleuth like Columbo.

The Lieutenant seems to be caught up in the electioneering excitement, applauds, and smiles, just like everyone else, when Nelson arrives at campaign headquarters. However, when asked who he'll be voting for, he admits that he's "still a little bit on the fence." Mrs. Columbo, of course, will be voting for Nelson, as she's "crazy" about him. Hanging around outside Nelson's office, amongst all the hustle and bustle, Columbo observes absolutely everything, while he waits patiently to talk to his man.

When Nelson eventually has time for him, Columbo talks in a rambling way about how the case is going and begins expounding his theories with plenty of sidetracking about sneakers and pencils. Nelson is impatient with Columbo's bumbling style, "Excuse me, Lieutenant, don't misunderstand," interrupts the politician, "You're a very nice man, I like you very much, but I would hate to have to depend upon you if I was in a hurry for something..." He asks Columbo to "get to the point" three times. Nelson is a very, very busy man.

Like many politicians, he is extremely charismatic and thinks he can fool Columbo by turning on the charm. When Columbo arrives at his house and admits that something is bothering him, Nelson announces, "You think I'm reluctant to talk to you. But you're wrong. I will talk to you as often as you want, for as long as you want, about anything you want!" He then dismisses his entourage and turns his full attention to the Lieutenant, asking him to sit down and offering him a drink. Columbo seems a little flustered by all of this and admits, "Gee, you make me feel so important, I forgot what I was going to say…" Then he throws what seems like a curveball into the mix, "Listen. Let me start by saying how much I like your jacket…" When the Lieutenant says that he's been to visit Nelson's tailor, the politician makes a joke at Columbo's expense, "I'm sure he was delighted, he loves a challenge." But Nelson has underestimated Columbo's attention to detail; this visit to the fancy tailor's has provided him with a very good lead.

Nelson stages an elaborate hoax to try and throw the Lieutenant off the scent, but of course, Columbo is one step ahead of him. When the Lieutenant reveals how he worked out the modus operandi for the murder, for the first time possibly in his entire adult life, Nelson Hayward has absolutely nothing to say.

Jackie Cooper was a lovable child star, and when you see his early films, it's hard to imagine him growing up to be a cold-blooded killer. But *Columbo* co-stars revel in going against type, so playing a politician hatching a complicated plan for murder must have been lots of fun for him.

Jackie was just a kid in the 1930s when he told recipe book compilers that this was a favorite recipe. "Whenever my mother wants me to have a dish that contains all the vitamins that are necessary for a young chap who is growing by leaps and bounds, this is what she serves me, and boy is it good."

Jackie Cooper's Curried Eggs and Macaroni

½ lb / 225g macaroni
4 tablespoons butter
4 tablespoons flour
½-1 tablespoon curry powder
Salt and pepper
2 cups / 480ml milk
6 hard-boiled eggs, cooled and sliced
Buttered breadcrumbs

Bring a pan of salted water to boil, place macaroni in and let cook until tender. Drain and wash with hot water until all the starch is removed.

Next, make a cream sauce. Melt butter and add flour, curry powder, ½ teaspoon salt and milk. Cook until thickened and add to the macaroni.

Place macaroni in baking dish, alternating layers of macaroni with layers of hard-boiled eggs, ending with the macaroni on top. Sprinkle with buttered breadcrumbs and brown under the broiler/grill.

Serves 4-6

Just one more thing... This recipe was much enjoyed by Columbo fan Ian Baxter and his family in Lancashire and he gave due credit to his fellow cooks, saying that although it was his idea to join in with the Columbo test cooking, it was his wife Gill and his three teenagers that actually made the dish. I loved Ian's summing up, "We shared it as a family of 5. We were a little skeptical of curried egg and pasta but were very pleasantly surprised. Turned out to be a tasty winter warmer that we'll certainly try again. Five clean plates!"

Samantha Ellis of Musings of a Classic Film Addict also really liked this dish. She wrote, "At first I was hesitant because I've often made dishes like this, just without the eggs and with lots of cheese. The taste of the curry was pretty strong fresh out of the oven, but once I had some leftovers, the flavors all blended together better and I really fell in love with this dish!" Her puppy loved it too, when a little bit fell on the floor it was gobbled up in double quick time!

Helen Coniam made a good point about the cooking of this dish, "The only major change I made was with the cooking at the end. Jackie's Mom just puts it under the grill. But if the eggs have been standing around for a while, they will be a bit cool. I baked it at Gas 7 for 15 minutes, which browned the breadcrumbs and made it all piping hot." Helen also helpfully provided a guide to making the buttered breadcrumbs for the topping. "If you don't have stale bread, toast 3 slices of fresh or frozen bread on both sides and allow to cool. Then put into the blender and whizz until the crumbs are of the required size. (I like mine to look a bit 'rustic.') Heat 25g of butter in a pan and when liquid, add the breadcrumbs. Stir well until all the butter has been absorbed. Then turn out onto a tray and allow to cool again. (This will give you the buttered breadcrumbs listed in the original recipe.)"

Helen's other half Dave, always makes me laugh with his verdicts on her celebrity-related cooking escapades. He thought this was real "comfort food" and said that "…if he got a flat tire, the rising damp reached the attic, and armed police closed the local pub, this would be what he would like for dinner."

DOUBLE EXPOSURE - 1973

Are you susceptible to advertising? I am. When I was young, I was fascinated by the concept of subliminal advertising and convinced myself that many of my 1970s purchasing impulses were due to this kind of brainwashing. Well, subliminal advertising plays a part in this plot, and as you'll see, it works!

Robert Culp plays a very convincing psychopath, Dr. Bart Keppel, in this episode. Not content with being a highly successful "motivation research specialist," he also enjoys a little recreational blackmail on the side.

Columbo recognizes early on, that his adversary is a man with enormous self-control. Steely and ambitious, he's famous for his groundbreaking techniques in advertising. He's experimenting with the use of subliminal cuts in films to promote products, and this is something Columbo finds fascinating. Our favorite detective often pretends to be interested in the passions of his adversaries, but this time, I think he is genuinely impressed. "You invented something I never heard of, and I'm over 40!" he exclaims.

Food is at the center of the first murder in this episode, and I love the way Columbo mine-sweeps the canapés when he arrives at the scene of the crime. "Excuse me," he says, "I missed dinner tonight, working late on that Hayward case" (a reference to the previous episode), but he drops everything when a colleague tells him that there is imported caviar (Royal Iranian Beluga, no less) in the other room, and goes straight to it with a teaspoon. His table manners leave something to be desired, but he stops shoveling the fish eggs into his chops when he finds out how much it costs; $80 a jar.

Dr. Keppel obviously believes that he is vastly more intelligent than the Lieutenant, and refers to him as "the little fellow in the rumpled raincoat." At one point, he begins weaving a little story designed to implicate the murder victim's wife in the crime. When Columbo asks Keppel if he thinks the murder victim's lover killed him, Keppel condescends, "You're a little less perceptive than I thought, Lieutenant. 70% of all murders involving married persons, turn out to have been committed by a spouse. It's a fact, look it up!" Cheeky man.

Keppel is also very condescending when the Lieutenant begins closing in on him. Columbo interrupts the Doctor's golf game, telling him how he believes the murderer has covered his tracks. Keppel replies: "I marvel, Lieutenant... I'm fascinated by your imagination, but as far as I know, a court of law in this country, requires some kind of evidence don't they?" Columbo admits that at this point, he doesn't have any. But in a moment of deep thought, the Lieutenant thinks of a brilliant way to get his evidence. It's subliminal!

You could push the boat out for this one and buy a whole bowl full of caviar for a dinner party and serve with teaspoons, although you'll have to know your guests well. It's not very hygienic to keep eating off a spoon and dipping it back in like Columbo does! Or, you could keep it simple and serve buttered popcorn which features in the subliminal advertising research. Keep a beady eye on your guests to see if Columbo mentioning popcorn gets them digging in. A third idea is burgers. Columbo admits that a shot of a burger inserted into a film about racing cars, really makes him want to eat one.

You could have a few thermos flasks filled with ice-tea to serve to your guests during proceedings, as this features in the plot. If you go for the caviar option, you'll need to have plenty of cold beverages on-hand. As Columbo admits, and something that's proved by this episode, caviar can make you very, very thirsty.

As I've had no luck in finding a recipe for Robert (didn't the guy eat?!), here's a recipe for the Columbo omelet seen in *Murder By The Book*. I wouldn't be surprised if the busy, busy, busy Dr. Keppel rustled himself up an omelet every now and then, just for fuel.

Lieutenant Columbo's Epic Omelet

In the first non-pilot episode of *Columbo*, the Lieutenant makes an omelet, breaking eggs like a professional. He knows what he's doing with eggs! I have guessed quantities in this omelet after watching this sequence many, many times!

3 eggs
¼ cup / 25g grated cheese
½ a medium sized onion
½ tablespoon butter

Break eggs into a large bowl. Grate cheese on the fine part of a cheese grater. Add cheese to eggs. Slice onion and add to the eggs and cheese (Columbo eats a couple of bits of raw onion as he prepares this dish).

Heat butter in a frying pan.

Alas, we don't see the finished omelet as the doorbell rings as the butter is warming up. Columbo is distracted, perhaps the omelet remains unmade. Shame.

When I make this, I put all the ingredients in a bowl except the butter and whisk it all up with a fork (the Lieutenant uses a wooden spoon). I have the butter on high heat until it's bubbling then pour in the egg mixture. Once the bottom of the omelet is nice and brown, I pop it under the grill to set the top. Simple and delicious.

Serves 1-2

Just one more thing... I have never met photographer Katya de Grunwald, but I am a huge fan of her work. It was so lovely to receive her test cook report, complete with wonderful photographs of the omelet she made to Lieutenant Columbo's specifications. Katya made this dish for her brother Tom, and mum Hope, using a red onion for extra flavor. Comments were, "Grilling it really helped." "Onions were pleasantly al dente." "Onion makes it nice and spicy, it's the big thing of the recipe." Katya added, I really enjoyed watching the appropriate scene before we embarked on the making of the dish. I had recently seen the episode for the first time, and it's good one!" Indeed it is!

I love the fact that the first omelet Samantha Ellis in Florida ever made, was a Lieutenant Columbo omelet! Samantha wrote, "I followed the recipe exactly, but I didn't have any pan that would be able to go into the oven, so I attempted and failed to flip the omelet. It was my first time making an omelet, so it sort of became a mess, but I tried my best!" Columbo would have been proud of you Samantha!

PUBLISH OR PERISH - 1974

For writers, writing about writers is always fun. There are several episodes of *Columbo* which feature writerly pursuits. These include two shows featuring the brilliant Jack Cassidy. In this episode, as in *Murder By The Book*, Jack's character, Riley Greenleaf has close ties to a talented novelist, in this case, played by real-life writer, Mickey Spillane. Alan Mallory is essential to Riley's livelihood. When Mallory abandons him, it's as much his ego as the potential loss of income, that makes Riley do the dastardly deed.

When Riley has some car trouble, the Lieutenant observes that fixing the paint damage will probably set him back "a hundred, a hundred and fifty." Riley is a show-off and informs Columbo that when you have a car as fancy as his, "It costs that much to merely to raise the hood." Ever helpful, Columbo offers to put him in touch with an extended family member, offering, "Listen, my wife's got a cousin in The Valley, owns a body shop, I mean if you want me to talk to him…" Riley smugly comments, "Well, that's very decent of you. You see, I have a cousin in Beverly Hills, he does all my work for me."

At the murder scene, Riley finds Columbo sitting at a typewriter and takes a crack at the Lieutenant's ambition to write about some of his cases. Columbo, holding his head, muses, "I wanna tell you something, this writing is not as easy it looks…" Riley loses his temper, feeling that Columbo is wasting his time, he tells Columbo that he doesn't give a damn about his story.

But it's all about the story, and in this case, about the ending of a story. An in-joke about Rock Hudson, who starred in *McMillan and Wife* (one of the other strands in the NBC Mystery Movie wheel) forms the crux of the Lieutenant's pinch (you may want to memorise the following phrase if you are having chums around to watch this episode), "For a hundred thousand dollars, you don't kill off Rock Hudson."

It is always comical when the Lieutenant finds himself in a fancy restaurant, in this case, the legendary Chasen's. When Riley's rivals, Jeffrey Neal and Eileen McRae, ask Columbo to join them for dinner, he is perplexed by the elaborate French menu. He asks the waiter, "Do you have any chili? With beans, without beans, either way, doesn't make any difference…" The waiter quite obviously thinks this request is beyond the pale. The Lieutenant further blots his copybook by asking for ketchup, and then crackers. He wants saltines, "if they have 'em." This is all a fun way of showing Columbo's lowly appetites, the irony being that Chasen's was, in fact, famous for its chili, the recipe for which is in the "Columbo's Chili and Other Delights" section.

There are three of Jack Cassidy's favorite recipes in this book, and I think that this is probably the one that Columbo, with his down to earth taste in food, would like best. It's a very traditional dish for a Thanksgiving dinner, according to my American chums. Some might turn their noses up at the use of canned mushroom soup for this recipe, but don't let's forget, it's a QUICKIE Green Bean Casserole, and very tasty it is too.

If you are hosting a party and you have the dough, I heartily recommend you invest in a red jacket with a red hat to match like Marietta Hartley, playing Eileen, wears in this episode. So very chic for Chasen's!

For British cooks - a 10½ oz can is actually equivalent to about 300g so you might not need a whole can of mushroom soup. Also, if you hunt for them, the larger supermarkets usually have tubs of French's Crunchy Onions - or similar. I'd never had these before I tried this recipe, now I love them! Good for sprinkling on top of all kinds of things… I make this in what I think of as my "lasagna dish" - a standard 9-inch x 9-inch square dish.

Jack Cassidy's Quickie Green Bean Casserole

2 x 15½ oz / 2 x 400g cans green beans, drained
2 tablespoons sweet/unsalted butter
Salt and pepper
One 10½ oz / 400g can cream of mushroom soup
One 3½ oz can / 100g French's Crispy Fried Onions

Preheat oven to 400 degrees F / 205 degrees C / gas mark 6.

Grease a large baking dish with butter.

Place beans in the dish, and dot with butter. Sprinkle evenly with 1 teaspoon salt and freshly ground pepper to taste. Spoon cream of mushroom soup evenly over beans, stirring so soup seeps into the lower part of the casserole. Top with crispy onions.

Bake uncovered in oven until beans are heated through (about 20 minutes).

Serves 6

Just one more thing... The first Thanksgiving dinner I ever went to, was at Battenburgbelle's in 2015 (it's not something we usually do here in the UK). She made an absolutely spectacular meal and the table was heaving with good things to eat. I took some of Jack's Quickie Bean Casserole. None of the ten guests there assembled, had ever had a green bean casserole before and there was much consternation when I revealed what was in it. I got rather drunk and the next morning found a little piece of paper in my bra upon which I had written, "Mike says that for the first post-zombie apocalypse, we can still have this for our Thanksgiving dinner as it all comes from cans and packets." Indeed, bring on the zombies!

MIND OVER MAYHEM - 1974

Do you know someone so lacking in any emotion, that they are a bit like a robot? Jose Ferrer's character, Dr. Marshall Cahill, is a super-brainy scientist, the Director of The Cybernetics Research Institute, and the kind of person who can say something like, "Einstein was the most modest man I ever met," with a straight poker face. When he invites his underlings out for a nightcap after work, you get the distinct impression that the evening is not going to be a barrel of laughs with him as the host.

Dr. Cahill's son, Neil, has been awarded a very prestigious science award, which makes his father very proud. But it's clear that Neil doesn't deserve the plaudit. He is passing off a dead man's work as his own, partly to impress his father. As another doctor at the Institute, Howard Nicholson puts it, "He stole the work of a giant, to win the approval of a tyrant." Howard is threatening to reveal the extent of Neil's plagiarism and Dr. Cahill challenges, "You resent me so much; you are willing to destroy my son." Howard replies, "Oh it's you who've destroyed him Marshall, but not with love, with browbeating domination."

Dr. Cahill is indeed a tyrant. He believes himself vastly superior to all of those who work around him, and naturally, underestimates Columbo's intelligence, too. When a young worker at the Institute helps Columbo with an experiment that might prove Dr. Cahill's guilt; the Lieutenant wants to avoid getting the youngster into trouble. They are discovered and he tells Dr. Cahill, "It was my fault, not the boy's." The murderer's response is a withering: "I doubt it. You haven't got the brains for it."

But for all Dr. Cahill's intelligence on the Cybernetics front, it is a simple analog item that puts Columbo on his trail. A used match.

There is no food at all in this episode, which is a shame! The boffins that work at The Cybernetic Research Institute, don't need to eat it seems, at least not in fancy restaurants. There are comedy moments though, mostly provided by Double M-Seven, the artificial intelligence robot that the Institute is developing. A very young member of the research team is tasked with programming the Double M-Seven. He's about 12 years old, but as he explains to Columbo, he's a "boy genius" named Steven Spelberg, (the name, of course, is a reference to another boy genius,

Steven Spielberg, who directed the first non-pilot episode of *Columbo*, *Murder By the Book*. I'm sure he would have been tickled by this in-joke). Artificial intelligence and computers are central to this episode. As we know, Columbo is often baffled by modern technology. His best line in this episode, eminently quotable, is when he has a sudden brainwave, puts his hand to his forehead, exclaiming, "something just computed!" I love it.

Jose's eggy potatoes are a nice dish to have for a pre-Columbo brunch. You could then watch this episode, have lunch, and then watch another Columbo!

Jose Ferrer's Eggs Ferrer with Fried Potatoes

2 medium-sized boiled potatoes, cold, thinly sliced
Salt and pepper
½ lb / 225g butter
1 egg yolk
2 whole eggs
1 tablespoon sweet cream/single cream
1 egg white

Preheat oven to 400 degrees F / 205 degrees C / gas mark 6.

Sprinkle the potatoes with salt and lightly brown both sides in butter in a hot frying pan. Place potatoes in an oven-proof dish. Whip together the egg yolk, the whole eggs, and the cream. Pour egg mixture over potato slices. Add a little salt to the egg white and whip to a frothy consistency; then pour over the potatoes. Cover and bake until the eggs are set.

Serves 1

Just one more thing... Undercooking alert! In the original recipe, José's instructions were to cook the eggs "no longer than 1 and ½ minutes." As my friend Greg Swenson put it, "In what kind of oven?... something from Dr. Cahill's mad scientist lab?" Haha - indeed. Both myself and test cook Kelli Cline baked this dish for a lot longer than recommended. Kelli tested this dish three times with different kinds of potato, what a trooper! Depending on the mightiness of your oven and the thickness of your potato layer, Kelli recommends at least 4½ minutes, probably more like 6. Just like the eggheads in this episode, experiment!

SWAN SONG - 1974

People are often surprised when I tell them that Johnny Cash is in *Columbo*. Most folks think of him as a singer and songwriter; but in fact, Johnny was in several films and TV dramas. He mostly played cowboys, but in *Columbo*, he plays gospel singer. Tommy Brown (who is not exactly full of faith).

Tommy's wife wants to build a tabernacle and already has two million dollars towards it in escrow, all thanks to Tommy's talent. He's getting heartily fed up with singing his heart out and having nothing to show for it, but his wife knows his guilty secret. He's therefore tied to her and will have to do something drastic in order to live the life of luxury and debauchery, away from the church, that he craves.

Tommy and Columbo bond, a little, over the fact that they were both involved in the Korean War. Our singing star was in the Air Force, and it makes him laugh heartily when he guesses that Columbo was in the MP (military police). Columbo sheepishly admits, "KP mostly" (on kitchen duty). After asking Tommy a lot of tricky questions at his home, Columbo leaves; returning after just a moment to add, "Just one more thing…" Tommy is startled, "You know Lieutenant, if that police career of yours ever fizzles out, you could always make it as a cat burglar." Tommy veers between being stroppy with the Lieutenant and being super-friendly towards him. When Columbo mentions he's got something else to ask, Tommy smiles, "ask away little buddy."

Our hero comes to see Tommy in the recording studio and informs him that he and his wife were at his concert the previous night. Tommy seems chuffed. He waves his walking stick, laughs, and yells, "You are really coming on Lieutenant!" But Tommy shouldn't think that the Lieutenant is on his side. While he is listening to the live recording they are working on, Columbo hears something that gives him another lead. In fact, it is Columbo's acute hearing that provides the crucial clue that allows him to catch his man.

If you know your Columbo, I expect that you've been waiting for a chili recipe… It's what the Lieutenant likes best, of course. He eats it whenever he gets a chance to. It feels like serendipity, that I have an excellent recipe for Johnny Cash's family chili in my collection, not least because the Lieutenant samples some of Tommy Brown's own version in this episode. Clever shorthand is used here to tell us something about the rags to riches nature of fame. When at an elaborate, al fresco party at Tommy's home, Columbo is encouraged to help himself. He has a taste and remarks, "Say that's delicious, I've never tasted chili like that before." His face is a picture when told that it's a "special recipe chili" made from squirrel meat. (You'll probably be pleased to hear that there's no squirrel in Johnny's very own chili recipe.)

I make half of Johnny's recipe, as I just don't have a pan big enough for the Cash family quantity. The chili in the adapted recipe below would feed 6 (so if you want to feed 12, as Johnny did, double away). I love the chunks of sirloin that are mixed in amongst the ground meat, like little treats! This looks like a very long recipe, but don't worry, it's quite simple really, and well worth it!

Watch out if you are using hot chili powder, ¼ cup seems quite a lot to me, but if you like your chili hot, go for it. I'm guessing that New Mexico chili powder (which I've never seen in the UK) isn't a "blow your head off" type of chili powder, but everyone has a different spice tolerance so it's up to you! For UK based cooks, the Schwartz Chilli con Carne mix is pretty close to a McCormick's Mild Chili Seasoning Mix ingredients-wise.

Johnny Cash's Chili

1 lb / 450g ground/minced venison (if available) or ground/minced beef (chuck or sirloin)
½ lb / 225g venison steaks (if available) or beef steaks, such as sirloin, or a rump roast, cut into bite-sized pieces
1 large onion, finely chopped
1½ cloves of garlic, peeled and chopped
1 tablespoon canola/rapeseed oil
24 oz / 680g canned tomatoes
1 large green bell pepper
½ large red bell pepper
2½ jalapeño peppers (optional)
½ habanero pepper (optional)
1 packet McCormick's Mild Chili Seasoning Mix (or your favorite brand)
Salt and pepper
¼ cup / 32g chili powder (New Mexico chili powder if available)
⅙ cup / 21g cumin
½ tablespoon sage
¾ teaspoon oregano
½ tablespoon cayenne pepper
15 oz / 400g can black beans, drained
15 oz / 400g can pinto beans, drained

15 oz / 400g can chili beans/kidney beans in chili sauce
12 oz / 340g can kidney beans, drained
6 oz / 170ml beer
⅛ cup / 25g sugar
A handful of self-rising cornmeal*

In a large pot, heat the oil over medium-high heat. Brown the steak in the oil in batches, draining off some of the fat if necessary. Remove from the heat and set aside. In a separate frying pan, brown the ground meat over medium-high heat. Drain off the fat and set meat aside.

With the oil remaining in the pot, brown half the onions and garlic over medium heat until they are caramelized. Now add the well-drained ground beef and steak. Stir and heat it all up. Add the cans of tomatoes, the bell peppers, hot peppers (if using), and the remainder of the onions and garlic. Heat to a brisk simmer, stirring often.

John Carter Cash says that his dad would normally add the spices in the following order, first the chili packet, followed by some salt and black pepper, chili powder, cumin, sage, oregano, and cayenne pepper. John advises tasting the chili and once the spicing it is to your liking, drain the cans of beans and add to the mixture. Now taste again, as the beans mellow the flavor of the chili. Once the chili is to your taste, pour in the bottle of beer. Stir well. Cover and simmer for at least 30 minutes, stirring occasionally. Add sugar to your taste. Simmer, covered, for at least another 30 minutes, making sure to stir so the chili does not burn. Now add the cornmeal and stir in.

* If self-rising cornmeal is unavailable, you can make it yourself. Just combine 1 cup / 160g of cornmeal, ⅓ cup / 40g all-purpose/plain flour, 1½ teaspoons of baking powder, and ½ teaspoon of salt. Put the leftover mix in a sealed container and save for your next batch of Johnny Cash Chili.

Serves 6

Just one more thing... Penny Armstrong is from a family of *Columbo* devotees. She told me that her mom, daughter, son-in-law, grandson and herself are "still talking about episodes over the miles in three states." Penny made this chili for a big family get-together and it got the thumbs up from everyone at the cousin summer splash party! "This family likes chili, and this chili didn't disappoint. Several of them had second helpings and even the kid's plates/bowls were scraped clean." She continued, "My daughter Katy highly recommends adding a dollop of sour cream, which I also like to do, especially if the chili is a bit spicy." Although Katy thought the Lieutenant would approve, her husband, Jesse, wasn't as convinced that Columbo would prefer this recipe over his questionable, diner-style chili to which he adds ketchup and crackers. "We didn't add the crackers this go round, but we sure used to eat saltines in our chili when were younger." With saltines or without saltines, it turned out Columbo-worthy according to Penny's daughter, "…his biggest fan!"

Helen Coniam of the fabulous Dinner With Zelda Manners really did me a kindness, by creating a veggie version of Johnny's Chili (which you will find in the "Columbo's Chili and Other Delights" section). It is just as delicious as the meat version.

A FRIEND IN DEED - 1974

Columbo nearly loses his badge in this episode. His antagonist is the Deputy Chief Commissioner of Police, Mark Halperin, and Columbo is already known to him. A murder is committed by a friend of the Commissioner, who begs him to help cover up the crime. The Commissioner hatches a plan and asks for Columbo by name. This is a silly mistake. He claims to have seen a suspicious man running from his friend's house, who might be a burglar, so why ask for a homicide detective?

Mark certainly comes up with a good scheme to get his chum off the hook for murder, but it comes at a high price. He decides that in return for supplying him with an alibi, The Deputy Chief Commissioner will kill his own wife, and his friend will have to provide an alibi for him. He is a very selfish man, and as he says himself, there's always got to be a quid pro quo.

From the moment Columbo arrives, he is apologizing to his superior, who says: "Ah Columbo, it's about time you showed up." The Lieutenant is having car trouble and explains how he tried to borrow his wife's car, with no luck. Later, when his car breaks down again, he begins telling Halperin that he's now got a problem with the generator. The Commissioner is in a hurry, and abrupt with the Lieutenant, stating that his limousine is waiting outside (which rubs it in a little).

Halperin tells Columbo off at one point when the Lieutenant is musing out loud over the possibility that this was indeed a homicide, rather than a burglary. The Commissioner is exasperated and speaks to Columbo as if he's a child, "You're wasting your time, and my time, and the department's time." He obviously knows the Lieutenant's success rate, but tells him, "Nobody can be right all the time." But the Lieutenant always is right of course. Even if he has to use some clever entrapment techniques, he always gets his man.

I haven't been able to find a recipe for any of Columbo's co-stars in this episode, but it was directed by Ben Gazzara, a great actor in his own right, and a great friend of Peter Falk's. I hereby propose his recipe for leg of lamb. This is really easy to prepare and very, very tasty.

If you don't have a meat thermometer, I would suggest checking with your butcher how long to cook your lamb and at what temperature. If you buy your leg of lamb from a supermarket, follow the timing instructions on the packaging. Ben's oven temperature is for a pretty slow roast - at this temperature, depending on the size of your leg, it could take around three hours. Your lamb will benefit from resting for half an hour after you take it out of the oven.

Ben Gazzara's Leg of Lamb, Sicilian Style

Leg of baby lamb
2 small cloves of garlic, finely sliced
Several sprigs of fresh oregano (or dried oregano)
½ lemon
Salt and pepper
⅓ cup / 80ml olive oil

Make incisions in the lamb and insert slivers of garlic and sprigs of fresh oregano (or dried herb) in the slits. Rub the outside of the lamb with the cut side of the lemon, 1 teaspoon salt, and ¼ teaspoon freshly ground pepper. Put lamb in a shallow pan. Squeeze the lemon half and mix the juice with the olive oil; pour this over lamb. Cover. Marinate for several hours in the fridge, turning several times.

Preheat oven to 300 degrees F / 150 degrees C / gas mark 2.

Drain meat, reserving marinade. Place meat, fat side up, in a roasting pan. Insert meat thermometer. Roast in preheated until thermometer registers 170 degrees F / 76 degrees C. Baste often with marinade.

Serve with a green vegetable, wedges of olive oil-browned potatoes and watercress salad.

Serves 3

Just one more thing... Mandy Wedgwood, a software developer in Leeds, West Yorkshire, had a bit of a Columbo shindig when she tested out four recipes at once. She told me it was so much fun, and that she fully intends making her Columbo Dinner Party an annual event, trying out other recipes from my book. What a fabulous idea! Ben's lamb was the main course, accompanied by Robert Vaughn's Stuffed Zucchini, with Shera Danese's Stuffed Peppers as a starter and Tyne Daly's Key Lime Pie as a dessert. What a feast. Mandy's feedback was, "The lamb prep was simple, the only addition I made, was to chop up an anchovy and place into the slits I made in the lamb for extra savory punch. The lamb created some amazing juices! I would eat it pinker if I made it again, and knock 15 mins off the cooking time (but that is just personal choice)." I loved the photos Mandy sent me of her dinner party, it looked like great fun and the food all looked utterly fabulous.

THE FOURTH SEASON
(1974-1975)

AN EXERCISE IN FATALITY - 1974

Do you belong to a gym? Do you actually go?

Robert Conrad is a fine figure of a man in this episode, but he's also a total health freak bore. He runs several health spas where the overweight and unfit are put through their paces, including Columbo at one point (for our general amusement). Robert's character is Milo Janus and as a mark of his egotism, his gymnasium chain is named after himself. Elevator music is piped through each one, sending out subliminal messages with lines such as, "Your new life is waiting to begin, at Milo Janus…"

It's kind of annoying when someone is super-fit. It's hard to keep up with them while they are diving into pools, swimming in the sea, shadowboxing, skipping with a rope, making smoothies and downing vitamins. It's pretty exhausting. Columbo admits that he's not keen on health food, explaining, "I happen to like a bowl of chili, I like a rare steak now and then…." And he would probably go on, telling Milo exactly all the other delicious, but not necessarily healthy, food he loves to eat; when he's cut off mid-flow. Mind you, later on, Columbo does appear to be making some life changes, after hanging around the health spas. Jogging on a running machine, he tells Milo that he's skipping beer, giving up the cigars and emphatically states, "No more chili!"

Later, however, when Columbo is closing in on his prey in a hospital waiting room, he lights up a cigar. Milo sneers, "Your health program didn't last very long, did it?" The Lieutenant stares at him and replies, "Long enough." Milo accuses Columbo of being a devious man, "I don't care what visions you see when you look at your cigar ashes because I am innocent… You can huff and puff on that rotten cigar until next July and you will never prove otherwise." "I wouldn't count on it," counters the Lieutenant. By pure chance, he spots a kid with his arm in a sling, giving him the clue he needs to prove Milo's guilt.

It's rather fun, that this most health conscious of Columbo's adversaries, counted Hangover Eggs as one of his favorite recipes. So in real life, I guess that he wasn't as squeaky clean as his character, hurrah! It's a pretty straightforward recipe, but when you've got a hangover, that's what you want, isn't it? I've tried these several times. It may be psychosomatic, who knows, but as far as I'm concerned, they work. To drink? Well, there is a lot of juice flying around in this episode. Milo's secretary (wearing a bikini) rustles up a Virgin Mary, and Milo gives Columbo carrot juice (which the Lieutenant is very suspicious of and doesn't drink). So it's up to you, if you are feeling healthy, go the whole juice route with your Hangover Eggs. If you have guests, give them carrot juice pretending it is orange juice and see if they make the same face as the Lieutenant.

Robert Conrad's Infamous Hangover Eggs

2 eggs
1 teaspoon sweet/unsalted butter
Salt and pepper
1 English muffin, split
2 slices beefsteak tomato

Break eggs, one at a time, into a saucer, slip carefully into melted butter in a frying pan. Cook eggs, without breaking yolks, just until the bottom begins to set. Add a scant teaspoon of water to the frying pan. Season with salt and pepper, then cover tightly and cook until eggs are cooked to desired doneness. Serve "hangover" eggs with toasted English muffin halves and sliced tomato. Robert says: "Consume at once, your hangover will disappear."

Serves 1

Just one more thing.... Some of the mightiest hangovers I've ever had, have been after a night of madness at my friend Sanja's house with her and her brother, Sasa. It seemed only right and proper then, to ask her to test this recipe for me. She emailed, "Made hangover eggs. Sasa had them, I had them, we loved them." After a night of lots of Japanese whiskey and beer, this hangover cure did the trick (though Sanja needed some chicken soup too). The need for an extra hangover cure, was blamed on the smoking (Sasa doesn't smoke). Sanja tells me that in their native Serbia, the traditional hangover cure is cabbage pickling liquid. Which sounds perfect to me as I love all things pickled. But this recipe definitely worked as a cure too, and she added, "I think I'll adopt this way of frying eggs, little bit of water and lid make it so easy to do it right."

NEGATIVE REACTION - 1974

We might have felt a little sympathy for Dick Van Dyke's character, Paul Galesko, in this episode, because his wife really is a dragon. However, he is very rude to the Lieutenant (and that just won't do). It's one of those episodes, where we see a preemptive, introductory sequence, Paul jokingly saying to Columbo, "You're a gem! You're a little flawed, and you're not too bright, but you're one of a kind!" Well, as his wife succinctly puts it, Paul is a silly man. Columbo? Not too bright? He'll definitely be changing his mind on that assumption very soon.

Dick Van Dyke rarely plays a villain. He's much better known as a cheeky chappie, a faithful husband, or a chimney sweep; so it's quite delicious to see him play a cold-blooded murderer. His character is a famous and successful portrait photographer, and it's ultimately his need to show-off, that gives Columbo the evidence he needs. Never underestimate Columbo's tendency to bone up on exactly the profession you excel at, and then trap you by pretending to know nothing about it!

At one point, Paul comes home to find Columbo in his living room trying to find an ashtray. He picks up suitable looking antique bowls and discounts them, eventually putting his cigar ashes in his raincoat pocket. I think this endears him slightly to his adversary, who apologizes to the Lieutenant for being abrupt with him. Columbo begins praising Paul's body of work, then blots his copybook by rambling on about what a terrible photographer he is himself. Paul gets a little impatient and seems irked when Columbo cheekily asks if he has a photograph in his collection of a cocker spaniel (to act as a pin-up for his lovesick "Dog"). Paul clearly is above taking animal portraits and his face says it all: he thinks the Lieutenant is a fool.

Eventually, pursued by the Lieutenant to a swanky, opening night exhibition of his photographs, Paul vocalizes his feelings, "Columbo, you are becoming very annoying, do you know that?" During a long conversation about a collection of Paul's photographs featuring inmates at San Quentin, he eventually loses his temper. He lets rip with, "You're like a little, shaggy-haired terrier who's got a grip on my trousers, you won't let go. I can't turn around without you staring up at me with that blank, innocent expression on your face." Columbo reacts with his usual grace when Paul threatens to, "...scream until the beams at City Hall shake," calmly stating, "That won't be necessary, I know I've been a pest, I'm just trying to do my job. I won't bother you anymore." We know of course that this isn't the case. This terrier will continue to go for Paul's trousers until he gets the proof he needs.

Columbo loves to learn about technology, and in a camera shop, he finds a technical quirk of photography that gives him a clever idea. He can trap Paul into admitting that he was the murderer. The Lieutenant is always open to new information and uses it wisely. He says with great pleasure, "Well I'll be a monkey's uncle! You learn something every day!" If Paul wasn't such a show-off, and Columbo hadn't realized this about him, he might have got away with murder.

There's a lovely comedy sequence in this episode, revolving around the legendary raincoat. When he visits a homeless shelter, a Sister of Mercy takes a liking to our Lieutenant and decides to find him a new coat. "I've had this coat for 7 years," he protests. "Oh you poor man," she replies. (Joyce Van Patten, the actress playing this part, will get a chance to shine in a later episode of *Columbo, Old Fashioned Murder)*.

When offering this recipe to a cookbook compiler, Dick commented, "Southern Fried Chicken is a favorite of mine, but how I love Breast of Chicken Florentine!" Well, I love it too. It's fairly simple to make, but impressive and delicious. Perfect to have before, during, or after *Negative Reaction* (and photogenic too)!

Dick Van Dyke's Breast of Chicken Florentine

4 whole chicken breasts, boned and halved
Flour for dredging
Salt and pepper
1 egg
Finely grated cheese, around ⅛ cup / 15g
¼ cup / 40g dry breadcrumbs
¾ cup / 180g butter, divided use
2 lbs / 900g spinach, cooked and drained
1 tablespoon lemon juice
Extra 2 tablespoons of butter
1 lb / 450g mushrooms, sliced
Chopped parsley

Remove skin from chicken breasts. Mix the flour with a little salt and pepper and dredge chicken breasts in the seasoned flour. Beat the egg lightly with 1 tablespoon of water and then dip the chicken into the egg. Coat with a mixture of cheese and breadcrumbs. Chill for 1 hour in the refrigerator.

In a large frying pan, heat ½ cup / 120g of butter, add chicken and brown on both sides. Lower heat and cook gently until tender, about 20-25 minutes. Meanwhile chop spinach coarsely and season with lemon juice. Pile spinach on a dish, arrange chicken breasts on top and keep hot. To pan, add ¼ cup / 60g butter and the mushrooms. Sauté until tender, then spoon mushrooms over chicken. Brown the extra 2 tablespoons of butter in a pan and pour through a fine sieve over the dish. Sprinkle with the parsley.

Serves 4

Just one more thing... Dick's recipe didn't include cheese in the ingredients list (an omission of the cookbook compiler I think). I used some finely grated Parmesan, and my lovely Bread Angel Juli Farkas, did too. She recommended 15g. Juli used her mum's method of making chicken in breadcrumbs, "I put a lid on the first half of frying time and took it off for the second side. This keeps more moisture in. I also cut up each breast into two pieces, as it would have taken too long to fry it whole and the outside might have burnt by the time the inside was done. I mixed olive oil and butter, half and half." Ooh, that is a top tip. Juli shared this dish with her daughter, Polly who loved it too. She announced, "I could eat this every day." How fabulous!

Itinerant ad-man and Hammerton bread enthusiast, Mike Nicholson tried this dish and said, "This is indeed a very simple recipe, though impressive-looking enough to roll out for casual guests, or for children with very high food standards." Like Juli, he recommended an olive oil/butter combo for the frying. His verdict, "Everyone loved the chicken. The coating has just the right amount of crunch, and the slow cooking keeps the meat very tender and moist. Combined with the mushrooms and spinach and served over rice, it was super (cali-frage-listic-expi-ali-docious)." It took me a while to get Mike's joke, a reference to *Mary Poppins* which featured Dick Van Dyke playing a cockney chimney sweep of course!

BY DAWN'S EARLY LIGHT - 1974

It's unlikely that Columbo ever attended military school. He's the complete opposite of the spick and span, highly disciplined square-bashers at the Haynes Military Academy. He's almost certainly everything that Colonel Lyle C. Rumford hates in a man: shabby, bumbling and with unruly thought patterns. But who is the smartest in the end?

Patrick McGoohan's character in this episode is so buttoned up, he's the antithesis of Columbo. The thin film of perspiration that appears on his face, when under stress, is a bit of a giveaway. He strains to keep control at all times. He's the ultimate military man and gets a kick out of turning boys into soldiers. Unfortunately, enrollments are down at the Academy, and the Colonel's worldview is being challenged. When his beloved institution is under threat of becoming a co-ed junior college the Colonel rages, "There are too many people set on destroying our country, and that is why institutions like this Academy cannot be allowed to die!" The grandson of the Academy's founder, however, has other ideas.

Columbo irritates the Colonel from the first moment he spots him at the Academy, scrabbling around the parade ground in his crumpled clothes, looking for evidence. When he picks something up, the Colonel barks at him, "Hey you. Mister. You'd better hand that over to the police… This is a restricted area. You'd better leave." He is very surprised to find out that the Lieutenant is in charge of the investigation. He doesn't get the same kind of reverence from our hero as he does from his cadets, that's for sure.

Columbo decides to stay the night at the Academy, and the Colonel is more or less forced to invite him to supper. He gets lost on the way to the mess hall and arrives late. The Colonel is impatiently waiting for him, having already finished his meal. Finally served his dinner, the Lieutenant doesn't get a chance to eat much, apart from a few peas, as his adversary is trying to coax information out of him. When Columbo asks for the butter, the Colonel playfully counters, "If I pass the butter, will you promise to tell me why the conversation was unsatisfactory?" Columbo is immune to the fake charm of course, and replies, "Actually sir, I'm putting on weight and I'm trying to cut down on the butter." He then gets a bit sidetracked, rambling on about how Mrs. Columbo uses margarine at home. Whisked away from his uneaten meal, Columbo quips, "Oh, I always have a light supper," then surreptitiously grabs a few bread rolls from the table and stuffs them in his coat pocket on the way out.

Questions are asked about strange behavior in the mess hall. Cadets make odd movements with their forks of food, eating on command, and they don't seem very happy about what they are consuming. Their chins almost touch their chests, it's very bizarre. When Columbo asks about this procedure, two cadets at the head table explain to the Lieutenant that they are not being punished; this method of ingestion is called "eating a square meal." You could make your dinner guests eat in a similar fashion, if you were that way inclined. A prize for the person who makes the most accurate face!

Try as I might, I've found no recipes attributed to Patrick McGoohan. I have it on good authority that he liked fish and chips, but that's about all I can tell you on the food front. For this episode, I therefore propose something Columbo might have eaten at home with Mrs. Columbo. Peter

Falk's very own recipe for a pasta dish. To drink with this episode? I would strongly suggest some cider, for reasons that will become clear as the story unfolds.

Peter Falk's Pumpkin Lasagna

12 oz / 340g jumbo shell pasta
Salt
2½ cups / 560g pumpkin puree, preferably fresh
⅔ cup / 70g slivered almonds, toasted and chopped
⅛ teaspoon ground nutmeg
Pepper
Olive oil
Topping (recipe follows)

Bring 2 quarts / 2 liters of water to the boil in a large pot, adding 2 teaspoons salt. Add the pasta shells, one at a time, to the water while stirring to keep the shells from sticking to the bottom of the pan. After the water comes back to a boil, cook the pasta for about 10 more minutes, continuing to stir occasionally to prevent the pasta from sticking to the pan. Move the pot of pasta to a sink where you can run cold water into the pot to cool the shells. Remove the pasta with your hand and set it aside to drain in a colander.

Preheat the oven to 350 degrees F / 175 degrees C / gas mark 4. In a large bowl, combine the pumpkin, almonds, and nutmeg, plus salt and pepper to taste. Put about two tablespoons of the mixture into each pasta shell. Arrange the shells, open-side up and about ½ inch apart, in a lightly greased (with olive oil) 9x13-inch baking dish. Cover with aluminum foil that has been oiled very lightly on the bottom.

Bake for about 30 minutes or until the pumpkin is heated through.

Topping

1 stick / 115g butter or margarine
½ clove garlic, crushed
½ cup / 30g soft breadcrumbs
1 teaspoon minced fresh sage
Fresh parsley
Freshly grated Parmesan cheese (optional)

While the pasta shells are baking, brown the butter in a frying pan over medium heat, stirring constantly and being careful not to let it burn. Add the garlic and sauté until it becomes translucent. Remove from heat. In a separate frying pan (with no oil), lightly toast the breadcrumbs. Add the breadcrumbs and sage to the garlic-butter mixture and mix thoroughly using a fork.

To serve, place the shells on heated plates. Top with 1 teaspoon of the breadcrumb mixture and garnish with parsley. Oh, and just one more thing: pass the Parmesan cheese at the table.

Serves 3 with, as Peter Falk puts it, "2 shells left over for the cook to nibble on."

Just one more thing... It is this recipe that graces the cover of this book (made and photographed by the wonderful food writer and photographer, my beloved friend, Joan Ransley). Joan made a pimped up version of Peter's dish, which you'll find on the Silver Screen Suppers blog. Joan felt that 4 pasta shells per person were plenty, "Even for a greedy guts!" It really made me laugh when she told me that her partner Nick, was known as the "Columbo of Gastroenterologists" when he was younger.

Ace cook Vera Roth in Berlin made her own spelt pasta for this recipe. Instead of making big shells and stuffing them, she "Made it like a classy lasagna: lasagna squares, filling, lasagna squares, filling, and so on." I'm very impressed! She and her husband enjoyed the dish, but agreed with Joan that there were too many almonds. "Best part, the topping tasted amazing!"

My chum, Michelle Kerry on the South coast of England, also loved the topping, "This would be good served with a sauce, maybe something cheesy, or slightly spicy like an Arrabbiata chili/tomato sauce." Michelle cracked me up with her comment about how tricky it was to find large pasta shells in her neck of the woods, "It's been quite a rigmarole down 'ere in 'astings!" But it's definitely worth seeking them out, they make this dish look so appealing and it's what Mr. Falk would have wanted.

TROUBLED WATERS - 1975

This episode of Columbo is fairly unusual, as we see the Lieutenant very early in the episode before a crime has been committed. He's on a competition prize holiday with his wife, but he arrives late for boarding and he can't find her anywhere on the ship. If you have doubts that Mrs. Columbo actually exists, the cute conversation he has with her on the phone might convince you that she does. In addition, the ship's officers mention having seen her on several occasions.

The ship's Captain is amused by the fact Columbo is wearing his trademark raincoat when he comes on board, asking, "Tell me, Lieutenant, do you expect inclement weather in the Mexican waters?" The eagle-eyed amongst you will be pleased to see another fan of the raincoat on board, Bernard Fox who played Detective Chief Superintendent Durk in *Dagger of the Mind*. I'm tickled by the fact that the Captain of the ship and his staff pronounce "Lieutenant," as "Leff-tenant," in the British style. They all have an appropriate respect for the "Leff-tenant," unlike the Robert Vaughn character.

Hayden Danzinger is being blackmailed by an ex-lover and has a carefully mapped out plan for getting rid of her. He's very impatient, when Columbo tries to engage him in conversation about room service, treating him like an idiot. He curtly tells him to go back to his cabin and "push the red button for the steward." When Columbo goes off on a tangent about how he's never been on a boat before, and how his wife has won this trip for them both, Danzinger cuts him off, "Push the red button. Push it," and walks away. Danzinger hasn't got time for small talk.

When they meet again later, Danzinger is in the sickbay; after staging a fake heart attack to establish an alibi. He's surprised to find out the shabby man, who was rambling away to him about room service is, in fact, a policeman. Danzinger is now slightly wary, but mostly he seems to stick with his original opinion of the Lieutenant, not being too bright.

There's a comedy moment on deck when Columbo joins his adversary in a traditional, onboard game of quoits. His quoit goes flying over the side of the ship. Danzinger thinks this is very funny and stops his game in order to quiz the Lieutenant about his investigation. Being a seasoned cruiser, he can, of course, play quoits and he knows a lot about cruise ships. When Columbo wonders why the murderer didn't chuck the murder weapon out of the porthole into the "biggest garbage dump in the world," Danzinger explains that the portholes don't open, they are purely decorative. When Columbo admits, "You probably couldn't tell, but I've never been on a boat before," Danzinger laughs, "I couldn't tell, no!" The murderer thinks he's got away with it, but of course, the Lieutenant is onto him, and he'll find a clever way of catching him out.

Mrs. Columbo likes cocktail parties apparently, but Columbo himself can take them or leave them. For fun, you could throw a little nautical-style cocktail party for this episode. If your male guests are so inclined, they could wear white suits with wide-collared shirts and patterned cravats. Ladies could dress in "formal wear" with corsages or long dresses with sparkly waistbands. It could be very glamorous indeed. Some cheesy, easy listening would be good on the stereo (with a version of the cruise entertainer's classic, *Volare*, a must).

Although Robert Vaughn's recipe doesn't sound particularly ritzy, it's surprisingly good. You have to carve the insides out of zucchinis, and they do, in fact, end up looking like little boats. You could have fun with your guests, seeing if they think they are boats or ships (there is a running joke throughout this episode about the difference). Robert appears in another episode of *Columbo* with a nautical theme, *Last Salute to the Commodore*, so you could serve his Special Fettuccine Alfredo instead, if you prefer. Happy sailing!

Robert Vaughn's Mushroom Stuffed Zucchini

6 medium zucchini/courgettes
2 tablespoons chopped onion
1 tablespoon oil
1 small clove garlic, crushed (optional)
4 oz / 115g mushrooms, sliced
2 tablespoons tomato puree
Salt and pepper
Pinch each of oregano and basil
¾ cup / 75g finely crushed cheese biscuits
¼ cup / 25g Parmesan cheese
1 oz / 28g butter

Preheat oven to 350 degrees F / 175 degrees C / gas mark 4.

Cut stems from zucchini, halve lengthwise, scoop out pulp and chop coarsely. Sauté onion in oil until tender. Add garlic and mushrooms and sauté 2-3 minutes. Stir in tomato puree, ½ teaspoon salt, black pepper to taste, oregano, basil, cracker crumbs and chopped zucchini. Spoon mixture into shells. Place on a greased baking dish, sprinkle with Parmesan cheese and dot with butter. Pour ½ cup hot water around zucchini and bake for 45 minutes until tender.

Serves 6

Just one more thing... These were a side dish to accompany Ben Gazzara's leg of lamb at Mandy Wedgwood's Columbo Dinner Party in Leeds. Verdict? "The stuffed zucchini were delicious! I wasn't sure what cheese biscuits were (lost in translation over the pond!), so just used a mixture of breadcrumbs and grated Parmesan to top them with." That sounds like the perfect thing for a non-US based cook to do, Mandy!

PLAYBACK - 1975

We can tell what kind of person Oskar Werner's character, Harold Van Wick, is right from the beginning of this episode. In the pre-title teaser, his wife, played the lovely Gena Rowlands, says very gently, "I think it would be best if I took over chairmanship of the company," to which he points his finger and shouts, "You think I would remain with the company in a subservient position to my wife?!"

It's actually quite difficult to see why Elizabeth Van Wick is so smitten with her husband, although he does have a certain sleazy, superficial charm. Obviously an inveterate womanizer; he flirts outrageously, at an art gallery event, with one of my favorite minor characters in *Columbo*, Marcy Hubbert. I just love the way she reacts to Harold's very stylish digital watch by exclaiming in a cut-glass English accent, "Oh, that's super!"

Harold is flattered by her admiration, as it is a watch he designed himself, for the electronics company he runs, (owned by his much-disliked mother-in-law). The animosity between the two is palpable, so it's no great surprise that when she tries to strip him of his position as the head of the company, he bumps her off.

Harold seems to be able to explain away many things that Columbo feels are incriminating, and he's very condescending to the Lieutenant. When Columbo finds a clever way to prove that the murder occurred earlier than it at first seemed, Harold finds a way of wriggling out of it, "I'm afraid Lieutenant, that your little parlor trick proved absolutely nothing." The exasperated look the Lieutenant gives him; one arm folded, one finger on his lip is classic Columbo. He goes out to get something to eat and to mull it all over. There he gets his big clue.

Oskar's Weiner Schnitzel is a wonderful sight to see if you garnish it exactly as he advises. It's delicious too. I get my butcher to bash out the veal slices for me, as this saves elbow grease.

There's a lovely chemistry between Peter Falk and Gena Rowlands. They were very good friends in real life. The classic Cassavetes film, *A Woman Under the Influence*, in which they starred together, was released in the same year as this episode. I think Gena's Cherry Torte, which is in the

"Columbo's Chili and Other Delights" section, would be lovely after Oskar's Weiner Schnitzel.

Burgers are an alternative meal you could serve up for this episode as Columbo has a brainstorm as he's about to eat one. He's in a diner looking for ketchup, going behind the counter because the staff are distracted watching a football game. When he gets his burger, he sees something on the TV that is a clue so good, he stops dead in his tracks. Does he ever eat his burger? I bet he doesn't…

Oskar Werner's Wiener Schnitzel

1 lb / 450g veal steak (cut from leg) cut ¼ inch thick
1 egg
Few drops of water or milk
Salt and pepper
½ cup / 30g fine fresh breadcrumbs
3 tablespoons sweet/unsalted butter (or half butter, half bacon grease)
Small beets/beetroot, cooked
Sliced lemon
8 anchovy fillets
Handful of capers

Pound meat with a wooden mallet to flatten. Beat egg with water or milk. Season meat well with ½ teaspoon salt and ¼ teaspoon freshly ground pepper. Dip steaks into the breadcrumbs. Shake off, then dip in egg, let stand 10 minutes. Dip again in breadcrumbs.

Heat butter in heavy frying pan and brown meat quickly on both sides. Remove steaks to heated platter. Garnish each steak with sliced beets/beetroot and a slice of lemon over which cross two anchovy fillets. Sprinkle with capers. Oskar suggests serving with mixed cooked vegetables (Brussels sprouts, asparagus tips, or green beans) and boiled (or mashed) potatoes.

Serves 4

Just one more thing... Cult filmmaker Jan Manthey (aka Fred Karno) tested this recipe for me in typical creative style. He couldn't get veal in his neck of the woods (Hounslow), so used pork loin steaks instead, bashing each flat to wafer thin-ness with a rolling pin. He told me, "Mrs. Karno is veggie, so for her I made Wiener Mushroom Schnitzel. Portobello mushroom put in the oven with butter for about 10 minutes to soften it. And then I carefully rolled it flat with the rolling pin. Then the recipe was the same as the regular schnitzel - tastes and looks good too." What a good idea! His aside, "Naturally Kaputnik was here for the free feed..." made me laugh. (Roger Kaputnik is the alter-ego of my ex-boyfriend Vic Pratt. Of course he was there for the free feed!)

A DEADLY STATE OF MIND - 1975

Is there someone in your life who makes you do things you don't necessarily want to do? Have they hypnotized you, and put ideas in your head when you weren't paying attention? It's possible. Even in everyday life, there are some clever folks who know how to mess with your mind without the use of drugs or years of training. The George Hamilton character in this episode, Dr. Mark Collier, does this for a living, however and is an expert in his field.

Everyone knows that trouble lies ahead when a doctor gets involved with a patient. Especially when the doctor is a psychiatrist, and his patient is an emotionally disturbed young woman who becomes dependent on him. Additionally, when he is behind schedule writing a book, and the publisher is hovering on his shoulder like a ravenous vulture, things start to get a little desperate.

The doctor has no respect for the Lieutenant and makes fun of him in front of his friends. "Brace yourself, Chuck, it's the law!" he says to a snooty friend (who seems surprised that someone so shabby looking could be a policeman). The Lieutenant crashes a house party thrown by Mark and the host puts on a silly British accent to make fun of our sleuth. When Columbo asks if it's okay to take a flint out of his lighter, Mark quips (in a very Sherlock Holmes fashion), "Most certainly Lieutenant. It's your case, do as you wish!" His guests all laugh. Columbo takes it in his stride of course, as he already has some of the evidence he needs to clobber the murderer.

I wonder what the cultural connotations of cream soda were in the 1970s? Columbo asks for one at Mark's get-together. If someone came to a party at my house and asked for a cream soda, I would think it very odd. Cream soda was more popular during the 70s I guess, but Mark does raise an eyebrow at this slightly bizarre request.

Unusually for him, Columbo refuses the offer of some nibbles, from a friendly partygoer. He says he's on a diet. Perhaps he really is? When Mark suggests a coffee at a later date, he says he takes it black, again mentioning that he's dieting. Maybe he overdid it on his cruise holiday a couple of episodes back?

George Hamilton's Ginger Snap Dandy is definitely not something to press upon guests who are on a diet. This makes a very big dandy, so you may wish to halve the quantities (unless you are having a big crowd over for a party like George does in this episode).

To drink? Well, cream soda I guess.

George Hamilton's Ginger Snap Dandy

3 eggs
1 cup / 175g chopped dates
4 cups / 950ml skimmed milk - divided use
¾ cup / 150g brown sugar - divided use
Butter for greasing baking dish
1½ cups / 150g Ginger Snap crumbs
2 teaspoons vegetable oil

Put the eggs, dates and half of the milk into a blender. Blend until dates are pulverized. Pour into a mixing bowl and add the rest of the milk and ½ cup / 100g of the brown sugar. Pour into greased baking dish and bake in a bain-marie at 375 degrees F / 190 degrees C / gas mark 5, for 40 minutes, or until firm like custard. Remove from oven and sprinkle topping over the custard. To make the topping, mix together the Ginger Snap crumbs, vegetable oil and ¼ cup / 50g brown sugar. Sprinkle this over custard and place in oven again for 5 minutes. Serve hot or cold.

Just one more thing... I am so lucky to have Helen Coniam from Dinner With Zelda Manners in my corner. For the life of me, I could not get George's pudding to set (but Helen cracked it). George didn't mention baking his dish in a bain-marie style, but Helen figured it out. My transcription of the original recipe just said to bake it for 40 minutes, but as Helen confided, "I'm guessing that George never made this ever in his life. When he was asked for a recipe, he probably phoned his mother and she dug this out for him. I have frequently found in these old recipes that the writer assumes that the reader is proficient with cooking techniques. An American custard is, of course, set and firm like we have a custard tart or a crème brûlée. So, I boiled the kettle, put the dish in a big baking tray, and topped it up with hot water. Then I put it back in the oven for another 20 minutes, and it set!" So, if you try this recipe, bake it in a bain-marie, and hopefully you'll have a lovely set pudding! Helen also made a version of this with brandy snaps rather than ginger snaps due to a purchasing error, by her other half, Dave. No offense to George, but Helen liked the brandy snap topping better.

THE FIFTH SEASON
(1975-1976)

FORGOTTEN LADY - 1975

The beginning of this episode gives a great big head nod to the classic movie musical, *Singin' in the Rain*. The plot may also put you in mind of another Hollywood classic, *Sunset Boulevard*. Janet Leigh plays the "forgotten lady" of the title, a former stage and movie star who wants to come out of retirement. Unlike the Gloria Swanson character in *Sunset Boulevard,* however, Grace Wheeler Willis looks as though she could make a plausible comeback. She is in great physical shape and slightly less deranged.

Columbo is very star-struck when he meets Grace. He reveals that he and his wife were big fans of hers when they were high school sweethearts. Grace seems charmed by this. She invites them both to watch a movie with her in her home cinema. The Lieutenant imagines his wife will "probably faint." Grace wants everything perfect. She tells her butler that as Mr. and Mrs. Columbo are old and loyal fans, she wants them to have, "an absolutely regal evening."

For reasons only made clear at the denouement, Grace isn't worried about the Lieutenant at all. There is no animosity between them, and she's completely oblivious to the fact that he suspects her of killing her husband. Unlike most of Columbo's foes, she's as nice as pie to him. When Columbo tests a theory, by climbing a tree outside her house and gets caught, Grace flirtatiously suggests, "I don't think you are being completely candid with me about your frequent visits." He scratches his head and is about to reply, when she interjects, "But I think I know the reason why you persist in popping up. You simply enjoy being around the *magic* of show business." Columbo does seem to always enjoy being in the company of actors and actresses, it is true.

This is definitely a film lover's episode, and we get a great insight into the Lieutenant's tastes in celluloid entertainment. He lists his favorite movie stars; Edward G Robinson; Humphrey Bogart; Jimmy Cagney; Alan Ladd; Paul Muni; and Eduardo Ciannelli. He thinks the fact he loved gangster movies so much when he was young, was the reason he became a cop. Could be!

We also see Grace watching her younger self in a film called, *Walking My Baby*. This is a real 1953 musical in which Janet Leigh starred alongside Donald O'Connor. This could make a fun double bill with *Forgotten Lady*. This recommendation does, however come with a warning: the "humor" in this film would now be considered very un-PC. I found it pretty cringe-worthy.

If you are feeling flush, you could invite a few guests 'round and present them with what was on offer at Grace's screening for Mr. and Mrs. Columbo; a 1968 vintage Champagne and caviar. Hire yourself a butler and a tuxedo, so you can look like Columbo all gussied-up for the event. If you aren't a fan of musicals, why not match this episode with one of the gangster movies the Lieutenant mentions; *This Gun's For Hire* or *Scarface*.

Janet's recipe is perfect for a solo Columbo session. Indulge yourself! It's easy to scale it up if you are watching it with others too. If you are in the UK, you probably won't be able to get Liederkranz cheese. The closest I could get was Epoisses. For American cooks, Liederkranz is a variety of Limburger cheese. I guess you could use whatever you have around the place, as long as it isn't mousetrap cheese!

Janet Leigh's Cheese Soufflé

1 tablespoon butter
1 tablespoon flour
A pinch of cayenne pepper
Scant ½ a cup / 120ml of milk
1 tablespoon grated Parmesan cheese
½ teaspoon mustard
1 egg yolk
1 stiffly beaten egg white
2½ oz / 70g Liederkranz cheese
Slice of toast

Melt the butter in a pan. Stir in the flour, a small pinch of salt, and cayenne pepper. Pour in the milk and stir over heat until the mixture thickens, but does not boil.

Remove and stir in the Parmesan cheese. Add mustard, egg yolk and beaten egg white. Spread Liederkranz on the slice of toast (Janet used whole wheat bread for "greater nutrition and no weight-gaining content"). Place in the bottom of a small, single serving casserole.

Gently pour the egg mixture over the toast and bake for about 20 minutes in a 375 degree F / 190 degrees C / gas mark 5 oven. Janet warns: "don't PEEK. If there is anything a soufflé can't stand, it is a sudden gust of air on the light mixture."

Serves 1

Just one more thing... Musicians, Ben Reed and his girlfriend Laura Groves, were keen to try this recipe and let me know, "We did the Janet Leigh soufflé the other night! It was very tasty. It did turn out a bit like posh cheese on toast though, haha. Laura took photos, and did 93% of the cooking." So which 7% of the cooking did you do Ben?!

I love the fact that milliner Lady Jane Fryers (who is a "can't cook, won't cook" type of Lady), made this when her other half (and definitely the chef de maison) was away in London. She loved it and proclaimed, "Delicious! I'm making this again! The recipe was easy to follow ... even for someone who's not really sure where the kitchen is and thinks the oven is for drying millinery flowers." Jane sent me a beautiful photograph of her dog Tia, patiently waiting to see if there might be a little sliver of leftovers for her. She was slipped a little slice of Epoisses which Lady Jane managed to source at the farmer's market in Rye, East Sussex. You can find Jane's amazing hats (including some made of fish leather) via her Facebook page Jane Fryers Millinery.

A CASE OF IMMUNITY - 1975

A seemingly emotionless villain is a difficult adversary for Columbo. There isn't much here for him to get his teeth into, as the Hector Elizondo character, Hassan Salah, is a very cold fish indeed. The homicide in this episode occurs in the legation of an imaginary Middle Eastern country, Suaria. The embassy and its grounds are effectively a foreign territory on American soil. Different rules apply and the concept of diplomatic immunity comes to the fore.

The King of Suaria is on a royal visit. He is intrigued by the Lieutenant and likes him very much, despite the two of them being worlds apart in status. The King is obviously a good egg. There is much amusement to be had from this episode, as Columbo tries to get to grips with Suarian culture, very different to his own. Our villain Hassan wears long flowing robes; Columbo accidentally stands on the hem of his garment, not once, but twice (the sound department supplies a great ripping sound effect on both occasions).

When the murder is committed and Columbo assigned to the case, Hassan recognizes him as the cop who ripped his robe on an earlier occasion. The Lieutenant explains how there was a mix-up over names; he shouldn't have been at the earlier meeting about security for the King's visit when the ripping incident occurred. It was all a mistake. "How amusing, and how co-incidental," states Hassan, stony-faced and obviously not at all amused.

Hassan is attempting to frame his colleague, Rachman Habib, played by Sal Mineo, for the murder; but Columbo knows that he didn't do it. "After 15 years in the business, I can still look at a person sometimes, and say, 'he can't be the murderer,'" claims our sleuth. Hassan asks how often he is right; Columbo admits to 20% or so, if that. He's being modest of course, Columbo is always right!

At one point in this episode, Columbo finds himself in the ligation kitchens, surrounded by food. He admits to being starved, as he forgot to eat. The Lieutenant transgresses etiquette, attempting to taste a beef dish that is being prepared expressly for the King; there is a bit of a panic. Hassan then insists the chef prepare several dishes of food for him. Columbo is a little surprised to find out, that rather than traditional Suarian food, the King favors French cuisine. He digs into a dish without knowing what it is, and looks slightly alarmed when told that it is "petits escargots." Snails of course.

To eat with this episode then, you could either have an elaborate French banquet (like the King of Suaria) or Hector Elizondo's simple, but delicious, Pasta Pomodoro.

Hector Elizondo's Famous Pasta Pomodoro

12 fresh plum tomatoes
¼ to ½ cup / 60-120ml olive oil
4 to 6 fresh cloves of garlic, peeled and crushed
1 can flat anchovies
1 tablespoon red pepper flakes
3 sprigs fresh rosemary (or 1 tablespoon dried rosemary)
Black pepper
1 lb / 450g uncooked spaghetti or linguini
Freshly grated Parmesan cheese

Put tomatoes in a pan of boiling water until skins crack.

Heat olive oil and sauté the garlic. Add anchovies and pepper flakes. Hector warns that it's important that you don't allow these to brown.

Peel tomatoes under cold water, so you won't burn your fingers. Drop tomatoes into sautéed sauce. Hector advised, "As you mix them in, sort of chop them - you want the sauce to be a little lumpy." Add rosemary and a dash or two of freshly ground black pepper.

Make pasta according to package instructions and drain. Pour sauce over pasta and add grated Parmesan to smooth out flavors.

Serves 2

Just one more thing... If you are a gamer, you may dispute my claim that Suaria is an imaginary country. According to WikiStates, "The Triple Republic of Suaria is a moderately large country located in the Brotherhood of Nod." OK then! Helen Coniam of Dinner With Zelda Manners thought that this was a quick and easy recipe to follow, and I agree. She concocted a modified version of this recipe for those who don't eat fish, substituting capers for the anchovies, which I think is a really good idea. Helen agreed that this recipe would easily serve two, but thought that it could stretch to serve 4 with a salad and some fresh bread. Agreed!

IDENTITY CRISIS - 1975

Patrick McGoohan plays the ultimate, haughty Englishman in this episode. He is extremely high and mighty in his general demeanor and obviously thinks Columbo is way beneath him, both intellectually and socially. As a Brit myself, it makes me cringe to hear phrases such as "my best to your lady," as it's the kind of thing I imagine ex-pats in the USA might say to cultivate an eccentric air of Britishness. Patrick's character is absolutely awful in this episode, with his patronizing air of colonial disdain. The repeated phrase, "Be seeing you," is an in-joke for fans of his cult classic television series, *The Prisoner.*

Patrick's character, Nelson Brenner, has a beautiful home with exotic staff; serving plates of elaborate hors-d'oeuvres to "droppers-in" at the drop of a hat. When Brenner invites Columbo to his house after lending him ten dollars for gas he tells the Lieutenant, "You rather fascinate me." Columbo has to decline the invite, but later, when he turns up unexpectedly; our villain is very hospitable. He asks the Lieutenant if he'd like a drink. When asked if he has any wine, Nelson replies that he has a cellar full. Asked what kind of wine he would like, the Lieutenant declines to show off his knowledge and simply says "red." Brenner gives direction to his manservant in some incomprehensible language along these lines, "Aobolwlgongallla balla balla Beaujolais, Columbo..." (The legendary Columbophile tells me that Patrick McGoohan made this up on the spot!) I would strongly suggest the appropriate booze for this episode would be lashings of Beaujolais. If you have guests; they should comprehend the joke, because the Beaujolais moment is so good.

If you *are* having chums around to watch this episode and would like to take on the persona of the villain when your guests arrive, you could enquire, "What would you like in the way of libation?" instead of, "Whaddya want to drink?" If you don't fancy cooking an elaborate meal, you could serve hot dogs and coffee. That's what Columbo chows down on in this episode.

If you fancy a little entertainment after the show, why not a game of Mah Jong, or backgammon, or another game of chance? You could play for money… for as Brenner observes, what else is there?

As mentioned previously, I can't find any recipes from the kitchen of Patrick McGoohan, so here's something that is really simple from Peter Falk instead:

Peter Falk's Avocado

Peter Falk liked his avocado sprinkled with lime or lemon juice, freshly ground pepper, and a few tablespoons of bottled French dressing or vinaigrette sauce.

Serves 1

Just one more thing... It made me laugh when my Shellac Sister and milliner extraordinaire, Lady Jane, offered to test cook this. She almost never sets foot in the kitchen (which is one of the reasons she is known as Lady Jane). If you too are a "can't cook, won't cook" type, you can still eat like Peter Falk with this recipe. (As recommended by a bona fide Lady!) I loved the fact that LJ got herself a Columbo DVD just for this project, "As I'd bought a double DVD to watch *Forgotten Lady* for my Janet Leigh recipe, I preceded my avocado extravaganza by watching *A Case of Immunity*. It was fabulous! The long-suffering (but obviously guilty) Hassan Salah (played by Hector Elizondo) was hilarious and I'm afraid I laughed out loud when Columbo trod on his traditional robe for the second time!!" That bit always cracks me up too!

A MATTER OF HONOR - 1976

I'm guessing that the part of retired, ace bullfighter Luis Montoya, was written specifically for Ricardo Montalban. Who else could play this wonderful role? In his late 50s, Ricardo's character is still svelte, upright, and sporting skin-tight trousers (that he could easily have been wearing 30 years earlier when he was king of the bullring). He's a magnificent looking man! There is a scene where this legendary matador is reliving his glory days; watching a 16mm film of himself as a young man in the bullring. This is almost certainly a scene from Montalban's 1947 performance as bullfighter Mario Morales in *Fiesta*. In fact, if you can get hold of *Fiesta*, it would make a great double bill with this *Columbo*.

The episode is notable for the Lieutenant's friendship with a Mexican cop (played by Pedro Armendáriz Jr.). Although they have never met before, Pedro's character, Commandante Sanchez, is a big fan of the Lieutenant; having read about him in the newspaper. Columbo's solving of the cruise ship crime, featured in the *Troubled Waters* episode, was big news in Mexico apparently. Columbo is worried about his car when it is towed away after an accident. He tells Sanchez, "I need the car, and it's very special." Sanchez replies, "*You* are very special!" The Lieutenant and his Mexican counterpart work together to solve the crime. Columbo rarely gets this kind of respect from senior colleagues in Los Angeles.

Retired bullfighter, Luis Montoya, is a legend in Mexico, and known as "the bravest of the brave." When Columbo suggests he could have murdered his assistant, Sanchez objects, "that's like saying the Pope did it!" Eventually, he comes round to the Lieutenant's way of thinking but takes a back seat. They joke together about the fact that Sanchez has to think about his pension, Columbo is a foreigner; he can afford to take more risks with the living legend that is Montoya.

When Montoya first meets the Lieutenant he tells him, "My house is your house," but when Columbo starts making a pest of himself (by sniffing around the ranch and asking tricky questions), he's not so keen. He certainly doesn't endear himself to the great matador when admits, "I'll tell ya the truth, I don't think I would enjoy watching a man kill an animal like that. As big and as mean as he is." Montoya inquires, "Perhaps you do enjoy the spectacle of two men in a ring, beating each other senseless, murdering an innocent deer with a rifle, or catching a fish with another one that is still alive… Our culture is different to yours Lieutenant." Columbo's Mexican counterpart feels obliged to apologize for the Lieutenant's meddling behavior. Montoya, with a serious tone and no hint of a smile, observes, "So inquisitive. I find him amusing."

Rather fitting for this particular episode (with calves and bulls running amok), is one of Ricardo's favorite recipes, "Mexican Calves Brain Soup, House of Montalban." A very grand title for a recipe that I'm not sure many of us these days, would want to make. I've selected something more benign for you to enjoy alongside this outing, but the calves brain soup recipe can be found in the "Columbo's Chili and Other Delights" section should you wish to tackle it!

To drink with this episode, it's got to be Mescal.

Ricardo Montalban's Cream of Asparagus Soup

6 tablespoons butter or margarine, divided use
½ cup / 75g chopped onion
½ cup / 60g chopped celery
2 cans (16 oz / 450g each) green asparagus spears
6 chicken bouillon cubes
¼ cup / 30g flour
1 cup / 240ml light/single cream
Salt and pepper

Melt 2 tablespoons of the butter or margarine in a saucepan over low heat. Add onion and celery and cook until tender. Drain, the 2 cans asparagus spears, reserving liquid. Cut tips and set aside. Dice stalks and add to cooked vegetables along with asparagus liquid plus water to make 5 cups; then add bouillon cubes. Bring to boil and cook for 5 minutes. Remove from heat and put through sieve or food mill. Melt 4 tablespoons butter or margarine in another saucepan over very low heat and stir in flour. Stir in the light cream, continuing to cook until thickened; stirring constantly. Add sieved asparagus mixture, asparagus tips, salt and pepper, and heat to serving temperature.

Makes approximately 1½ quarts (about 1700 ml).

Just one more thing... Judy Gelman, co-writer of the deliciously good, Unofficial Mad Men Cookbook, made this for her husband who liked it and proclaimed it to be tasty! Judy used 1 lb fresh asparagus, cooking the soup for 30 minutes rather than 5, and whizzed the soup up in her blender. The photograph of the finished dish that she sent me looked absolutely delicious.

My favorite food blogger Emily Brungo, aka Yinzerella of Dinner is Served 1972 made this for herself and her boyfriend. She thought it was, "yummy" and he liked it so much, he had seconds. Mr. Sauce Esq. commented, "fantastic," and "a really good blend." I thought the best quote from their evening in Baltimore was, "It has the appearance of a grasshopper (the cocktail) but instead of minty - it's whatever that flavor is." Perhaps we should invent an asparagus flavored cocktail? By the way, I am putting some money on Yinzerella being the person most likely to attempt Ricardo Montalban's Calves Brain Soup.

NOW YOU SEE HIM - 1976

I have decided. Jack Cassidy is my favorite Columbo villain. He's in three episodes, and this particular one is my favorite of them. He plays a magician, and I love magic.

The action takes place at The Cabaret of Magic, the kind of dinner venue I do so wish still existed. Crystal cut glass, waiters in red jackets with yellow carnation boutonnieres, high-backed, velvet upholstered chairs, round tables with teeny weeny lamps in the center - all utterly fabulous. Plus, there is a magic show par excellence, involving a Houdini-esque stunt, where Jack's character, "The Great Santini" is locked in a box and suspended in a tank of water. Can he escape before the sand in the enormous egg timer runs out? We shall see.

Santini's plan for the perfect murder involves the classic technique of misdirection, he is not where he appears to be when the murder takes place. Columbo seems to be impressed by the illusionist's magic tricks. He watches Santini performing a sleight-of-hand trick and observes, "I've always wanted to know how those things were done… I guess you have to have dexterous hands." Santini flatly responds, "How astute of you." Columbo looks at his own hands, "You see, my hands wouldn't conceal, anything, too small." But as he often does, the Lieutenant tries to get into the mind of his villain by studying their specialty. He learns a magic trick himself and challenges Santini's escapologist skills with a set of police handcuffs.

He clearly bugs Santini, who alternates between being smarmy and friendly with him or being snappy and super-protective over the secrets of his magic tricks. When Columbo crashes Santini's dinner date, the illusionist is peeved, "Lieutenant, what is it about me that you find so irresistible?" Columbo questions him about his many stage names, and Santini finally admits that this is not the name he was born with. Affirming that he once used the surname of Washington, Columbo asks for a first name. Santini delivers the withering reply, "Martha," which gets a wry smile out of the Lieutenant.

Santini, of course, underestimates the Lieutenant. At the very end of the episode when Columbo has his "gotcha" moment, Santini acquiesces, "..and I thought I'd performed the perfect murder." The Lieutenant responds: "Perfect murder sir? Oh, I'm sorry, there's no such thing as a perfect murder. That's just an illusion." Perfect!

For dinner, here are a few ideas. Firstly, if you are the kind of person to own an enormous, silver tureen you could serve shrimp (flown in from Yucatan) on a bed of ice, accompanied by a decanter of rosé (as this is the final meal of the murder victim).

When Columbo turns up at the scene of the crime, he is wearing a brand new raincoat and has his dinner in a brown paper bag. It's greasy chicken. Generous as ever, he offers a piece to his colleague, the legendary John J. Wilson. We don't see Columbo eat any of the chicken, but knowing the Lieutenant as we do, he almost certainly won't get around to it.

But here is my big recommendation. I had never heard of City Chicken until I saw Jack's recipe for it in a newspaper from 1969. He said that was a specialty of his wife (at the time), actress Shirley Jones. City Chicken is a very strange dish, but it's great fun to make (and as Columbo has a bag of chicken in this episode, I think it's entirely appropriate). If you don't fancy making Jack's dish, why not just get some tasty fried chicken from your local takeaway and serve it from brown paper bags so you can be like the Lieutenant?

Jack Cassidy's City Chicken

1 lb / 450g veal
1 lb / 450g beef, lean
1 lb / 450g pork loin
Salt and pepper
1 egg, beaten
1½ teaspoons milk or water
1 cup / 150g fine dry breadcrumbs (or cracker crumbs)
¼ cup / 60g sweet/unsalted butter (or margarine)
1 tablespoon finely chopped onion
A few tablespoons of water or beef broth

Preheat oven to 325 degrees F / 160 degrees C / gas mark 3.

Cut meat into 1½-inch cubes. Sprinkle with 1 teaspoon salt and freshly ground pepper. Arrange beef, veal, and pork on 6 skewers. Press pieces of meat closely together, forming the shape of a drumstick.

Beat egg with milk or water. Dip drumsticks into this mixture; then roll them in breadcrumbs (or cracker crumbs). Melt butter or margarine in a frying pan and brown drumsticks on all sides, then remove and place in baking dish. Lightly sauté the onion in pan drippings. Add water (or beef broth) to cleanse frying pan. Pour this over drumsticks in baking dish.

Cover, place in oven until meat is tender (about 1 hour).

Jack suggests serving these with baked potatoes and broccoli with butter sauce.

Serves 6

Just one more thing... Rebecca and Jim, who work at the amazing cake and chocolate company, Choccywoccydoodah in Brighton, made this with their daughter Connie to share with friends and family. I loved Rebecca's comment, "Very meaty! Old school meaty dinner." Ann's verdict was, "Loved the coating, really, really nice," and Jim and Connie both found it pleasing and enjoyable to make. I agree this is a fun recipe to make, and a fun one to eat too! As an internet commentator once put it, "My grandma used to make this, but simply called it Meat on a Stick." That's what we call it at Silver Screen Suppers Towers, too!

LAST SALUTE TO THE COMMODORE - 1976

When you watch a lot of *Columbo,* you begin to realize that how a murderer reacts to the arrival of the Lieutenant, is crucial to whether they are immediately the sole focus of his suspicion (which they usually are). There are many episodes where Columbo knows right from the get-go, who the murderer is. He just has to find a way of tripping them up. Keep an eye on Columbo's general demeanor in this one, when he unceremoniously turns up to announce that "The Commodore" has jumped ship. He's a bit bemused.

This is possibly the most controversial of all *Columbo* episodes for the die-hard fans. It deviates from the formula because we do not see the perpetrator of the crime commit the deed. I don't want to give too much away, but let's just say that the denouement is more like an Agatha Christie than a traditional *Columbo*. There are many theatrics and a fair amount of comedy thrown in. This is a playful episode, and all the more enjoyable because of it.

Columbo, in a nautically themed episode, is always a humorous thing to see. He bumbles around and tries to get to grips with cleats, booms, mizzens, marine paint, and the ship's log. We get the feeling he half admires those who enjoy life on the ocean wave, and half thinks it's a ridiculous waste of time. The Lieutenant is not to be bamboozled by unfamiliar surroundings and terminology of course. He always gets his man, or woman…

Unlike many of Columbo's adversaries, Robert Vaughn's character, Charlie Clay doesn't try and get chummy. He is a man of few words. When the Lieutenant offers him a cigar, "Smoke?" Charlie's reply is, "Intermittently." The scriptwriters didn't give Vaughn much to work with throughout this episode, and unless he is talking about boats, he keeps it zipped. Because he doesn't give anything away, he's a very tough nut for the Lieutenant to crack.

I'm not telling if Robert Vaughn committed a murder in this episode, or not. I'm just saying that his Fettuccine Alfredo is an excellent dish to serve before, during or after this episode. If you are having a get-together, make sure that you have a watch that ticks about your person, so that you can re-enact the "Commodore's watch" scene after dinner. It's classic *Columbo* hokum!

If you would like a dessert, I suggest a box of donuts (as these are what the cops offer the group of murder suspects at the end of the episode). I think everyone gathered together is just too posh to have one…

Robert Vaughn's Special Fettuccine Alfredo

¼ lb / 115g butter
2 cups / 480 ml heavy cream/double cream
¼ lb / 115g prosciutto, cut into ¼ inch cubes
1 lb / 450g Parmesan cheese, freshly grated
1 lb / 450g plain fettuccine noodles, cooked, drained and hot
1 lb / 450g spinach fettuccine noodles, cooked, drained and hot
1 cup / 150g green peas, cooked and hot
Salt and pepper

TO GARNISH

Fresh parsley or basil leaves

Cherry tomatoes

In a large pot, heat butter and cream until butter melts. Add prosciutto, cheese, plain and spinach noodles and peas. Toss until mixed. Add salt and pepper to taste.

Spoon onto individual plates or place in a large serving bowl. Garnish with parsley or basil, and tomatoes.

Serves 8

There is an absolutely genius clip from a cookery show on YouTube featuring Robert preparing this recipe with host Robert Morley. Do seek it out, it's hilarious.

Just one more thing... Columbo fan, Kiran Kaur, sent positive feedback about Robert's recipe, "The dish was the perfect meal for a cold autumnal night. If I could make a suggestion, it would be probably to up the amount of prosciutto to 200g - for a Christmas version, 300g prosciutto, and I'd also include the zest of a couple of lemons." I do like that idea! Kiran continued, "I watched *Troubled Waters* after I'd made this, and I laughed at the thought that Robert Vaughan probably wouldn't need to fake a heart attack after all that cream and cheese in the recipe!" Quite so!

Fellow film archivist and neighbor across the back lawn, Corinna Reicher, made this dish for Vic and I one summer night, and we were absolutely stuffed! Corinna reported, "This dish mainly consists of all things that your GP has recommended you cut from your diet as much as possible: gallons of double cream and mountains of butter and full-fat cheese. Yummy! I'd say you still have plenty of stuff that is bad for you in the dish if you only use about a third of the amount stated in the recipe." Haha - so true. I loved Corinna's advice to think of the health factor, "Summing up, this dish is perfect for lazy cooks who enjoy all that is truly bad for you. If you are prone to guilt, hang on to the pea, Vaughn's special ingredient."

THE SIXTH SEASON (1976-1977)

FADE IN TO MURDER - 1976

If you offered a friend an alcoholic drink and they refused it, saying they had been on the wagon for eight months, what would you do? You wouldn't cajole, "One drink isn't going to turn you into a pumpkin, you know," and fix them one anyhow, would you? I sincerely hope not. But the William Shatner character, Ward Fowler, does this because he's an egotistical bully.

This is a very clever episode. Ward is an actor who plays a television detective, and there is much fun to be had seeing our favorite *real* television detective at loggerheads with a *fictional* television detective. What do you mean they are both fictional? Don't be daft.

Ward thinks he understands police procedure, through his primetime role as America's favorite detective. His television persona is so ingrained, that it blurs with who he is off-screen. Columbo says that he never misses the Lieutenant Lucerne show, and admires a character who is ultimately very much like himself. When Ward offers to assist Columbo in his investigation, it tickles Columbo pink. He feigns the humbleness that we love about him, and replies, "Oh, that would be an honor! Detective Lucerne helping me? Wait 'til I tell my wife!"

When the two first meet, Ward has Columbo's number immediately. He knows that the Lieutenant is being disingenuous and points out: "They don't send a police detective, stumbling around, asking silly, fake, innocent questions, on a routine check. I know that from my show…" He gets a wry smile when he explains what he means by silly, fake, innocent questions, effectively imitating the Lieutenant's questioning style. Columbo laughingly admits, "Well, you're absolutely amazing sir, you're right!" Later, when Ward expounds on a theory, trying to put the Lieutenant off his scent, that the murderer was a robber with no intent to kill anyone; Columbo pretends to be impressed. "It's brilliant, sir. That's very impressive. No wonder you solve more crimes than I do, sir."

There's no animosity between the two "detectives," it's very easy for Columbo to play along with the idea that the two of them are going to solve the crime together. Ward is greatly amused when during a gap in filming, he returns to his trailer and finds the Lieutenant posing in Lucerne's trademark hat. They drink brandy together and fool around with Ward's video camera, Columbo acting along and pretending to be one of Lieutenant Lucerne's adversaries. Ward obviously thinks, for a while, that Columbo is a fool, but soon realizes that the Lieutenant is also playing a role, and is just as good an actor as he is himself.

So when Columbo starts asking Ward some tricky questions, Ward gets a little uppity, "Why don't we stop pretending that I'm brilliant and you're simple for one moment." He definitely thinks he has the upper hand, but the trouble is, Ward makes a very silly mistake and Columbo catches him. Realizing he's done for, he delivers a great line justifying his error and showing his blurred sense of reality, "I've had no rehearsal as a murderer, I am, after all, a detective."

I love the scene where Columbo visits Ward, offstage at home. He's relaxing in an open-necked shirt, wearing a lot of jewelry, and holding the biggest brandy glass I have ever seen. Later in the episode, the two drink brandy together, so this would be an appropriate tipple to sip during your screening. Especially if you can get humungous glasses to drink from.

William's steak dish is simple but surprisingly delicious.

William Shatner's Steak Picado

2 green peppers
1 large onion, peeled
4 ripe tomatoes, peeled
1 tablespoon olive oil
2 lbs / 900g lean, top sirloin steak
2 teaspoons chili powder
Pinch dried oregano
1 clove garlic, crushed

Cut peppers, onion, and tomatoes into ½ inch pieces. Sauté in olive oil until onion is transparent. Cube steak into bite-sized pieces. In a separate pan rubbed with olive oil, sear the meat quickly until brown outside, but rare inside. Add sautéed vegetables, chili powder, oregano, and garlic. Season with salt and pepper to taste; mix well. Cover and simmer for 10 minutes. William suggests you serve at once, either alone or with side dishes of rice, tortillas, a green salad tossed with vinegar-oil dressing, and dry red wine.

Serves 6-8

Just one more thing... My excellent desk-mate and co-editor of *Holdfast Magazine*, Lucy Smee, tried this recipe and felt it needed more chili. Lucy's capacity for chili is legendary however, so if you are weedy, maybe try it with 2 teaspoons and see how you feel about it.

Emily Brungo aka Yinzerella of Dinner Is Served 1972 felt that this dish did have a "Latin" flair to it because of the chili, but didn't peel the tomatoes because she thinks that's a "pain in the ass." I am definitely in agreement with that.

Journalist and Rock Musician, Jez Fielder, agreed with Lucy that this recipe needed more oomph. He said, "It didn't boldly go anywhere, taste-wise. I think it needed a lot more oregano and a lot more garlic." However, I loved the fact that Jez followed the recipe as written, observing, "Shatner has visited loads more galaxies than I have so I didn't mess with his specifications!"

OLD FASHIONED MURDER - 1976

Joyce Van Patten's character isn't a complete battle-ax in this episode, but she certainly knows what one looks like (especially if it was once used by William the Conqueror in 1066). She plays Ruth Lytton, the spinsterish curator of a small museum which has fallen on hard times. Family members consider her old-fashioned because she has immersed herself in the history of relics and artifacts, rather than getting out and about and finding a beau. But as Ruth points out to Lieutenant Columbo, an old maid is someone who has never been married, not necessarily someone who has never been engaged.

As usual with a female combatant, the Lieutenant has a certain respect for the perpetrator of the crime in this episode. Eagle-eyed Columbo viewers might recognize Joyce Van Patten from an earlier episode called, Negative Reaction where she plays a nun with just a few, but seriously brilliant, lines of dialog. I like to think that Peter Falk suggested Joyce for the lead in Old Fashioned Murder, after enjoying her earlier work. It's possible.

Joyce plays her role with great restraint, and we can see that Columbo has respect for a woman who has such a deep understanding of history. "Very nice, very nice little things you have standing around, very nice," he muses about the priceless antiques in Ruth's home. She thanks him and asks, "Are you interested in figurines, or has there been a homicide?" The two of them treat each other very gently and very politely; to begin with. "Your delicacy does you credit," she tells him. But her attitude changes when Columbo begins to ask tricky questions. "Is it part of your job to trip people up? Or to see if you can?" She warns the Lieutenant not to underestimate her, "I don't in the least mind you playing tricks, but you are going to have to be a little cleverer aren't you?" She is quietly confident that she's not going to get pinched. But of course, she does.

Columbo continues to treat her courteously right to the end though and is quite happy to lend her his arm when she asks him to; as she goes off to meet her fate.

Celeste Holm plays Ruth's more glamorous, cocktail quaffing sister, who always has a man's arm when she needs one. A great comic actress, Celeste provides much of the fun in this episode, fainting left, right, and center, and haughtily calling Columbo "Lieutenant Columbus." A classic, clumsy Columbo moment occurs, when he accidentally stands on the flowing scarf of one of Celeste's elaborate gowns, ripping it with a terrific sound effect (an echo of the same blunder in the A Case of Immunity episode).

Alas, I haven't been able to find a recipe for Joyce, so here's a lovely one from Celeste. She calls this "a heavenly entree" - indeed it is! Montmorency cherries are difficult to get in the UK (I've never seen them), so I use sour cherries from an Iranian grocery shop that is a bus ride away from where I live. I go there about once a year just to stock up on tinned sour cherries.

Celeste Holm's Celestial Chicken

2 chickens, jointed
Butter for sautéing the chicken joints
2½ cups / 565g Montmorency cherries
2 tablespoons cornstarch/cornflour
Salt and pepper
2 tablespoons sherry
1½ cups / 285g wild rice
Parsley

Sauté the chicken pieces in butter in a large frying pan (not par-boiled - do not use flour). When browned, place them on a serving platter.

Place the cherries and juice in the same frying pan in which chicken has been cooked. Add a little butter if necessary. Cook down and add cornstarch to thicken. Salt to taste, and add sherry.

Put rice in a sieve and rinse. Place in a separate pan, pour cold water over rice until it is about one inch above. Cook slowly until almost dry.

Place rice around the chicken. Pour sauce on top. Decorate with parsley.

Serves 6-8

Note: after I have fried the chicken pieces, I pop them in an oven preheated to 375 degrees F / 190 degrees C / gas mark 5, for about 20 minutes to cook through.

Just one more thing... Bethany B. in Michigan, really helped out with this dish (as Celeste's recipe was rather vague). She points out that some folks might like to reduce the amount of fruit in this recipe, reducing the amount of cornstarch in turn. She also wondered how it would taste to sauté some garlic and onions up after you remove the chicken from the pan, "I bet it would be a nice addition." I agree! Bethany and her mom thought that fresh or frozen tart cherries would be nicer than tinned ones if you can find them, concluding, "I would make this again though, it's a nice elegant meal."

It tickled me that my pen-pal, esteemed food writer Orlando Murrin, reported of his tinned cherries, "I found them in what I think of (perhaps unfairly) as the 'old lady' section - tinned fruit, jelly, and blancmange." Orlando offered a nice recipe tweak, "There is plenty of sauce, and it's rather sweet. Another time, I would drain the cherries, add 1½ cups/ 450ml chicken stock to the pan. The easy way to correct the thickness would be to dissolve 2tbsp of cornstarch in 2tbsp cherry juice, then whisk in as much as you need to the boiling stock in the pan until thickened to your pleasing. I also added a squeeze of lemon as well as the sherry, to cut the sweetness a bit." Yes, I agree and I'm going to try that next time I make Celestial Chicken. Thanks, Orlando, see you in the "old lady" section.

THE BYE-BYE SKY HIGH I.Q. MURDER CASE - 1977

Do you know your IQ? I've been dying to find out mine, ever since I first saw this episode. I'm pretty sure it would be low though. Any kind of mathematical problem drives me insane.

A conundrum is posed in this episode, in order to test Columbo's IQ. It fairly made my mind boggle trying to work it out myself, as it involves several sacks of real gold, several sacks of phony gold, and a penny scale. I don't think I understood the answer to it, even when the Lieutenant explained how he and Mrs. Columbo had worked it out. No matter what the Lieutenant's IQ is though, he's definitely smarter than everyone else in this episode. Naturally.

The Sigma Society is a club for those who are in the top 2% of people in the world, intelligence-wise. But despite their impressive intellects, most members have childish tastes; including train sets, silly word games, and ice-cream. Mind you, Columbo himself likes a sugary treat and misses a vital clue running after an ice-cream vendor in this episode. Later on, he tries to get away with eating a doughnut in a restaurant that he has bought elsewhere. A severe waitress, brilliantly played by Jamie Lee Curtis, soon puts a stop to that.

Theodore Bikel's character, Oliver Brandt, explains to Columbo how it's not all fun and games, being born smart. He reveals to the Lieutenant that he had no real childhood, he was an "imitation adult" and hid his genius because most children despise smart kids. He thinks out loud, "I wonder if all those early, bitter memories had something to do with my recent discovery that I simply no longer care, even for my fellow intelligentsia in this club." He finds them to be "eccentric bores."

But Columbo can't feel too sorry for him. The Lieutenant in return tells him that over the years, he's met a great many people much smarter than himself. There were many kids at school much clever than him. However, when he joined the force, he figured out that if he worked harder than those around him, read the books, and kept his eyes open; he'd make it to Detective, even if he wasn't the smartest of the bunch. "I really love my work, sir," Columbo explains.

Oliver thinks that the people he works with and the other members of the Sigma Society are dunces. He thinks he's smarter than them all. When Columbo explains how he believes the crime was committed, giving credit to another member of the Society for working it out. Oliver's ego cannot bear for another man to be credited with more intelligence, and he falls into the Lieutenant's brilliant trap. Our humble sleuth's gumshoe thinking beats a high IQ every time!

Theodore's meatloaf is utterly delicious. What makes it glorified? The raisins I guess... I use a big, 1-kilo loaf tin for this meatloaf, and I would say you can easily feed 8 people with this dish accompanied by some baked potatoes (I do mine in the oven while the meatloaf is cooking) and other veggies on the side. Of course, you can always serve this to fewer people and have leftover meatloaf to enjoy later in the week. I know which option I would go for, but I am greedy!

Theodore Bikel's Glorified Meatloaf

2 lb / 900g minced beef
1 green pepper, cut into small pieces
Dehydrated onions, amounting to one or two onions, Theodore says, "… depending upon one's taste."
1 cup / 240ml red table wine
1 cup / 150g raisins
1 cup / 150g seasoned dry breadcrumbs
2 tablespoons Worcestershire Sauce
1 teaspoon garlic salt
1 teaspoon seasoning salt
1 egg

Mix all ingredients together.

Form into a loaf, then bake in a preheated, moderate 325 degrees F / 160 degrees C / gas mark 3 oven for 45 minutes to one hour.

Serves 8

Just one more thing... Sarah Bailey of Sarah's Cooker-ebook thinks that this recipe would serve more than 8. She made a version halving all the ingredients, and said "We had ample for a meal for two, plus four rounds of sandwiches." Personally, I have never had meatloaf in a sandwich, but I really, really like the idea! I do know from previous experience that this meatloaf freezes very well, and it's always nice to find a big chunk of it in the freezer when I am least expecting it!

Kelly Patterson, of the wonderful Velveteen Lounge Kitsch-en, also rustled up this dish and proclaimed, "It was delicious! I didn't expect to like it as much as I did." She continued, "I shared it with my husband and he really liked it too. He commented that it was very moist. That might be owing to the cup of wine in the recipe (which no doubt contributed to our enjoyment)." Do check out Kelly's super-stylish blog and YouTube channel for fabulous recipes - especially cocktails!

THE SEVENTH SEASON (1977-1978)

TRY AND CATCH ME - 1977

If I ever went to a *Columbo*-themed party and had to act out my favorite scene from the series, I would probably dress up as Ruth Gordon and grab a set of keys from a sideboard. It's one of those magical moments when a *Columbo* co-star really shows how nobody in the whole, wide world could have done a scene any better.

Ruth Gordon is magnificent in the role of Abigail Mitchell. Chic and composed in her smart suits and very tidy, but super-ornate, hairdo. Abigail is a little old lady with a magnificent presence and a razor-sharp mind. I would love to have her life. I could sit behind a massive desk, splurging out my crime novels into a Dictaphone and suggesting to my secretary that my nephew might like to take me for a walk along the beach at 2 pm. Wouldn't you? She merely raises an eyebrow slightly, when asking Columbo how many lumps of sugar he would like in his tea, "One? Two?", he plumps for three.

If pressed, I would probably say that this is my favorite *Columbo*, because Ruth plays a great villain. Plus, "Dog" makes an appearance, and it is written by Stephen Bochco. These three things, in my humble opinion, make for a very good Columbo indeed.

Not only is Abigail Mitchell a famous novelist, she specialises in murder. There is an immediate mutual respect between the writer and the detective. Columbo tells Abigail that his wife is a huge fan of her books, and she in turn, seems very interested in the work of a police detective. At the home of the murder victim, she hovers close by as he looks around, observing, "What a pleasure to watch a consummate professional at work. You may ignore me, proceed to detect!"

Columbo thinks the reason Abigail is such a great crime writer is that she puts herself in the position of the detective, rather than the murderer. This, of course, gives her great insight into a cunning way of staging a murder of her own. She has planned it meticulously. But like most crime novel villains, she makes a few schoolgirl errors.

When Columbo turns up at a talk Abigail is giving to "The Ladies' Club," he already suspects her of being the guilty party. She inveigles him up to the podium and invites him to speak in her place. The Lieutenant tells his appreciative audience how much he loves his job, and reassures them that the world is not full of criminals; it is full of nice people. He expands, "Even with some of the murderers that I meet, I even like them too. Sometimes." He holds up a finger for emphasis, "like 'em and even respect 'em. Not for what they did, certainly not for that, but for that part of them which is intelligent, or funny, or just nice. Because there's niceness in everyone. A little bit anyhow." He sends a significant look in Abigail's direction of course.

There's a lovely scene down on the pier, where Abigail and Columbo bond over, "Dog" and his love of the sea. They discuss Abigail's loss, and Columbo sympathizes, "I'm beginning to be very fond of you Lieutenant," Abigail admits, "I think you are a very kind man." "Don't count on that, Miss Mitchell," counters the Lieutenant, "don't count on it." Columbo is sympathetic about why Abigail committed her crime, and he is indeed a kind man, but he is also a consummate professional. So he pursues her until he gets his proof.

Ruth's Zucchini Omelet is simple and delicious. It could be made just for one, for a self-indulgent brunch and *Columbo* combo. If you have a big omelet pan, however you could make a larger one, slice it up and invite some friends. If you fancied something a little more substantial, you could try the Chicken Wonderful recipe, supplied by Ruth's onscreen assistant (played by Mariette Hartley), which you'll find in the "Columbo's Chili and Other Delights" section. You might have to do some belly dancing later, to work off the calories!

Ruth Gordon's Zucchini Omelet

1 cup / 150g chopped zucchini/courgette
3 tablespoons diced onion
3 tablespoons diced green pepper
3 tablespoons diced celery
3 tablespoons butter
4 eggs, beaten
Salt and pepper

Heat butter in frying pan then sauté zucchini, onion, pepper, and celery until tender.

Slowly add beaten eggs and cook as for omelet.

Add salt and pepper to taste.

Serves 2

Just one more thing... My lovely friend, actor Clive Smith, had a go at Ruth's omelet and proclaimed it to be, "Delicious with a CAPITAL D."

He said that he usually makes an omelet with cheese, but SO didn't miss the cheese in this variation. I quote, "…it had a creaminess and gorgeousness that I can't put my finger on," and I agree. This is one of those recipes that is greater than the sum of its parts. Clive's tip, is to sauté the pepper, celery, and onion for five minutes longer than the zucchini/courgette (as it takes less time to soften).

MURDER UNDER GLASS - 1978

For foodies, this is the ultimate *Columbo* episode. Food and drink are central to the plot, central to the action, central to the murder, and central to everything! Just like in real life!

Louis Jourdan plays famous food critic Paul Gerard, who makes money from many sources. He has a regular TV cookery show, presents recipes on the radio, reviews restaurants, is paid to promote products such as Bon Snax (which look suspiciously like Ritz Crackers), and does a little bit of extortion on the side.

When Paul first meets Columbo, the Lieutenant is tucking into a massive bowl of Cioppino at a restaurant where there has just been a poisoning. Paul pretends to be concerned for the Lieutenant's health, but Columbo is very much enjoying the Cioppino, exclaiming, "It's terrific," and explaining to the food critic that Chef Albert, "…uses a freshly grated lemon peel to give it that extra zing!" He reveals that Mrs. Columbo is no great shakes as a cook, but that she has many other talents.

As in many episodes, Columbo soon begins to show a specific interest in the specialized subject of his suspect. He asks Paul about a particular sauce from his radio show that he wants to, "…spring on Mrs. Columbo." The Lieutenant can't seem to remember the name of the sauce. Paul wonders if it is Béchamel? Remoulade? Hollandaise? Naively, Columbo clarifies, "it's some kind of a French name."

Throughout this episode, the Lieutenant is presented with many delicious dishes to sample. The murder victim was a well-respected restauranteur and many chefs in Los Angeles were fond of him. When they realize Columbo is investigating the murder, they feed him up. He samples champignons farcis au crabe, caviar, smoked salmon and foie gras. There are hints throughout this episode that the Lieutenant is a quite a gourmand on the quiet, and knows a fair amount about fine dining. But he hides this light under a bushel when it comes to Paul, pretending, as usual, to be a bit of an ingénue.

When the Lieutenant crashes a rather special, Japanese-themed dinner party Paul is hosting, Paul, feigning formality, asks if he has eaten. Columbo admits that he's been eating a lot lately, but his appetite for a free meal is always present; waving his hands in the air, 'Well, maybe a small bite!" Paul is reluctant for the Lieutenant to try the fugu sashimi, "It's a developed taste. I think the Lieutenant would prefer one of the cooked dishes…" But Columbo tries it and likes it, announcing, "Gee that's funny, I thought the fugu was gonna taste like tuna fish!" The special Japanese guest at Paul's dinner party laughs heartily and gives the game away, explaining that fugu can poison a person if not prepared in the correct way. "Holy mackerel!" exclaims our hero. Utterly brilliant.

Margaux! It's the only wine to drink with this episode. If you have guests coming, would it be rude to ask them to bring a bottle of Margaux each? No, because you can then shout MARGAUX at the appropriate point in the build-up to the crime (in sync with the restaurateur who bites the bullet). You'll need some for the recipe too, so save your pennies up and buy a couple of bottles in advance, you won't regret splashing out on all of this, I promise.

If you have any loose change left over after buying the veal and Margaux, you might wish to get hold of one of the air driven cork removing devices that feature heavily in this plot. Just type Spong Corkette into eBay and you'll find one. You can make a very grand show of using your Corkette to open all the bottles of Margaux before and during dinner, without giving away to your guests that you have bought this as a prop, especially for this episode of Columbo. They will love you for it, I'm sure.

This recipe is Columbo's recipe. Not Peter Falk's you understand, but Columbo's. He cooks this for the perpetrator and we watch him every step of the way. Just as in *Any Port in a Storm*, where Columbo impresses a wine buff with his surprising knowledge of red wine, the Lieutenant surprises Paul Gerard with his prowess with a frying pan. He's self-deprecating of course, admitting, "I do a little cooking sir, nothing fancy."

I have watched this episode many times to work out exactly how Columbo cooks this dish, and have transcribed his recipe below. It is absolutely delicious - just as Paul says it is. The duo eat it served alongside a simple tomato and onion salad, with a mustard vinaigrette made by Paul. Accompanied by Margaux of course.

An alternative meal to have with this episode is Cioppino. Vincent Price's marvelous Cioppino recipe can be found in the entry for *Murder: A Self Portrait,* if you would like to try this dish. Make sure you add some freshly grated lemon peel to give it extra zing as the chef in this episode does.

Don't feel like cooking? You could have a Chinese takeaway. Columbo enjoys some Chinese food in this episode, but don't forget the egg rolls and fortune cookies. You could also have Japanese food. Just don't risk the fugu, whatever you do!

Whatever you eat, be sure to practice reciting Paul's catchphrase: "Bonjour and Bon Snax!"

Lieutenant Columbo's Veal Scallopini (aka Escalopes de Veau aux Cèpes)

2 veal escalopes, cut into long thin pieces if large
Approximately 1 tablespoon sweet/unsalted butter
Dash of olive oil
Salt
White pepper
2 shallots
½ cup / 25g dried, wild mushrooms, soaked in boiling water for 20 minutes and chopped
½ glass / 75ml red wine (Margaux!)

Heat the butter and olive oil in a frying pan. Season the veal with salt and white pepper (Columbo observes that white pepper "…somehow looks better on veal,"). When butter is bubbling, place veal in the pan and cook until browning on the edges, turn over and cook the other side. Columbo's veal is in the pan for approximately 1.45 seconds - but the cooking time will depend on how thin your escalopes are. Put the veal on a plate in a warm place.

Add shallots to the pan, "…two should be enough," until they caramelize and then add the mushrooms. Let them "…bubble around" for a minute. Then add wine, and stir around for a moment until getting hot. Put the veal back in the pan for approximately 40 seconds to warm through.

Serves 2

Just one more thing... Classic movie fan and amazing food illustrator, Miriam Figueras in Barcelona, shared this dish with her lovely mum, a lover of Columbo, who said that "the real mystery was why we hadn't cooked veal escalopes like this before! If only Columbo could see us!" The medium of television had to compress the cooking a little, so I really did appreciate Miriam's tweaks to the recipe, "Shallots should cook first for a bit so that they caramelize, and then add the mushrooms. It is a personal suggestion as I like to cook onion that way, I feel it adds more flavor. I also think that the mushrooms should cook a little bit longer than a minute and the same for the wine, it should fully evaporate its alcohol." Miriam suggests adding salt and pepper to the shallots and she really bumped up the amount of mushrooms in this dish, using a whole 350g tray of fresh rather than dried ones. Miriam really enjoyed trying out this recipe and I love her comment, "From watching the episode again to actually making the recipe, it has been a beautiful experience for me." Ah, that makes me so happy, Miriam!

MAKE ME A PERFECT MURDER - 1978

When you are a bustling, busy, beautiful, television executive, there is little time for pleasantries. When the Trish Van Devere character, Kay Freestone, is asked by her PA if she'd like some lunch, she bluntly demands: "Shrimp Salad." No please and thanks to top and tail it, like most polite folks would do. She's almost at the top of the television tree and she demands the utmost respect for her talents and tenacity. Telling a colleague that he'll have to work overnight on some figures for her, there is definitely some glee behind her throwaway comment, "Condolences Junior, comes with the territory." She has worked her way up in a man's world, through hard graft and bloody-mindedness and now she's got her eye on a further promotion.

Like many of Columbo's adversaries, however Kay is a little too sure of herself. When her secret lover breaks it to her that she's not going to get the job she wants; her face is a picture. He tells her she's not good enough, because, "You don't make decisions, you make guesses." This is not how she sees herself at all, and his flippant attitude to their affair, as well as her career, doesn't help. "In the end, all we really owe each other is a little affection," he states, "nobody was keeping tabs." Well watch out lover boy, Kay was definitely keeping tabs, and now you're for the chop.

This crime is timed to the second, meticulously planned and executed. As in many cases though, the Lieutenant seizes upon a seemingly insignificant anomaly, involving a seemingly insignificant object; the victim's spectacles. As he explains to Kay, "Interesting isn't it? How you can work these small things out if you just think about it? Like you've got a tiny voice, whispering right in your ear, trying to tell you who did it." Smiling, Kay replies, "You're a very attentive listener Lieutenant." To which his response is, "Oh yes ma'am. Well, that's all we've got to go on. Listen and look. Look and listen." Which fairly sums up the Lieutenant's technique.

Kay seems to genuinely like our sleuth, and she pays him several compliments. When Columbo asks her if she was attracted to the murder victim, she eventually admits that she was, saying that he was an attractive man, in his way. She follows this up by telling Columbo, "You are an attractive man in your way too." But the Lieutenant lets this veiled compliment pass on by; he's already got Kay's number. Columbo plays the role of someone impressed by the glossy world of television very well. But our indecisive murderer should have realized much sooner; Columbo doesn't make guesses, he makes decisions.

I'm sure the Lieutenant would have loved a bowl of Trish's chili with some crackers. There is something nice about knowing from the get-go that you are going to have this chili on the stove all day. I have cooked it successfully in a slow cooker/crock-pot too. You won't need as much stock if you cook it this way, as the liquid doesn't evaporate. Alternatively, you could make it with the same amount of stock but thicken it up towards the end as Johnny Cash does with cornmeal (see the entry for *Swan Song*).

As mentioned in the entry for *The Conspirators*, I've never seen condensed beef stock here in the UK. When I make this chili I use one can of Campbell's Beef Consommé, you can buy this via the internet. If you want to replace this with ordinary beef stock, I would suggest using less water than your box of stock cubes suggests for a more condensed beef flavor, or making the full amount and reducing it down.

Trish Van Devere's All Day Chili In The Pot

3 cups / 525g dried kidney or pinto beans
3 tablespoons fine grade olive oil
3 large onions, peeled and chopped
2 large cloves garlic, crushed
3 lb / 1350g lean, chopped, beef chuck/beef mince
1 teaspoon salt
⅛ teaspoon cayenne pepper (more if desired)
3 Spanish chili pepper pods (or 3 tablespoons fresh chili powder)
3 cups / 600g chopped, fresh tomatoes
1 cup / 240ml undiluted, canned beef stock

1 teaspoon cumin seeds

Trish doesn't mention this, but if you are using dried kidney beans these should be soaked overnight. If you use pre-cooked, canned beans, skip the first part of the recipe and use approximately 1320g drained beans.

Wash and pick over beans, cover with cold water in a vast pot and bring to the boil. Reduce heat. Remove from the heat, let stand one hour. Add water to cover, bring to boil again, lower heat, simmer slowly. Stir from time to time.

Meanwhile, in large Dutch oven or saucepan, sauté onion and garlic in olive oil until onion is golden. Remove onion from the cooking dish with a slotted spoon. Add meat to pan drippings and cook slowly over low heat, stirring with a spoon until meat is crumbly and light. Add meat and pan drippings to the large cooking pot with beans. Add remaining ingredients, including sautéed onions and salt.

Cook over very low heat, stirring with wooden spoon to blend and mix well. Keep on a low simmer, stirring often to prevent burning. Add more liquid (beef stock) if required to keep beans covered, and continue cooking until beans are tender but not mushy. Just before serving, taste to correct seasonings.

Trish suggests serving in bowls, garnished with minced, raw, sweet white onion, shredded lettuce and/or grated, aged, sharp Cheddar cheese if desired. Chili can also be served over hot, cooked rice.

Serves 10 to 12

Just one more thing... My hero, Lieutenant Columbo aka Columbophile, tested Trish's recipe for me, which was such an honor. He is the recognized expert on Columbo, and if you don't follow the Columbophile blog, you definitely should! He reports, "So it was an easy decision to opt for Trish Van Devere's chili when Silver Screen Suppers came a-knocking. After all, it pretty much looks after itself once it's all lobbed into the slow cooker, so the only issue is whether it'll be spicy enough to keep me keen." After his first bowlful, he decided to add a couple more teaspoons of chili powder, which made this dish exactly to his taste. I love LC's final summing up, "All in all I'd give Trish's chili a good old-fashioned thumbs up. You can't really go wrong with a chili recipe, and this backs up that assertion. So please whip up a batch with confidence." I'm sure that your eight selected dinner guests detailed in the foreword to this book would love your spiced up chili. Thank you, Columbophile!

HOW TO DIAL A MURDER - 1978

This episode of *Columbo* has special significance for me. It's the first one I can remember seeing. It's possible I saw it when it first aired on UK television, or it may have been later. Whichever it was, I clearly remembered the ferocious dogs and the clever use of the command word, "Rosebud."

It is also a dream episode for movie buffs, like myself. Nicol Williamson plays a rather self-satisfied psychologist called Dr Eric Mason, who collects cinema memorabilia. His dogs are called Laurel and Hardy, and he lives in a house that used to belong to silent movie star Theda Bara. If you have seen *Citizen Kane*, the word "Rosebud" will ring a bell with you, as it subsequently rings a bell to Laurel and Hardy. As the theme of the episode is so closely linked to *Citizen Kane*, why not have a double bill? We know from the Lieutenant that Mrs. Columbo thinks the movie is a masterpiece…

Columbo is full of admiration at Mason's collection of movie artifacts. He recognizes a photograph of W.C. Fields and enjoys shooting a few balls on Fields' pool table, smiling at Fields' own curved comedy pool cue. Mason is suitably wary of him. When a discussion about his wife's suspicious death gets him on the back foot, he remarks, "You're a fascinating man Lieutenant." "To a psychologist, sir?" the Lieutenant asks. "You pass yourself off as a puppy in a raincoat, happily running around the yard digging holes all over the garden," explains Mason. Only, you're laying a mine field and wagging your tail."

Columbo drinks a large glass of wine with the perpetrator during this episode, remarking "This is terrific wine, sir." Since the *Any Old Port in a Storm* episode, Columbo has a more refined taste in fine wines. But of course he's also partial to a more down to earth beverage, so when a young Kim Cattrall, playing Mason's lodger Joanne, asks the Lieutenant if he'd like a hot chocolate, he replies, "Oh I'd like that very much. Very much."

When Columbo begins to close in on the murderer over a friendly game of snooker, he tells Mason, "I must say, I found you disappointing. I mean your incompetence. You left enough clues to sink a ship. Motive, opportunity, and for a man of your intelligence sir, you got caught in a lot of stupid lies, a lot of 'em!" This challenge riles Mason's intelligence and he tries to set his dogs on the Lieutenant. But as always, Columbo is one step ahead; and we should never forget that he loves dogs and they love him.

Nicol was Scottish, so it's appropriate that one of his favorite meals involves "stovies." This is a great, hearty dish which is especially pleasing on a cold winter's night. I'm not sure hot chocolate would necessarily be the thing to have alongside your steak and stovies, but a terrific bottle of red, like the one Columbo shares with Dr. Mason in this episode, would be very good indeed.

Nicol Williamson's Steak Mince and Stovie Potatoes

4 large potatoes, peeled, sliced into large pieces
1 tablespoon butter (or bacon drippings)
1½ lbs / 675g ground/minced, lean, top quality steak
1 medium-sized onion, peeled and chopped
Salt and pepper
4 carrots, peeled and chopped finely [you might wish to parboil the carrots]
About ½ cup / 120ml water/stock or beef broth
1 beef bouillon/stock cube (optional)
Butter (optional)

Preheat oven to 300 degrees F / 150 degrees C / gas mark 2.

Parboil potatoes a few minutes in boiling water. Drain and reserve.

Melt butter or bacon drippings in a frying pan and sauté steak and onion, just until meat begins to turn brown. Take off heat and remove meat-onion mixture from frying pan, reserving the pan drippings.

Grease a large baking dish with butter (or bacon drippings). Arrange a layer of meat-onion mixture on the bottom of a casserole dish. Sprinkle lightly with salt and pepper. Top with a layer of carrots. Repeat these layers until all ingredients have been used, seasoning with salt and pepper as you go - Nicol suggests using 1¼ teaspoons of salt in total, pepper to your taste.

Heat water (or stock or beef broth) in the frying pan in which meat and onions have been cooked. For added flavor, dissolve bouillon cube in water (or stock) in the pan. Pour heated liquid over the vegetables in casserole dish.

Arrange potato slices on top of vegetables and mince to form a "fence" [I am guessing by this Nicol means to arrange the slices in rows so that they overlap with each other, covering the top of the other ingredients]. Salt and pepper lightly. Dot butter on top of potatoes if you wish.

Cover. Bake for 45 minutes. Remove cover and allow to cook for 30 minutes longer or until potatoes are browned and tender.

Serves 4

Just one more thing... Jessica Maitland of the Colmworth Micro Bakery reported, "We really loved this dish, it was easy but super tasty. I especially liked the flavor of the mince, the seasoning was just perfect! I actually made the dish during lunchtime nap and then baked it for dinner, so I think you can probably put it together a day ahead and it would be fine to pop in the oven for a kitchen supper with close friends or family. I am sure it will be a regular for my family." Ah, that's great Jessica!

Host of the brilliant Museum of Soho radio show, Mark Brisenden really enjoyed this dish too. I liked his description of the potatoes, "Thickly sliced to form a croftie style roof to the mince," Mark called this, "…a classic mince and spuds affair just right for a November night and some comfort TV watching." He watched *How To Dial a Murder* of course! Recipe feedback ended with, "I supped alone, but that was because I don't have Kim Cattrall's number, although I doubt she would have been able to make it at such short notice anyway." I'm sure Kim would love to share this dish with you sometime Mark, if you give her enough notice.

THE CONSPIRATORS - 1978

There is a lot of booze in this episode. Clive Revill plays Irish writer, Joe Devlin, who definitely has the gift of the gab. He loves his beer and he loves his whiskey. Columbo joins him in a fair few drams, just to get into Joe's good graces.

At first, it seems as though Columbo really enjoys the company of this particular adversary. Joe has a flowery, poetic way of speaking and at one point declares, "The mind flags, temporary exhaustion, deprivation of nourishment… Will you be my guest at lunch Lieutenant?" They get a little tipsy together, drinking beer at an Irish pub, where it turns out Columbo is pretty good at darts. Arrested at the age of 14, Joe is wary of the police, informing Columbo, "Even today, when I spot a gentleman of your persuasion, my instinct is to flee." The Lieutenant counters, "we're not that bad, sir, once you get to know us."

Columbo has done some reading up on Irish poetry, and Joe is impressed. Later in the episode, they have another chummy, bonding session over more beer and whiskey. They act like two old muckers in the pub, getting squiffy and making each other laugh with limericks. They both take great pleasure in a rhyme; however it is Joe's quoting of poetry that really gives Columbo food for thought and a particular drinking custom that provides the Lieutenant with the ultimate proof of his involvement in a murder. Joe is quoting from Lewis Carroll when he realizes that the Lieutenant has a lot of evidence against him, "You can charge me with murder, or want of sense, we are all of us weak at times. But the slightest approach, to a false pretense, was never amongst my crimes." But Columbo knows all about Joe's pretenses. Joe uses that old excuse for many crimes, "Politics makes liars of us all, Lieutenant."

How I wish I could recommend that you get yourself a bottle of Full's Irish Dew, Joe's preferred whiskey, and a bottle of which is the key to solving the crime. Alas, it seems the brand was created for the program. I guess they couldn't be seen advertising a particular product. Tullamore Dew could be a good match (one that is aged for 12 years), or another fine, old, Irish whiskey. If you are a not a fan of the hard stuff, beer also flows freely in this episode, in traditional, tankard-like glasses with handles. You can keep requesting, "Two ales, celebration size!" as Joe does.

If you *are* going for the whiskey option, be sure to wear a diamond ring, so that you can mark the bottle each time you are about to drink from it, proclaiming, "This far, and no farther." But remember what Joe says, "Easy beginnings, prudent endings. The trick is knowing when to stop."

Jeanette Nolan is almost unrecognizable in this episode if you remember her as the wonderful Mrs. Peck in *Double Shock*. She plays the regal Kate O'Connell, the matriarch of an Irish dynasty. As I have no recipe for Clive Revill in my collection, here's Jeanette's unusual, but delicious, way of serving liver.

We can't get condensed canned consommé for love nor money in the UK, so I got some via the internet when I first made this dish. Also, steak sauce is tricky to get here. For a Brit based version of the Sizzling Livers, I used a Knorr Beef Gravy Pot (you'll find these in supermarkets near the Bisto, similar to a Stock Pot but the resulting sauce is thicker) I also substituted HP Sauce instead of steak sauce. It was just as delicious as the authentic version. Personally, I don't salt the walnuts as I find everything else salty enough for my taste.

Jeanette Nolan's Sizzling Livers and Walnuts

1 cup / 100g walnut halves
Cooking oil for frying
Seasoned salt
1 lb / 450g chicken livers
1 cup / 240ml soy sauce
3 tablespoons dry sherry
2 tablespoons brown sugar
2 cloves garlic, peeled and halved
1 cup / 240ml condensed, canned consommé (undiluted)
2 tablespoons cornstarch/cornflour
2 tablespoons bottled steak sauce
A little flour to dust the chicken livers with
1 cup / 120g chopped scallions/spring onions

Sauté walnuts in a small amount of cooking oil until golden; drain and salt lightly. Parboil the chicken livers in salted water to cover for 2 minutes and drain. Mix together the soy sauce, sherry, brown sugar, and garlic; pour over the chicken livers. Marinate chicken livers for one hour in the fridge; turning several times in the sauce.

Drain the marinade into a saucepan. Remove and discard the garlic. Add consommé, cornstarch and steak sauce, stirring until ingredients are well blended. Heat mixture a few minutes over low heat; stirring constantly, until the mixture begins to thicken.

Dust chicken livers lightly with flour. Heat a small amount of cooking oil in a frying pan; sauté chicken livers a few minutes only (they should be moist in the center). Add chicken livers to the hot sauce, mixing well; turn into a chafing dish. Pile the walnuts in the center. Decorate the edges with the scallions. Jeanette suggests serving with assorted breads or hotcakes/pancakes.

Serves 3-4

Just one more thing... My lovely chum Michelle Kerry, living by the English seaside on the South coast, also made this with a Gravy Pot, even though she, "didn't really want to buy it, as the ingredients list looks a bit scary." We both agree that this dish would be best made with a reduced beef stock if you have the time to do this. Using a low salt soy sauce is also recommended by both of us. One *very* good thing came from test cooking this recipe for Michelle, "I do like the Fino sherry I bought for this recipe!" Result!

THE EIGHTH SEASON
(1989)

COLUMBO GOES TO THE GUILLOTINE - 1989

The 1970s *Columbo* episodes are generally viewed as the classic era, but I firmly believe that there is much fun to be had from later episodes too. This is the first of the 1980s episodes to be screened, and I think it holds up very well. Just imagine how wonderful it would have been in 1989, to see the Lieutenant again after an eleven and a half year break! The production team must have had this in mind when filming the scene where we first see our old hero. He's on a dark and moody street; sitting in his car with the lights off. His familiar face is revealed as he lights his cigar; to the accompaniment of a cheeky, jaunty soundtrack. He's back! It's been a long time, but we are reassured that it's the same old Columbo when he cracks a hard-boiled egg on the wall of the murder scene.

The plot of this episode involves a bunch of psychics and a magician (who makes it his mission to expose the mind-readers as charlatans). Those familiar with the work of James Randi, whose book entitled, *The Truth About Uri Geller* was published in 1982, will be able to see where some of the ideas in this episode came from.

Although Columbo, as usual, plays along with the killer who's a renowned mind reader; it's clear that the Lieutenant doesn't use psychic powers to solve his crimes. He's much more logical. When the Anthony Andrews' character, Elliot Blake, claims to be able to feel vibrations of suicide at the magician's place of death; Columbo is firm in his belief that it cannot be suicide. Why? Because he has found a grocery bag at the scene of the crime containing cabbage and corned beef. As he puts it, "Why would a man go to the market and buy himself a three-pound corned beef and pick out two head of cabbage, and then go home and cut off his own head?" He's got a point; I can see the logic in that, can't you?

I'm sure it would tickle your guests if you served corned beef and cabbage after a screening of this episode. If that's not to your taste though, here's a recipe from Anthony Andrews for Chicken in a Brick. A brick is a covered, terracotta cooking pot that was hugely popular in Britain and the USA in the 1970s. If you can't procure one of these, Anthony says you can cook your chicken in a large casserole dish instead (but you would need to pre-heat your oven and adjust timings accordingly).

Anthony Andrews' Spicy Yogurt Chicken Cooked in a Brick

1 chicken
1¾ scant cups / 400g plain/natural yogurt - divided use

2 tablespoons fresh mint
2 x 1-inch pieces of fresh ginger
1 large clove garlic
1 teaspoon turmeric
1 tablespoon cumin seeds
1 teaspoon chili powder
1 teaspoon brown sugar
1 teaspoon mixed spices [pre-made mix in the UK of spices such as cinnamon, coriander, caraway, nutmeg, ginger, cloves]

Put just over 1 cup / 230g of the natural yogurt into a blender and add all of the ingredients that follow. Process.

Pour mixture over chicken and marinade in the fridge overnight (or during the day for an evening meal).

Put chicken and sauce in a chicken brick, pre-soaked in water, and place in a COLD oven. Switch temperature to 400 degrees F / 205 degrees C / gas mark 6 and cook for one and a half hours, basting occasionally.

Slice or quarter chicken and keep warm. Pour juices and sauce from brick into a blender; add remaining yogurt and blend. Warm gently on top of the stove and pour over chicken.

Anthony suggests serving with brown rice or new potatoes and a green salad.

Serves 4

Just one more thing... Make sure your chicken isn't too big to fit in your chicken brick! Author of fabulous cookbook *Tonight at 7.30,* Kristen Frederickson attempted this recipe for the first time (like me, investing in a chicken brick just to try this dish), she couldn't fit her chicken in! So, trooper that she is, she carried her chicken brick to the butchers to make sure the second chicken she bought would definitely fit. Such dedication from a strong-armed test cook! Feedback from Kristen, who used sour cream in place of yogurt was this, "The sauce was INCREDIBLY delicious, perfection, and I would say that you could skip the step of passing the cooked sauce and the reserved sour cream through the blender again. It just didn't seem necessary and I had already washed my blender! The sauce as it came from the cooking dish was perfectly smooth and I just whisked it together with the reserved sour cream in a little saucepan to heat. Perfect." Glad you enjoyed it Kristen, worth buying a chicken brick for, I think.

MURDER, SMOKE AND SHADOWS - 1989

Wouldn't it be great to have a secret hangout? A "goof-off place" that you could fill with all the things you love; like a Coke machine, a jukebox, beanbags, arcade games and bubble gum dispensers? If you are a special effects whizz kid who has "made more super hits than anyone in Hollywood history," you can have whatever you want, it seems. Fisher Stevens is suitably boyish in the role of young film-maker Alex Brady. He zooms around the studio in a little golf cart; bounces around in general; and bosses everyone about, with the over-confidence of youth. But of course he has a dark secret, and someone from his past is planning to turn his little world to garbage.

Alex has a secretary called Rose, who is "of a certain age." She and Columbo have a conversation about how very young the wunderkind director is. Columbo observes, "When I was a young policeman, the Inspectors - they all seemed very old." Rose replies, "When I was a young secretary, all the great directors and producers seemed very old. Now that I'm an old secretary, they got very young." She continues with her rant, "Film children! They know every foot of film ever shot, but they think the most important date in the history of the world is their own birthday."

Alex is indeed, very self-centered and busy, busy, busy. He tries to avoid talking to the Lieutenant, believing himself to be too important and all wrapped up in his movie. At one point, high above a film set on a crane, he bellows through a megaphone, "I'm afraid I'm a bit busy up here at the moment Lieutenant!" The Lieutenant persists and asks for a trip on the crane. Comedy ensues as he goes a little green-around-the-gills flying high through the air, above the film set. Columbo doesn't like heights.

There is more comedy to be had from the Lieutenant, trying to get comfortable in Alex's den. Alex pretends that the Lieutenant is, "…the answer to a film-maker's prayers." He tells Columbo that he's interested in hearing everything about the life of a homicide detective; claiming that he's been thinking of making a detective picture. The Lieutenant seems flattered and mentions that he's been made to feel very warm and welcome (but it's plain to see he's having a hard time coping with the groovy form of seating that is Alex's low-level beanbag). Alex asks if he'd like to try lying on the waterbed instead. The Lieutenant reveals that Mrs. Columbo had recently tried to get him interested in this unusual form of furniture. He's never tried one before, but after having a go declares that it "…feels all swimmy." Laying on it makes him wonder what Mrs. Columbo had in mind…

Alex feigns chumminess with Columbo, but when he is finally confronted with evidence of his crime, the boy wonder shouts, "Do you really think some underpaid policeman is going to arrest me with all that circumstantial claptrap?" But the Lieutenant has been very clever indeed. Using all the techniques of a film director, he has staged a scene with actors to glean evidence. Entrapment? Perhaps, but he's just playing the "maestro" at his own game.

Alex has a fully stocked soda fountain in his boy's club ("the boy's club for one boy!" as his secretary Rose puts it). Columbo visits Alex's den early in the episode, and using his powers of detection, works out that Alex has been drinking a Black and White Ice-Cream Soda. Columbo delights in making himself one, with canned, whipped cream and a cherry on top. Ice-cream sundaes also make an appearance in this episode.

I couldn't find a recipe for Fisher Stevens, so here's a recipe for a classic Black and White Ice-Cream Soda. It's traditional to serve this kind of affair with a long-handled spoon and a straw. Hope that you get as much of a kick out of this as Columbo obviously did.

Columbo's Black and White Ice-Cream Soda

3 tablespoons chocolate syrup
¼ cup / 60ml milk
2 scoops vanilla ice-cream
1 teaspoon vanilla extract
7 oz / 200ml club soda/seltzer/fizzy water
Canned, whipped cream/squirty cream
Cherry - preferably with a stem!

Pour the chocolate syrup into a tall glass, mix with the milk, vanilla extract and one scoop of ice-cream. Fill the glass, nearly to the top, with club soda/seltzer/fizzy water. Top with the remaining scoop of ice-cream and a dollop/squirt of whipped cream. Place the cherry on top.

Serves 1

Just one more thing... My lovely friend, film-maker extraordinaire Sarah Akrobettoe, has a super-sweet tooth and makes the most amazing chocolate puddings I have ever eaten. I sent her this recipe and a photograph, because I thought she would be the perfect person to test the recipe for me. Her response made me laugh for about ten minutes,

"Looks yummy, but I don't like the idea of the soda." Yes! Why add water to ice-cream and chocolate?!

SEX AND THE MARRIED DETECTIVE - 1989

You can tell from the title of this one that sex is going to play a big part in the plot. This new season of Columbo definitely features more sex and violence than the earlier ones. I'm still reeling over the Lieutenant mentioning in the previous episode, that Mrs. Columbo wanted to invest in a waterbed. "I don't know what she was thinking about." He's equally coy about his home life with Lindsay Crouse's character, Dr. Joan Allenby when she asks him if "…everything is alright at home". Dr. Allenby is a sex therapist and she likes to play games.

Columbo gets off on the wrong foot with the Doctor when they first meet in an elevator. He's smoking a cigar and she fans the smoke away; giving him several dirty looks until he puts it out. It's a great example of the subtleties to be found in the series.

But Dr. Allenby's attitude to the Lieutenant softens as she gets to know him a little. Their interactions become a little playful. After the Lieutenant quizzes the Doctor about her relationship with the murder victim, she, in turn, asks, "Can you tell me about your own primary sexual relationships?" Columbo looks very uncomfortable and laughs out loud, "I'm a married man Ma'am" making a swift exit after refusing to elaborate. The therapist laughs in a sympathetic way; she's obviously playing with Columbo.

Behind the scenes though, Dr. Allenby, a seemingly super confident, sexually liberated woman is a right jittery-pants. She jumps out of her skin a few times and has a little freak out in the ladies' powder room when she can't find something she hid there earlier. Columbo stages an elaborate sting at the end of the episode; rattling the Doctor into admitting that she is indeed "the woman in black."

You could create a slightly sleazy cocktail bar atmosphere if you were having chums over to your place for this episode. Put a "Buckets" sign up and invite the ladies to dress all in black with fedora hats. You can welcome your guests with the classic phrase used by our villainess, "Hello sailor, do you come here often?"

If you are making a romantic dinner à deux, I strongly suggest Bavarian Chocolate Cream Pie for dessert rather than Rice Pudding, both play a part in the plot. You can bring the chocolate pie to the table after asking your loved one the killer question that makes everything kick off for Dr .Allenby, "If I were a dessert, what kind of dessert would I be?"

To drink? I suggest cocktails including Shirley Temples (which feature in this episode; there's a recipe in the "Columbo's Chili and Other Delights" section).

Bavarian Chocolate Cream Pie

1 envelope / 7g unflavored, powdered gelatin
1¾ cups / 420ml full fat milk, divided use
⅔ cup / 130g sugar
6 tablespoons cocoa powder
1 tablespoon light corn syrup/golden syrup
2 tablespoons butter
¾ teaspoon vanilla extract
1 cup / 240ml whipping cream, cold
1 x 9-inch pie crust or crumb crust, baked and cooled
¼ cup / 60ml chocolate syrup

Sprinkle gelatin over 1 cup / 240ml milk in a medium-sized saucepan; let it stand for several minutes to soften. Stir together sugar and cocoa; add this to the milk mixture. Add the corn syrup/golden syrup. Cook, stirring constantly until mixture boils. Remove from heat.

Add the butter; stir until melted. Stir in remaining ¾ cup / 180ml milk and vanilla. Pour into large bowl. Cool. Refrigerate until almost set.

Beat the whipping cream in small bowl until stiff. In a stand mixer, beat the chocolate mixture on medium speed until smooth. Then on low speed, add whipped cream to chocolate mixture, beating just until blended. Pour into the prepared crust; refrigerate until set, at least 3 hours. Just before serving, drizzle each pie slice with chocolate syrup.

Serves 8

Just one more thing... Battenburgbelle says of this most delicious of all pies, "If you want your dinner guests drooling and sighing a lot, this is a recipe for you - it's most gratifying to watch them keep going back for "just a little more". It even got the teenage seal of approval from Missy B and this is not handed out lightly!" Bear in mind that, "The choc mix needs to chill for three hours, so a bit of planning is required." If you are using gelatin leaves rather than powdered gelatin, six leaves should do the trick. BB's recipes for sweet pastry and a crumb crust are in the "Columbo's Chili and Other Delights" section.

GRAND DECEPTIONS - 1989

It is always fun to see Columbo interact with military types. When the Robert Foxworth character, Frank Brailie, first lays eyes on the Lieutenant, he's on his hands and knees performing a fingertip search of a woodland area. Frank is standing stiffly upright; his hands behind his back watching the search. He's a Colonel, and upon learning of Columbo's rank, offers, "We seem to be fellow officers Lieutenant, you know the responsibilities of leading your men." Self-effacing as ever, Columbo admits, "Well mostly the men I lead - that'd just be me, sir."

As well as training civilians to "get ready for the time of anarchy" at a boot camp, Frank runs a think-tank called the First Foundation for American Thought. When Columbo wonders aloud what they think about there, he's told, "Our country's problems, Lieutenant." Quite a tall order. The Colonel is a classic example of arrogant self-aggrandizement. My favorite line in the episode is when he orders his secretary, "Marsha, please remind Professor Galt that I'll need to see the Dalai Lama before my trip to Tibet." Yes, sir!

It's often easy to see whether Columbo likes or dislikes his adversaries, but he rarely voices his feelings out loud. In this episode, however he makes things plain. As the Lieutenant is moving towards proving Frank's culpability, he asks many questions. Frank always replies in the affirmative. Columbo observes, "You know Colonel, the way we always agree with one another, that's amazing. Considering the fact that we don't really like one another. Would you agree with me on that?" Frank acknowledges that this is true. Columbo then begins to explain his process of deduction. Frank thinks he has planned a murder with military precision, but he hasn't bargained for the Lieutenant's knowledge of strategic thinking. A seemingly insignificant soldier, found where he shouldn't be, gives Columbo the clue he needs to blow the murderer's alibi wide apart.

I don't have a recipe for Robert Foxworth, but this is the kind of dish I could imagine Frank Brailie rustling up in his bachelor pad for his secret lover, Jenny Padget, in this episode. This is Peter Falk's very own recipe for Veal Scallopini. I was so excited when I found this recipe, spotting a nice synchronicity with Columbo rustling up a dish with the same name (although with different ingredients) in the episode *Murder Under Glass*.

Peter Falk's Veal Scallopini and White Wine

1 lb / 450g veal scallopini (1-inch squares)
Flour for dusting
¼ cup / 60ml olive oil
1 clove garlic, crushed
1 onion, finely chopped
3 cloves
1 bay leaf
Juice of 1 lemon
½ cup / 120ml white wine
Saffron rice to serve

Dust veal with flour and brown in oil with the garlic. Remove veal and sauté onion in the same pan. Add rest of ingredients plus ¼ cup / 60ml water and veal. Simmer 45 minutes covered. Serve over saffron rice.

Serves 3-4

Just one more thing... My very own beau, DJ and vinyl archivist, J T Rathbone, tested this dish for me, and he used Mr. Vincent Price's recipe for saffron rice as an accompaniment (you can find this in the "Columbo's Chili and Other Delights" section). Mr. Rathbone bought veal from his local butchers and cooked it up by himself in the P&Q of his kitchen without me interfering. I then went round to his cabin in the sky (he lives on the 13th floor) to try his version of this dish. I thought it was utterly delicious. Just one more thing? I rather think he'd prefer just one less! He said that if he made it again, he might use two cloves instead of three and a little less lemon juice, but I thought it was perfect.

THE NINTH SEASON
(1989-1990)

MURDER: A SELF PORTRAIT - 1989

This episode begins with a comedic turn, as Columbo attends a dog show with his beloved basset hound. "Dog" wins a rosette in the "dogs rescued from the pound" category. "If they ever gave an award for the loving department," boasts Columbo, "he would win the grand prize. When it comes to loving, this dog, he's the champion, aren't you sweetheart?" "Dog" responds to this compliment by biting him. The dog show has nothing to do with the events that follow (apart from possibly acting as a contrast between the down to earth lifestyle of Columbo, and the glamorous lifestyle of the rich and famous artist who is the protagonist of this episode).

Patrick Bauchau plays famous artist, Max Barsini; a superstar in the art world and known simply by his surname, like Warhol or Dali. Barsini is blessed with two wives and a mistress who all live more or less together, right beside the sea on the coast of California. On the surface, the three women are fairly content with the situation they are in, and naturally enough, Barsini himself is very happy with it. The women cook for him, keep his house in order and satisfy him in bed. But one of them knows his secret, and he'll soon have to do something drastic to prevent it being revealed to the world.

Columbo knows the artist by reputation and seems a little star struck. When Barsini asks if he can paint the Lieutenant, he seems dead chuffed. "Wait 'till I tell Mrs. Columbo!" he exclaims, thrilled. But in spending time sitting for his portrait, our detective is able to get inside the mind of the artist. They listen to tape recordings of Barsini's ex-wife's dreams, and the artist's secret is slowly revealed. Columbo offers some dream analysis. As the Lieutenant begins to get closer and closer to the truth, Barsini has a tantrum. He stops painting and shouts: "Your portrait bores me! It's become grotesque. Like this totally pointless dream game that leads everywhere and goes nowhere." But Columbo's musings about dream symbolism will lead him to the truth, no matter how dotty it seems.

Barsini loves Cioppino. Early on in the episode, his first wife rustles up an enormous pot of it; which this strange family group all eat together. This would be a great dish to accompany the episode, so I'm proposing Vincent Price's excellent recipe for Cioppino. This extravaganza is good for a chatty crowd, for as Barsini puts it, "Cioppino is never to be taken in silence." Serve with huge chunks of bread for dipping.

Vincent Price's Cioppino

2½ lbs / 1125g firm white fish, cut in pieces (such as striped bass, halibut, and barracuda; a variety is desirable).
1½ lbs / 675g fresh shrimp [prawns to us in the UK]
2 dozen clams
2 dozen mussels
1 large Dungeness crab or 1½ lbs / 675g frozen King crab legs in the shell
1 large onion, chopped
1 large green pepper, chopped
2 stalks celery, chopped
2 large cloves of garlic, finely chopped
¼ cup / 60ml olive oil
1 x 1 lb, 13 oz can / 820g tinned tomatoes
2 x 8 oz cans / 450g tomato sauce
2 cups / 480ml white or red wine
Salt and pepper
¼ teaspoon dried oregano
¼ teaspoon dried basil
½ cup / 15g minced, fresh parsley

Preheat oven to 300 degrees F / 150 degrees C / gas mark 2.

Wash the fish; shell and clean the shrimp; scrub the clams; wash the mussels and remove the beard; crack and clean the crab. To make the sauce, sauté the onion, green pepper, celery, and garlic in oil until golden. Add tomatoes, tomato sauce, wine, 1 teaspoon salt, freshly ground pepper to taste, oregano and basil. Cover and cook for 15 minutes. Arrange the fish, shrimp, and crab in layers in a large casserole. Sprinkle over the parsley, saving a small amount to sprinkle on before serving. Pour in the sauce, cover and bake in for 30 minutes. Add the clams and mussels and bake, covered, until they open, about 6 to 10 minutes. Sprinkle with remaining parsley and serve at once.

Serves 6-8

Just one more thing... With Battenburgbelle's assistance, I made this for Vincent Price expert, Peter Fuller, and it was a great success. Peter proclaimed, "WAS DELIZIOSO GRAZIE"!

Vincent Price fan, Kelli Cline, made me laugh with her comment after making this dish, "I was chocked full of briny goodness!" adding, "...the recipe turned out great. Very tasty soup!" Kelli and her husband invited three friends to share their soup, all of them *Columbo* fans and they watched the episode that featured Vincent Price after dinner. Kelli reported, they were "…excited to come for a nice meal and a chance to watch the show together. I was just happy because I was able to also share a Vinnie recipe with friends!" That's what it is all about Kelli, how lovely!

COLUMBO CRIES WOLF - 1980

Bachelor's World. What a wonderful place to be in 1990, a world designed purely for the pleasure of the single man. Ah, those were the days! But of course, there is trouble in this Playboyesque paradise. The pool parties, glamorous photo shoots and shopping sprees for the Bachelor's World live-in "nymphs", are all going to come at some kind of cost.

Ian Buchanan plays a Hugh Hefner type, Sean Brantley, living in a world of beautiful women. He's a photographer who runs a highly successful glamour magazine business with a female business partner, and he has his pick of the bunnies. He has fallen for the Nymph of the Month, much to the displeasure of his partner. Now she's threatening to sell her 51% share of the business.

I think it is fair to say that Sean is the sleaziest character in the whole Columbo oeuvre. He thinks himself a real charmer in his peg trousers and orange jackets (with shoulder pads as big as feet). When he and Columbo first meet, he almost flirts with the Lieutenant. Sean is sitting on a sofa with a beautiful woman wrapped around him, as Columbo inquires, "Is it alright to talk in front of the young lady?" Bradley responds, "Yes of course, but let's get on with it. As you can see, I have better things to do." Public displays of affection between the two lovebirds continue. Snogging in front of Columbo? Not very respectful.

Sean also has the cheesiest grin in the glamour business, and he's like a Cheshire cat when he tells Columbo, "It's all an act with you isn't it? You're not the naive, bumbling detective you pretend to be." How true. Indeed he is not! Checking the impressive display of firearms at the Bachelor's World Chateau, the Lieutenant asks his suspect when he last fired the Beretta. Sean quips, with a smile, "I've never fired a gun in my life, Columbo. These are all just toys for boys: bric-a-brac for the sophisticated bachelor."

Columbo often professes not to understand modern technology. He's baffled by mobile phones, fax machines, and pagers; but this is one episode where he quite brilliantly uses technology to his advantage - gotcha!

I haven't been able to acquire a beloved recipe by Ian Buchanan, but as his character is such a playboy, here's the kind of thing I can imagine Sean Brantley ordering up on a regular basis. This recipe has been adapted from one in the Playboy Wine & Spirits Cookbook, published in 1974.

Playboy's Stewed Pheasant in Champagne with Dumplings

1 pheasant, about 3 lbs / 1350g
Salt and pepper
6 tablespoons butter - divided use
½ cup / 75g finely minced onion
2 tablespoons finely minced shallots
1 teaspoon extremely finely minced garlic
1 tablespoon very finely chopped, fresh chervil or 1 teaspoon dried chervil
1 small bay leaf
3 tablespoons cognac
3 tablespoons flour
2 cups / 480ml chicken broth or stock
1 cup / 240ml brut Champagne
1 large fresh tomato, peeled, seeded, finely chopped
1 cup / 120g all-purpose / plain flour
2 teaspoons baking powder
1 tablespoon extremely finely minced fresh chives
⅓ cup / 80ml milk

Cut up pheasant for stewing. Sprinkle with salt and pepper. Melt 3 tablespoons of the butter in Dutch oven or heavy stew pot over a very low flame. Add pheasant pieces, and sauté until light brown. Add onion, shallots, garlic, chervil and bay leaf. Continue to sauté, keeping the pot covered, until onion is tender. Add cognac and set ablaze. When flames subside, stir in flour, blending well. Add chicken broth, Champagne, and tomato. Simmer slowly 1 to 1½ hours or until pheasant is tender. Skim gravy, and season with salt and pepper. While pheasant is simmering, prepare dumpling dough.

Sift together flour, baking powder, and ¼ teaspoon salt. Cut in remaining 3 tablespoons butter until the mixture resembles coarse meal. Add chives. Slowly stir in milk with a fork to form a dough. Use more milk if necessary. If the dough feels wet, dust with flour. Very lightly knead dough about ½ minute. Roll dough to ¾ inch thickness. Cut with small round biscuit cutter, 1½ inch diameter if possible. When pheasant is tender, place pieces of dough on top of pheasant. Cover with lid. Simmer over low heat 10 minutes longer.

Serves 4

Just one more thing... Battenburgbelle reminisced, "The dumplings brought back fond memories of both my grandmas, who used to make good old-fashioned stews. I always much preferred the dumplings to the meat (which I often couldn't identify…) As far as the pheasant itself was concerned, my brother Patrick observed that "Little game birds are always hard work, but I love them". He also said he found the dish very rich and 1970's. He couldn't particularly see what the cognac and champagne brought to the party and would have preferred them out of the casserole and in a glass (not together, obviously)."

AGENDA FOR MURDER - 1990

Patrick McGoohan plays a pompous and snooty spin doctor with an overblown way of speaking, in this excellent episode. Oscar Finch is the puppet master behind a political campaign for Congressman Mark Mackie, and neither of them is squeaky clean.

Oscar loves the sound of his own voice and doesn't mince his words. He calls the Lieutenant's car a "decomposing rattletrap" and an "oxidized relic." When the Lieutenant begins pressing him with some tricky questions, he tries to baffle him with his highbrow question, "What o'clock do you have?" Columbo looks bemused, "I beg your pardon?" Patrick very precisely reiterates, "My timepiece says 10:09 and counting." He explains that he detests being late, and detests repeating himself. The Lieutenant is obviously beginning to annoy him.

Oscar thinks the Lieutenant is harmless at first. He tells his partner in crime, "The guy's got an act he could take on the road! He's harmless, a jumped-up boy scout." Later, when Columbo starts closing in, Oscar observes, "You're rather subtle for a man who seems so overt." Columbo isn't sure if this is a compliment or not.

Like many of Columbo's adversaries, Oscar thinks he is pulling the wool over the detective's eyes. Columbo begins moving in for the kill, informing him, "I think you did it, sir." Oscar responds with, "I'm very disappointed in you… I thought we had a nice relationship going." Columbo tells him that although the evidence is mounting up against him, he cannot quite place him at the scene of the crime. Oscar counters, "All you have is a load of unsubstantiated, circumstantial poppycock!" But of course, Columbo has something very clever up his sleeve that proves Oscar is guilty.

I don't want to give anything away, but food is central to the plot. In an example of how closely Peter Falk was involved in many aspects of the production of Columbo, he got the idea for the essential clue for this episode from a magazine that he read in a dentist's waiting room. It's one of my favorite plot twists and I love the idea that Falk was behind this one. It would be my advice, never to chew gum around the Lieutenant.

The perfect accompaniment for this episode would be an elaborate cheeseboard. You must have a great big wedge of Parmigiano-Reggiano amongst your selection, for reasons that will become clear during your screening. Columbo LOVES Reggiano!

There are no recipes in my collection for Patrick McGoohan, or Louis Zorich (who played his victim), but Louis is married to one of my favorite actresses, Olympia Dukakis, and she has a great recipe for meatballs.

Olympia Dukakis' Greek Meatballs

½ lb / 225g ground/minced beef
½ lb / 225g ground/minced veal
½ lb / 225g ground/minced lamb
1 large egg
¼ cup / 60ml milk
1 large onion, chopped
2 teaspoons Dijon mustard
1 teaspoon tamari (or soy sauce)
1 teaspoon dried oregano, divided use
¾ teaspoon salt
½ teaspoon garlic powder
2 drops red-wine vinegar
⅓ cup / 50g plain, dry breadcrumbs (or cornmeal)
½ cup / 15g chopped, fresh parsley, divided use

In a large bowl, combine the beef, veal, and lamb. Add egg, milk, onion, mustard, soy sauce, ½ teaspoon of the oregano, salt, garlic powder, vinegar, and breadcrumbs. Gently mix with your hands until combined. Shape into walnut-sized meatballs. Olympia suggests making smaller meatballs for a buffet or for the kids.

Heat a 12-inch nonstick frying pan over a medium heat. Add half the meatballs and sprinkle them with ¼ teaspoon of the remaining oregano and 2 tablespoons of the parsley. Cook, gently turning the meatballs as they brown, 5 to 7 minutes. Transfer to a platter, keep warm and repeat with remaining meatballs, oregano, and parsley. Transfer the last batch to the platter with the other meatballs, sprinkle on the remaining parsley and serve.

Makes 36 large meatballs

Serves 8

Just one more thing... Ace textile artist, Ptolemy Mann made these for her book group and reported, "Everyone liked them very much!" Ptolemy used fresh garlic, rather than garlic powder, and added a little oil to her frying pan to help the meatballs caramelize. The photographs she sent me were drool-worthy.

The Burrow Family in Walthamstow liked these too, and Olympia was right in her suggestion that they might appeal to youngsters. Rob announced, "They were delicious! The kids loved them too, especially Nicholas, he ate four!" I did like Rob's serving suggestion, "We ate them with spaghetti and homemade sauce (gravy). I'm Italian-American. It just felt appropriate. And they totally worked, especially with Parmigiano-Reggiano, as suggested." Wonderful, so you can definitely tie the meatballs into this episode with Columbo's much-loved Parmesan!

REST IN PEACE, MRS. COLUMBO - 1990

Some people think that Mrs. Columbo doesn't exist. They believe, that as we never see her in any of the 69 episodes, she could just be a figment of the Lieutenant's imagination. If a suspect is famous, Columbo usually claims that his wife is a fan. He often drops her into the conversation when he's getting to know a murderer. She likes Bette Davis; she enjoys paint-by-numbers; she likes Italian food; all her houseplants die. But some claim she's just another weapon in Columbo's bag of tricks and that he makes all this stuff up.

But I firmly believe that she does exist. My main evidence for this is several phone calls throughout the series where the Lieutenant chats to his wife. These conversations often revolve around food. Who else would be asking him to pick up some Chinese food on the way home? Or a head of lettuce and two quarts of milk?

In this episode, we get the closest proof that there really is a Mrs. Columbo (unless the whole police department is on Columbo's fantasy life too). We get a peek into what appears to be Columbo's home and see a photograph of what appears to be his wife. It's all part of an elaborate plot to trap the killer, but we don't know that at first.

Vivian Dimitri, played by Helen Shaver, has a grudge against Columbo. He was involved in the arrest of her husband for murder. She blames Columbo for his subsequent death and she wants retribution, "...a balancing of the books," for the loss of the love of her life. She hatches an elaborate plan to make Columbo suffer. It includes marmalade.

Vivian is a good actress; she cozies up to Columbo, being charming, friendly and getting his sympathy, or at least she thinks that she is. But Columbo is very suspicious of her interest in his wife.

When Columbo arrives at Vivian's house one morning, she offers him an English muffin with lemon marmalade. She boasts of the marmalade, "It's English, it's very, very good." Well personally, I'm English and I've never seen lemon marmalade in my life, but Columbo is impressed. "You know who would love this? My wife," the Lieutenant continues, "that woman's crazy about marmalade. Me, I can't stand the stuff." He likes raspberry jam though, and boysenberry. So if you are not in the mood for cooking, why not have some muffins and preserves? The lemon marmalade is pretty central to the plot.

Ian McShane plays Vivian's love interest, Leland St. John, and if you fancy something more substantial, here is Ian's recipe for salmon. As Ian puts it himself, "It's very simple, it's very tasty". This recipe was used in an advert to promote a British supermarket, and you can find it on YouTube (search for Sainsbury's - Ian McShane), it's rather fabulous. My friend Greg let me know that fromage frais might be an unfamiliar product to most Americans. Sour cream or crème fraîche might be an appropriate substitute. This amount of fromage frais makes a lot of sauce, so be prepared to have lots left over if you make this amount (nice on a baked potato!). I'm not sure how big a pack of watercress was in 1992 when Ian presented this dish, so I'd suggest checking the advert so you can see the proportion of cress to dairy.

Ian McShane's Salmon Steaks with Watercress Sauce

Butter for greasing foil
Half a medium onion, thickly sliced into rings
Dill, two sprigs

2 salmon steaks
½ lemon
2 knobs of butter
Salt and pepper
¾ cup / 180g fromage frais
Pack of watercress
New potatoes to serve

Preheat oven to 350 degrees F / 175 degrees C / gas mark 4.

Lightly butter two pieces of cooking foil. Place two slices of onion on each piece of foil next to each other. Place a sprig of dill on top of the onions. Place the salmon on top. Squeeze a little lemon juice over each salmon steak. Add a knob of butter and a little salt and pepper. Wrap the salmon up in the foil like a parcel, and bake for 20 minutes. Meanwhile, empty fromage frais into a bowl, finely chop one pack of watercress and add to fromage frais. Mix thoroughly and season with salt and pepper to taste. Remove the salmon from the foil and serve with new potatoes and the watercress sauce.

Serves 2

Just one more thing... Film historian and writer Vic Pratt comments, "I'm by no means a natural in the kitchen. However, Ian's tasty recipe was straightforward enough that even a saucepan simpleton like me managed to knock this up for a party of four, and nobody complained. I did discover, though, that in the health conscious 21st century, it's not quite as easy to buy full-fat crème fraîche as it was when this recipe was originally written in the 1980s. I had to shop around until I found it – but it's imperative that you use the real stuff - because a man's man like Mr. McShane would surely never accept a reduced-fat option." I am sure you are right Uncle Vic.

My birthday buddy and writer chum, Sarah Wenban, also tested this dish and proclaimed, "I thoroughly recommend this recipe – it's easy peasy and delicious." She added, "It all went very well together and was an 'excellent' (according to my dad) treat for two." It appears that it's not always easy to find fromage frais in the UK either. Sarah made me laugh with this comment, "I did have a minor panic attack in the supermarket when I couldn't find the fromage frais. I started to think that maybe it was a really '90s thing that you couldn't get any more. I eventually found it on my second attempt, all on its lonesome, squeezed in-between rows and rows of every permutation of Greek yogurt you'd care to think of." Search well my friends, it's worth it!

UNEASY LIES THE CROWN - 1990

James Read plays dentist, Wesley Corman, and is as cool as a cucumber in this episode. I'm guessing it is easier to distance yourself from murder if you are not actually there when the person you have murdered, snuffs it. This episode reminds me a bit of *A Deadly State of Mind*, where George Hamilton also murders by remote control. *Murder With Too Many Notes* is another. This one is a classic example of a *Columbo* where the murderer has a very clever and unusual modus operandi, and it's one that people often remember.

Wesley has an excellent alibi for the time of death; he's playing cards with an all-star cast at a friend's place. The Lieutenant gets very star-struck when he meets them all a few days later. It gradually dawns on him, that they are all famous in one way or another. Nancy Walker is one of the card sharks, a brilliant character actress who is most remembered by me, as the mother in the TV series *Rhoda*. There's a great in-joke for longtime viewers of the series; Columbo recognizes her and asks, "Are you Nancy Walker? From the Rock Hudson show?" Nancy played the maid in the TV series *McMillan and Wife,* which starred Rock Hudson. It was one of the original three series in the NBC Mystery Movie rotation wheel of the 1970s with *Columbo* and *McCloud.*

When Columbo wants to meet with the murderer; he phones him to suggest meeting at Barney's Beanery. Wesley doesn't like that idea and suggests Club 5th Avenue which is a much more hip establishment, full of the beautiful people. Perhaps he thinks Columbo will feel out of place. We can tell by the detective's smile when he strolls in, that he digs it. Wesley's brother-in-law issues a warning about the Lieutenant, "Remember, he's a lot sharper than he appears." This is, of course, very true.

At the race track, Wesley thinks he is very clever by ordering Columbo a Scotch, and himself a glass of milk, proclaiming it to be his lucky drink. He laughs in the Lieutenant's face when Columbo admits that he doesn't have any proof as to his guilt, but it will be a combination of a laundry accident and a kid's chemistry set that helps Columbo get his man. Nobody is smarter than Columbo!

I don't have a recipe for James Read, but I love Nancy Walker so much, I'm suggesting her lovely Chicken a la Nancy to have with this episode. You might want to serve margaritas made in a blender too (as they feature in this episode).

Nancy Walker's Chicken a la Nancy

Fresh asparagus (boiled for only 5 minutes)
6 chicken breasts (boned)
1 cup / 240ml cream
4 tablespoons butter
1 cup / 75g fresh mushrooms, sliced
½ cup / 45g grated Parmesan cheese
Paprika to taste

Preheat the oven to 375 degrees F / 190 degrees C / gas mark 5.

Place asparagus in a buttered, oblong baking dish. Place boned chicken breasts on top of asparagus, cover with cream, butter, mushrooms, salt and pepper to taste, and then sprinkle the top with cheese. The final touch is to dust with paprika. Bake for 30-45 minutes until the chicken is no longer pink and cooked through.

Nancy suggests serving her chicken with a crisp green salad of various kinds of lettuce and hot buttered French crusty bread. Yum yum!

Serves 4-6

Just one more thing... The lovely Orlando Murrin thought this would make a nice luxury supper dish, served with rice. He doubled the mushrooms when he tried this dish, feeling that Nancy's quantity would make them a bit of a non-event. As someone who fears the fungus, this would never have occurred to me, but of course, if you are a mushroom lover, feel free!

MURDER IN MALIBU - 1990

Do you know someone who always says the right things and does the right things? Are they a bit too good to be true? Andrew Stevens' character in this episode, Wayne Jennings, is a real smoothie. He's a ladies' man, who charms every woman that crosses his path. Even those who think they hate him, actually love him. Women just can't resist him. When his romance novelist girlfriend arrives home after a six-week book tour, he's done all the right things. He's got the hot tub all heated up; he's planning to give her a massage, and he's planted some bluebonnets in the garden because the color matches the dress she was wearing on the day they first met. What a guy, right?

Columbo gets the measure of this no-good playboy immediately upon meeting him. He sees Wayne's room in the lady novelist's home, and exclaims: "Boy, she sure fixed this up nice for ya!" Looking at all the fishing trophies, photographs of Jennings mountaineering, skydiving and yachting, he observes, "Boy, I mean, for a man as young as you, and to manage to do all these things, and still find time to earn a living and all…" The Lieutenant's implication that Wayne is a kept man, is not far wrong. He's an out of work actor who appears to be living off his very successful girlfriend. There's a life insurance policy that he might benefit from too.

Wayne puts on a really hammy act for Columbo, pretending to be distraught at the death of his girlfriend and going absolutely berserk when he is being arrested for her murder. The Lieutenant isn't fazed by the overacting though, telling another cop: "I never saw a guy unwind that fast!" Later in a private hospital room, Wayne is having an elaborate silver service lunch and offers the Lieutenant a glass of wine. Columbo declines as he says he's just had a root beer. He looks at the silverware on the table and jokes, "Boy, this is sure different from my hernia operation!"

Our villain is confident that he's got away with murder, but he made a schoolboy error. Despite his thinking he knows all about women, there is a teeny tiny fact that has escaped his notice. Not the Lieutenant's though; he knows all about ladies' panties!

Brenda Vaccaro plays the sister of the murder victim, and she's suitably brusque with the Lieutenant. I love Brenda's way of cooking sausages. They really are T-E-R-R-I-F-I-C!

Brenda Vaccaro's T-E-R-R-I-F-I-C Italian Sausages

1 lb / 450g sweet Italian pork sausages
Salt
2 tablespoons fine grade olive oil
1 onion, peeled and chopped
3 large sweet peppers (green, red or yellow), diced
2-3 Italian plum tomatoes
1 cut lemon

Separate sausages into individual links. Spread a thin layer of salt evenly on large iron frying pan; heat over high flame. Add sausages. Reduce heat, cook sausages slowly until brown and crisp on all sides. In a separate frying pan, heat olive oil. Add onion and peppers; cook over low heat, stirring. Cut and seed tomatoes and press the through a sieve. Add to frying pan with peppers. Cook over moderate heat, stirring until thickened and nicely colored. Season to taste with salt and pepper. Drain cooked, hot sausages on absorbent paper, removing excess salt and grease. Serve sausages on a plate, squeeze lemon juice over sausages. Serve sauce hot, on the side, or spoon over the sausages.

Serves 2

Just one more thing... Peter Fuller's verdict? "Is it Terrific? Well yes and no. Yes if you use great sausages. They are the hero of the dish, so I hunted down some Salsiccia from an Italian deli in Soho. They were delicious with or without the sauce which doesn't taste like a traditional ragù which was what I was expecting. All those peppers make it more like a sautéed pepper side dish." Peter would have liked more seasoning, saying "I was missing my garlic and herbs that I like in a pasta ragù. But it was nice nevertheless."

Bethany B. in Michigan, "...found the salt step unnecessary, as the salt browned instead of the sausages. Next time I make them (and I will definitely make them again, as they were great) I would just leave out that step and brown them like normal and serve with the sauce." I loved Bethany's time-saving tip, "I also seeded and chopped my tomatoes because, no matter how I tried, they would not go through a sieve. I actually don't think sieving is even necessary, perhaps not even seeding the tomatoes. It still cooks down into a nice topping." I agree, Bethany. Plus, I love this serving suggestion, "I would really like to try this on a warm sub bun and top the sausage with the sauce, I bet it would be great." Definitely!

THE TENTH SEASON AND SPECIALS (1990-2003)

COLUMBO GOES TO COLLEGE - 1990

Frat boys. We don't really have these in the UK, but we know what they are, through films like *Animal House* and *Porky's*. The two main characters in this episode are over-privileged and self-important college students. They have all the latest gadgets in their lives, including something probably considered pretty space-age at the time, a button that will lock and unlock a car door from a distance. They are studying law, but they both consider themselves to be outside of it. They have a heavy case of, what in the modern day parlance might be called, self-entitlement.

With the arrogance of youth, Justin Rowe and Cooper Redman (played by Stephen Caffrey and Gary Hershberger) poke fun at Columbo's clothes, his car, and his detection skills. But he's always one step ahead of them, of course. Despite their gadgets and gizmos for remote controlled devices and surreptitious recording of conversations, Columbo uses old-fashioned gumshoe techniques; nabbing them with a bit of forward planning. Some might consider the way he catches them to be entrapment, but Columbo is not above this as we have seen in many previous episodes. He hints at the fact that he doesn't always play strictly by the book, in a lecture he gives to the two suspects and their classmates about the clever way he solved a particular crime (the killing in *Agenda For Murder*). These lucky students have Columbo as a visiting speaker, and he's asked by one of them if the police ever make up evidence. He talks about how he once went surreptitiously looking for a piece of gum through an attorney's wastepaper basket; avoiding admitting to any real kind of derring-do or actually planting evidence. When he's challenged about sidestepping the issue, he confesses, "I know what you're asking and I'm trying to avoid the question." The students laugh. "I follow my nose, and when I get the scent, there is very little I wouldn't do in order to solve the case."

He picks up the scent very quickly in this episode, but it will ultimately be a fluke of 1990s television technology that delivers the concrete proof he needs. For those of you too young to remember videotape and obscure television channels, don't worry too much. As the Lieutenant puts it, "Timing is important, and luck. You gotta be lucky."

We can see where the main culprit in this crime, Justin, gets his cocky attitude from; his mother calls Columbo a "rumpled little dumbbell" and his father (played by Columbo stalwart Robert Culp) obviously thinks the Lieutenant is a dimwit, accusing him of not knowing "which end is up." But at the very end of the episode, Justin states, "You got lucky, you caught a fluke. Don't count us out Lieutenant, because my father doesn't like to see me fail." Columbo's face says it all. Too bad frat boy, you are going down!

I don't have a recipe for either of the two villains of this piece so here's something I imagine frat boys might like to eat. Some seriously delicious ribs prepared Peter Falk style. I don't cook my ribs exactly as Peter suggests (although I love the idea of the magnetic hooks), I simply plonk them on the oven rack with the grill pan lower down in the oven underneath them to catch any drips.

Peter Falk's Barbecued Spare Ribs, Chinatown Style

2 teaspoons minced ginger root (or ½ teaspoon ginger)
Scallion/spring onion (white part only), minced
Small clove of garlic, crushed
1 tablespoon chili sauce
2½ tablespoons Hoisin sauce (or hot tomato catsup/ketchup)
2 tablespoons soy sauce
2 tablespoons dry sherry
1 tablespoon light brown sugar
½ teaspoon salt
2 lbs / 900g of lean, baby pork ribs, fat removed
1 tablespoon honey

Prepare marinade by combining all ingredients except ribs and honey; blend into a thick paste. Place ribs in a shallow pan, brush both sides with marinade, place in the fridge for two hours. Halfway through the two hours, turn once, basting both sides with honey.

Preheat oven to 275 degrees F / 135 degrees C / gas mark 1. Ribs are cooked in a suspended position, either by attaching magnetic hooks to ceiling of the oven or by means of double hooks which may be fashioned by bending the ends of small metal skewers into hooks. One end of the skewer is hooked into the fleshy part of ribs and the other end is looped over an oven rack set as high as possible in the oven.

Place a foil-lined pan filled with a little water below meat to catch drippings and moisturize meat. Roast meat for 30 minutes, then turn oven up to 300 degrees F / 150 degrees C / gas mark 2 and roast for another 30 minutes. Turn oven up to 400 degrees F / 205 degrees C / gas mark 6 and bake for 30 minutes or until ribs are crisp but moist. Serve hot or cold by cutting between each rib.

Peter suggests serving with duck sauce or hot mustard sauce.

Serves 4 as hors-d'oeuvre.

Just one more thing... Silver Screen Suppers blog reader, Vera Roth in Berlin, recommends wrapping the ribs in foil and letting them rest in the oven for ten minutes after you have finished cooking them (so that the meat softens as it is kept warm). Vera's butcher recommended spare ribs that included the chop, these "came out really juicy" said Vera. She let the meat marinate for a night and a day, so that all the flavors really permeated the meat. Delicious!

Even though he only marinated the ribs for an hour, as he was "too hungry," fellow archivist Chris Scales in Peckham, thought these were "Very tasty." He used fresh red chilies instead of chili sauce and "mushed it all together" in his NutriBullet. How very modern! I'm sure Peter Falk would have done the same, if such a thing had existed in his day.

CAUTION: MURDER CAN BE HAZARDOUS TO YOUR HEALTH - 1991

Suave George Hamilton plays super-confident, television crime show host, Wade Anders, in this episode. He appears to be squeaky clean, but he has a dirty secret. I am pretty sure that George is the only *Columbo* murderer to crack a joke immediately after snuffing someone out. It's a clear sign of how secure he feels (as the presenter of *Crime Alert)*, that he's never going to get caught. The top brass at the television station love him, his production team invite him to their parties, and he's got many fans in homes all around the country (including Mr. and Mrs. Columbo). The Lieutenant tells Wade that it's a real pleasure to meet him and that his wife recently thought that one of their grocery clerks looked like one of the suspects on his show. Wade's response is, "Well, that's part of our appeal Lieutenant, the audience likes to get involved in catching the criminals." Wade is so sure of himself, he offers his services, "By the way Lieutenant if I can be of any help to you, you'll let me know..." He then makes himself laugh by adding, "and, tell your wife, we'll look in on that grocery clerk!"

Later, as the Lieutenant begins to close in on him, things become less friendly between the two. Wade finds Columbo in his dressing room, sitting in a chair, just about to get a haircut from the TV host's own personal barber. Wade is not amused by this. Columbo confides in him, that he has some theories about the murder. Wade jokes, after finishing his trim, "That's very good! Maybe *you* should host the show! Fix his hair!" Everyone laughs as the Lieutenant is leaving the trailer, "He's got a great sense of humor," Columbo comments, "Yes, he does," agrees the barber (but we get the strong feeling that neither of them actually think that this is the case).

Columbo is famously perplexed by modern technology. "Anybody know how to work these things?" he asks as he crouches down, staring at a computer screen in the murder victim's house, "These machines, they baffle me!" But even though Wade thinks he's been very clever (covering his tracks by fiddling around with the victim's computer to plant a fake news story) there is a tiny detail he has overlooked; which of course Columbo picks up. Ultimately, it's another bit of machinery that gives Columbo his real proof of Wade's culpability. A surveillance camera.

If you are having a bit of a party for this episode, you could rustle up some Black Beans and Demon Rum. This is the dish Wade is hoping for at one of the shindigs he's invited to. Alternatively, you could make George's own Smoky Chicken and follow this up with his Ginger Snap Dandy, the recipe for which you'll find in the entry for *A Deadly State of Mind*.

I cannot find frozen orange juice for love nor money here in the UK. So sometimes I use a cup of ordinary orange juice, boosting the flavor up with a tablespoon of orange flower essence. If I am feeling fancy I use Cointreau instead for an extra kick. Also hickory seasoning salt is something I have never seen here. I use Maldon smoked sea salt. Liquid smoke can be bought via the internet fairly easily even if it isn't barbecue season!

George Hamilton's Smoky Chicken

5 lb / 2250g chicken, jointed
½ cup / 60g flour
Salt and pepper
1 teaspoon olive or salad oil
1 can or bottle of beer
1 chicken bouillon cube
2 teaspoons honey
1 cup / 240ml undiluted frozen orange juice
⅛ teaspoon liquid smoke
¼ teaspoon hickory seasoning salt
¼ teaspoon garlic salt

Shake the chicken pieces with the flour, 1 teaspoon of salt, and 1 teaspoon of pepper in a paper bag. Brown the chicken in heated oil in a large frying pan that has a lid. After chicken is browned on all sides, pour off all the oil and add the beer. In a separate pan, heat the chicken bouillon cube, honey, and orange juice together until the cube is dissolved. Add the liquid smoke, hickory salt, and garlic salt. Then pour over the chicken. Cover frying pan and cook the chicken over a low heat for about two hours or until done.

Serves 6 to 8

Just one more thing... Test cook Bethany B., really had to do some deep thinking about this recipe, as George's original was rather vague and included a typo (beat rather than heat). Thanks to her, this slightly modified version of George's recipe works much better than the original. It's recommended to cook the chicken in batches to avoid overcrowding, and I agree with Bethany, you will probably need more than one teaspoon of oil, more like 2 tablespoons if you make the whole recipe. Bethany shared this with her mom, and their verdict was, "We both agreed that the flavor was great and we would absolutely make this again, but we didn't like the skin on the chicken. To us, it made it slimy. We would just use boneless, skinless, chicken breasts next time. It makes it a lot faster and a lot easier. I would definitely make it again though, the flavor is just superb. I also recommend boiling the sauce down for a few minutes to thicken it. This dish also reheats very well and it results in a very tender chicken." I agree, Bethany, this is an unusual recipe, but I really like it, especially with the Cointreau!

COLUMBO AND THE MURDER OF A ROCK STAR - 1991

It doesn't matter how many times I watch this episode, I still don't understand the killer's alibi. I won't issue a plot spoiler, but let's just say, if someone asked me to do what Shera Danese's business associate asks her to do, I'd want to know what the hell was going on. She appears to have done something very strange, without asking why he would want her to do such a thing. However, she gets a law firm partnership and a marriage proposal out of it, so hey-ho, wouldn't you?

I get a big kick out of the fact that John Finnegan who has played Columbo's favorite chili emporium boss, "Barney," several times, appears in this episode as the Lieutenant's superior, Chief Quentin Corbett. He drags Columbo over the coals about the fact he's not playing ball with a very influential lawyer, but the banter between the two of them soon turns to food. Columbo is told that the restaurant where he's going to meet the suspect serves the best steaks in town, New York Steaks. The Daryl Club is very fancy, and as usual, our sleuth seems a little out of place in these rarified surroundings. Hugh Creighton (played by Dabney Coleman) is having a light lunch of chicken noodle soup, as he's not very hungry. Columbo hesitates for a moment, saying he's not very hungry either, then proceeds to order New York Steak (medium rare), asparagus with hollandaise sauce, roast potatoes, a shrimp cocktail to start with, a Caesar salad and a piece of sweetcorn. Greedy! Mind you, as we see later in the episode, Columbo's usual lunch al-desko is the much less hoity-toity peanut butter and raisin sandwich.

At the crime scene, Columbo is bothered by the fact that it seems as though two bottles of Champagne were opened in the kitchen, rather than the bedroom. This doesn't fit with his understanding of how couples behave in a romantic situation; coyly put, "When there is sex in the air". He expounds, that couples, "…want to share the pop and the spritz. That's what Champagne is all about. Why else would you drink champagne, if it's not for the pop and the spritz?" So if you can afford it, champagne would be a perfect tipple to accompany this episode. Just for fun, you could draw two stars on the bottom of the popped corks when your guests aren't looking, as this detail forms the basis of a big clue in this episode.

New York Steak Dabney Coleman

In Los Angeles, there is a restaurant called Dan Tana's that has a dish on its menu called "New York Steak, Dabney Coleman". At the time of this writing, it costs $68 (about £50), I am saving up to visit. Surely this dish was named shortly after this episode aired, in tribute to Dabney and the Lieutenant's newfound penchant for New York Steak? It would be fun to prepare it for this episode.

Here's what I know about the "New York Steak, Dabney Coleman" served at Dan Tana's. It is 20 oz (about 560g - that is a whopper!). The restaurant has their steak sent to Los Angeles from Kansas City. You can have spaghetti or fettuccine on the side, or as someone who's been there and done that says: "if you'd rather go healthy you can get it with sliced tomatoes."

So for this episode why not get yourself the fanciest steak you can afford - a New York Strip steak (also known as a Kansas City strip steak), or if you are in the UK or Australia, a sirloin or porterhouse steak respectively. A frequent visitor to Dan Tana's says that the steak is served "very basic, no potatoes or anything, just seared with some salt/pepper and oil with a little fresh parsley and a small order of pasta."

Spaghetti? Fettuccine? Sliced tomatoes on the side? - your choice!

Just one more thing... I don't know anyone who lives in Los Angeles so couldn't get the New York Steak Dabney Coleman tested in person. Perhaps someone reading this book will use this as an excuse to go to Dan Tana's? Do let me know if you go and sample this steak. When I replicated this recipe for myself, I bought the best quality steak I could find (not 560g worth though!) and had it with some roasted tomatoes and a baked potato on the side. I am British, and the idea of serving pasta with steak just does not compute! It was utterly delicious, as expensive steak always is. Treat yourself!

DEATH HITS THE JACKPOT - 1991

Do you play the lottery? I do. Do you always think you are going to win when the numbers are announced? I do too. How would you feel if you actually won the jackpot? It would be brilliant, wouldn't it? But what if you were on the verge of a messy divorce and you didn't want to give up half of a $30 million win to your former significant other? You'd be in a quandary, right? That's the issue at the center of this episode.

"Touch it, feel it…" when we meet the Rip Torn character Leon Lamar, he immediately seems seedy. He's trying to persuade a couple to spend a large amount of money on a necklace from his upmarket jewelry store. The woman handling the piece is swooning over it, but her husband rolls his eyes at the sales pitch. Leon looks (to me) like a man not to be trusted. But blood is thicker than water and his nephew turns to him with his lottery win conundrum. This proves to be his undoing.

When we first see the Lieutenant in this episode, he has a chimpanzee in his arms. We know by now that Columbo loves cats and dogs, but obviously, he's quite at home with chimps too. The chimp appears to be wearing a skirt, but as with Louella the puppy in a later episode, the Lieutenant persists in calling it a "he." Maybe because his dog, "Dog" is a boy, he thinks of all pets as male. Watch this chimp, he's going to provide a crucial clue for Columbo.

Columbo is on the scent of the killer and makes a nuisance of himself at an auction. Leon is buying some very expensive jewelry. There is a wonderful comedy moment, when Columbo accidentally bids $450,000 for an "heirloom, 40-carat diamond necklace of exceptional quality," while he is trying to get Leon's attention by waving his auction catalog. As our hero begins to focus in on his suspect, they share a little joke together about how the guests at Leon's party thought Columbo was wearing a costume (when he was just wearing his normal clothes). But the murderer is beginning to get rattled. The Lieutenant catches him in a lie, and then the case is solved. All because of a chimp.

It seems as though the *Columbo* production team had a few crates of Champagne left over from *Columbo and the Murder of a Rock Star* (as bottles with the same label turn up in this episode too). The murder victim cracks one open to accompany, what looks like, a cheese sandwich. So why not have yourself a little solo supper with sarnies and champers (sandwiches and champagne to non-Brits). You could throw in some mixed nuts too (as the murder victim Freddie does for his guests).

Here is Rip's recipe for a Mexican-themed filling to an omelet. I make half of Rip's recipe and scoff the lot myself for a hearty brunch, but I am greedy. If you make the full amount, you can share it with friends!

Rip Torn's Omelet Mexicali

2 teaspoons butter
½ cup / 75g finely chopped onion
½ cup / 75g chopped green pepper
1 or 2 finely chopped, hot green peppers (or chopped, canned, mild green chilies to taste)
2 medium ripe tomatoes, peeled, chopped
1 teaspoon canned red taco sauce
½ teaspoon monosodium glutamate
Salt and pepper
½ cup / 50g grated American cheese/cheddar
1 small ripe avocado, peeled, diced
Chili powder

Melt butter, add onion and green pepper. Cook until vegetables are tender over low heat. Add hot peppers, tomatoes, taco sauce, monosodium glutamate, plus salt and pepper to taste. Simmer 20 minutes over low heat until sauce is the consistency of a thick puree.

While the top of the omelet is still runny, top with grated cheese and avocado. Spoon sauce over all. Sprinkle with chili powder to taste. Serve omelet open face-style, cutting into pie-shaped wedges.

Rip Torn's Omelet

6 eggs
Pinch of white pepper
3 tablespoons sweet/unsalted butter - divided use

Separate yolks and whites of eggs. Beat yolks until thick; whites until stiff. Fold whites into yolks, adding ½ teaspoon salt and the white pepper. Heat 2 tablespoons of the butter in heavy frying pan. When butter is sizzling, but not brown, add eggs. As the eggs begin to set, reduce heat. As omelet cooks, push back from the edges and keep adding butter. Cook until golden brown on the bottom but slightly runny on top. Remove from heat, loosen the edge of half the omelet from frying pan with a spatula. Add filling, fold one half over the other. Turn upside down on a heated dish. Lightly brush top with absorbent paper to remove excess butter. Serve at once.

Serves 3 or 4

Just one more thing... Greg Swenson, author of the fabulous *Recipes for Rebels: In the Kitchen with James Dean* cookbook and glorious website of the same name, tested this recipe for me. He admitted that the "one teaspoon canned red taco sauce" was a complete mystery to him! I agree. It seems pretty crazy and wouldn't really bring much to the party. Greg suggests that you omit this altogether, or add a whole lot more (to your taste). Alternately, he recommends replacing with chili sauce (as he did), hot sauce, or taco seasoning. Slave to a recipe that I am (and living far from the Mexican border), I actually made some taco sauce myself, just for that one teaspoon!

NO TIME TO DIE - 1992

This is an unusual *Columbo*. It breaks the formula in a number of ways. Firstly, we actually get to meet one of the many members of Columbo's much spoken about extended family; his nephew Andy, who is the victim of a crime. It is also different because, in almost every episode of *Columbo*, we see a murder being committed; in this one, the storyline revolves around a kidnapping. This introduces an element of jeopardy not seen in other episodes. Will the Lieutenant work out who the kidnapper is, in time to prevent something awful happening? What do you think? Also, it's the only *Columbo* I can think of, where there is no interaction between our hero and the villain. The only moment they are in the same place is at the very end; and it's not Columbo who gets his man, it's Andy.

Although this one doesn't follow the normal rules we *Columbo* fans love so much, there is still lots to enjoy. First and foremost, we see Columbo dancing! The Lieutenant is quite a mover. I just love his samba walk. Also, despite his nephew's new bride being in imminent danger, the Lieutenant doesn't allow a doughnut go to waste. He is calm and collected throughout the whole investigation, despite the mounting panic of his nephew (who is also in the police force). Since many of the wedding guests are cops, there are plenty of hands on deck to help out. This one involves teamwork, but of course, it's Columbo who does the deep thinking. He finds a witness who saw the getaway vehicle, and as the Lieutenant explains, sometimes people see more than they think they see.

Fabulous British actress Juliet Mills has a small guest role in this episode, so I am recommending her recipe for Hoppin' John. Sounds weird, tastes good! This episode also begins with a wedding, where the Champagne is flowing freely, so fizz would be an appropriate tipple. Does Hoppin' John go with Champagne? Why not? If you don't fancy booze, cookies and Darjeeling tea also make an appearance. If you are having a salad, oil and vinegar would be appropriate on the table. As you will see from the kidnap victim's resourcefulness, oil and vinegar have many uses…

Posh, modern sausages might night yield too much fat so you could add a tablespoon or so of cooking oil to sauté the green pepper in. I cut my sausages into quarters and remove the skins, it makes lovely meatball-like chunks to place on top of the rice mixture.

Juliet Mills' Chive-Sausage Hoppin' John

1½ lbs / 675g sausages
1 green bell pepper, chopped
1 x 15 oz can / 400g can kidney beans, drained
3 cups cooked rice (about 1 cup/190g uncooked)
¼ cup / 12g chopped chives, plus 1 tablespoon for garnish
Salt and pepper
6 oz / 170g can tomato paste/puree
1 lb / 450g canned, chopped tomatoes

Fry sausages until lightly browned. Sauté green bell pepper in ¼ cup of sausage drippings. Combine green pepper mixture with remaining ingredients, except the 1 tablespoon chives. Add salt and pepper to taste. Pour mixture into large casserole dish. Top with sausages. Bake at 400 degrees F / 205 degrees C / gas mark 6 for 25 to 30 minutes, or until hot and bubbly. Sprinkle the top with additional chives.

Serves 6

Just one more thing... Liz Wilson, aka Ma Baker, made this dish for her hubby and what do you know? Turns out he's a massive *Columbo* fan! Excellent! Liz reported, "…most of the meal was spent reminiscing about his favorite episodes." How brilliant! The verdict on the dish, "We loved this! So very easy and completely delicious, though it did need salt and pepper. Would be a great recipe for students. Filling and not too pricey. Only fed three (hungry we were....but I think 6 is ambitious. I'd say 4). We ate it with lashings of red wine and my daughter had the leftovers later that evening." So pleased you enjoyed it and had a good *Columbo* reminisce over your Hoppin' John, lovely Liz!

A BIRD IN THE HAND... - 1992

The minute we see Tyne Daly's character, Dolores McCain, we know that she's a lush. Standing with a large glass of spiked orange juice in her hand; when she sees that her toy-boy lover has turned up, she drunkenly fluffs up her hair a bit. She's a sassy southern belle, married to the very rich manager of an American football team. At one point we see her half-heartedly watching a game and hungover (behind very large sunglasses even though she's not outdoors). Don't be fooled though, underneath her fluffy, boozy demeanor, she's a focused, determined woman who has designs on her husband's money.

There's an element of ambiguity to this episode, as Dolores' young lover (her husband's nephew, Harold) also has reason to bump off the wealthy football manager. He's got gambling debts and Dolores is getting tired of bailing him out. It's a little difficult for Columbo to see which one of this pair is the guilty party. Each as bad as each other it seems.

There's no real flirtation between the Lieutenant and Dolores, unlike when we see Tyne appearing in a later, bonkers episode, *Undercover*. Dolores flirts with all the young bucks in this episode though. She's a strange mixture of coquettishness and practicality. When the Lieutenant finds some suspicious cotton gloves that smell of petrol in her trash can, she claims they are hers, "I threw them out just the other day… They're stinky!" She explains that she always carries gloves like these in her car, for when she pumps her gasoline. When the Lieutenant expresses surprise that a wealthy woman like her would pump her own gas, she responds, "Full-service, Lieutenant, was invented to cheat women and old folks."

When Columbo goes through all the evidence he has against her, Dolores pretends to be incredulous, imploring, "There has to be a reason for murder. I have none." Glamorous to the very end, once she realizes she's been rumbled by the Lieutenant, Dolores puts on a magnificent hat and raises a glass towards him in a toast. As she leaves the room with a flourish, she gives the young police officer who is holding the door open for her a sexy look and a Southern Belle, "Why thank you." So regal!

Tyne was recently asked for her favorite recipe for a cookbook being compiled to raise funds for the Riverland Domestic Abuse Service in Australia. Tyne's response was classic, "My dears, I no longer cook and I hope you are in that position too one day." Such a brilliant reply. Luckily for us, in the 1990s Tyne contributed a recipe for Key Lime Pie to the *Cop Cookbook*.

In this episode Tyne is almost permanently attached to a large glass of orange juice which we can assume has vodka or some other spirit mixed in. I think, therefore, you would be perfectly justified in serving just booze with this episode (if you can't be bothered to cook).

Tyne Daly's Key Lime Pie

3 egg yolks
1 x 14 oz / 397g can sweetened, condensed milk
¾ cup / 180ml lime juice
1 x 9-inch baked and cooled pie shell (or chilled crumb crust)
1 cup / 240ml heavy cream/double cream or whipping cream

In a large bowl, whip the egg yolks and sweetened condensed milk. Gradually beat in the lime juice. Pour into the pie shell and chill for 6 hours. Whip the heavy cream and spread over the pie.

Alternate Meringue Topping

3 egg whites
6 tablespoons sugar

Preheat oven to 425 degrees F / 220 degrees C / gas mark 7.

Whip the egg whites until they form stiff peaks. Whip in the sugar 1 tablespoon at a time. Pile on top of the pie. Brown for 3 to 4 minutes in the oven. Let cool.

Serves 8

Just one more thing... Writer Sarah Broughton in Cardiff, made this for her book group and comments included, "Nice and zingy" and "Properly limey." Sarah's verdict? "The filling is very runny – I would recommend putting it on the most accessible level shelf in the fridge – the slightest tilt and it goes everywhere! But it tastes DELICIOUS!" Sarah's niece Jess and boyfriend Jon were lucky to get a slice each too, I loved Jon's comment, "I give it a "D" – for delightful!"

IT'S ALL IN THE GAME - 1993

It is well worth bearing in mind when watching this episode, that it was written by the great man himself, Peter Falk. It's the only *Columbo* episode he wrote, and by golly, he did a good job.

Falk obviously had a lot of fun writing so many flirty scenes for himself to play with his co-star, and it's easy to wonder whether he already had Faye Dunaway in mind when he was writing. We know that Peter loved Faye in real life (he says so in his autobiography) and they have great, on-screen chemistry. But it's nice, that although Columbo makes a good show of being wooed by Faye's character, Lauren Staton, it is, of course, all an act. But is it an act on Lauren's part? You can see how she would be attracted to the Lieutenant, especially when he is spending the police department's money on a huge bunch of red roses and a cozy steak dinner for two at the chef's table chez Barney's Beanery.

The first time we get the sense of a frisson between Lauren and the Lieutenant is when he asks her if she minds cigar smoke; she says she likes it. This seems to tickle him pink. He's just been telling Lauren all about how he sweats a lot, and how because of this, he's got soft feet. It's hardly the usual chit-chat that would get someone romantically interested in you, but Lauren is an unusual woman, and the Lieutenant is an unusual man.

It's a shame so few men wear ties these days; it gives us women less opportunity to flirtatiously select a new one and pop it around their neck for them. We've already seen Anne Baxter's character using this technique in *Requiem for a Falling Star*, and Lauren does this too. As she's sliding off the Lieutenant's old tie she suggests, "This tie is for older men, and you're not old. Why do you want to appear old? What I should do is buy you a new suit. But I don't know you well enough for that. Maybe someday…" Later, she tells her co-conspirator that she bought the Lieutenant a tie. When asked if he liked it, she reports, "he liked that I bought it, men like that."

Over a counter lunch at Barney's Beanery (chili, I am guessing), Columbo tells Barney that a "beautiful woman" (Lauren) is making a play for him. He seems to be quite pleased about this. Barney brings him down to earth, informing him, "Listen, she knows what she's doing, she has her motives. You know, you're not exactly Robert Redford." which makes the Lieutenant laugh.

But he plays along with the romancing, and although it seems that he might be getting a little too close for comfort to Lauren, he is a professional through and through. If there was any doubt in the viewer's mind that the Lieutenant may have been tempted by the glamorous Lauren, this is punctured by his last words at the end of the episode; announcing that he's off to take the wife bowling.

If you don't feel like cooking when you plan to watch *It's All In The Game*, why not just make yourself (and guests if you have any) a peanut butter and raisin sandwich. Columbo constructs himself one of these in this episode. It consists of two slices of white bread, butter, peanut butter and approximately 45 raisins (I counted). Jam is optional.

I haven't been able to find a recipe for Faye, so here's my version of a lovely cocktail invented in her honor by Jonathan Humphrey, the bar manager at the Drake Hotel in Toronto. This was created in 2011 to coincide with the 36th annual Toronto International Film Festival and it is really delicious!

The Faye Dunaway Cocktail

1½ ounces vodka
1¼ ounces fresh mango juice
¾ ounces lime juice
½ ounce agave syrup
3 pickled Jalapeño slices (two in the shaker, one for garnish, seeds removed if desired)
2 dashes orange bitters

To make the Faye, simply pop all the ingredients (reserving one Jalapeño slice) into a cocktail shaker with a few ice cubes, shake vigorously and strain into a classic coupette. Garnish with the remaining Jalapeño slice on the side of the glass.

Serves 1

Just one more thing... The Tuesday Club in Hastings tested this recipe. The evening was hosted by artist Olivia Bishop, in her beautiful, converted, artist's warehouse by the sea. In attendance were Katya, Lady Jane, Trix, Rose, Olivia, Philippa, Eleanor, Amil and Tanya. According to Olivia, "A rush for the second batch said it all. The hint of chili was a big success." She added, "We definitely wanted ice … we added cubes to the cocktail shaker."

Lovely, lovely food blogger Taryn Fryer of Retro Food For Modern Times, made this and reported, "I made it yesterday and it is divine! Just the right blend of sweet, sour and spice!" I'm in total agreement, the Faye is currently the favorite cocktail at Silver Screen Suppers Towers and no doubt will be for some time.

BUTTERFLY IN SHADES OF GREY - 1994

William Shatner is great as the villain in this episode, and it's one of my favorites of the later seasons. Fielding Chase is a bombastic talk radio host and a borderline bully when it comes to matters relating to his adopted daughter, Victoria. She works for him on the show and he hates the idea of her trying to "bust loose from her cocoon," trying to make it as a writer. He does everything he can to scupper her literary ambitions; this, of course, involves a murder.

We know what little respect Fielding has for those who phone into his radio show when we hear one of his links. He introduces himself as, "Your obedient servant Fielding Chase, ready and able to chat with the brightest of you. Fuzzy brains and the inarticulate need not bother dialing in. The valuable time of my tens of millions of listeners is far too precious to waste on chatting about your latest gall bladder operation or your Uncle Willie's baseball card collection…" Fielding believes himself to be very important and influential indeed. He cannot bear the thought of losing control of his daughter; at one point, telling her that she's still just a child. She protests, "For God's sake, I'm 25 years old!" She is ready to fly the nest and he'll do everything he can to prevent it.

When Columbo firsts meets Fielding, the radio show host is sitting in his convertible making a call on a mobile phone. The Lieutenant hovers beside the car, and Fielding breaks off his conversation, barking, "Would you mind? This is a very important call!" The Lieutenant is suitably chastised and ostentatiously pretends not to be listening to his call. Mobile phones were a fairly new thing in 1993, and there is much fun to be had with Columbo deciding to get all modern and try one out. Ultimately, it's new telecommunications technology that helps Columbo to get his man. It's one of those great era-specific details that crop up in the series every now and then. For those of us that are old enough remember; in the early days of mobile phones, there were many signal black-spots. I used to live on a houseboat and couldn't get a signal at all unless I held the phone out of the window… The Lieutenant's unfamiliarity with new technology, but his willingness to give it a go, ultimately gives him the lead he needs.

Fielding believes himself superior to those around him, including Columbo of course. When Columbo delivers the classic line, "There is sir, just one more thing." Fielding snaps: "With you Lieutenant, there's always just one more thing. Do you have a problem with short-term memory? Maybe you should consult a physician." How very rude! But when the Lieutenant stages a sting, involving cyclists, a mobile phone, and a gun, Fielding Chase has to admit that he underestimated the Lieutenant, "You know Columbo, I think possibly, I may have misread you." Columbo's response? "Possible sir, possible."

There is a fun scene in this episode where Columbo shares a table at a posh restaurant with Fielding. He asks for a cup of tea with honey, as he's got a tickle in his throat. He asks the waiter, "Would that be too much trouble?" When the tea arrives he says that it smells terrific, but he's bemused by the fancy slotted honey spoon that arrives with it. Fielding, obviously amused by this perceived class difference, condescendingly advises him how to use it. "Twist it." Columbo chuckles and admits, "Never saw that before!" and then observes to himself, "You live and learn!"

So you could have a nice cup of tea with some honey while watching this episode, plus here is a really tasty way of preparing chicken a la William Shatner. Easy, and delicious!

William Shatner's Lime-Garlic Broiled Chicken

3 lb / 1350g chicken parts
1 large clove garlic, halved
1 lime
4 tablespoons melted butter or margarine
¼ cup / 60ml sweet vermouth

Salt and pepper
Oil for greasing
Lime slices

Rub chicken well with garlic halves, then crush or mince the garlic. Grate rind from lime, then halve lime and rub the chicken with cut sides. Squeeze lime juice into a bowl, add 1 tablespoon of the grated rind and all the minced garlic. Blend in the vermouth, 1 teaspoon salt, and ¼ teaspoon pepper. Place chicken pieces on a lightly oiled rack in broiling pan/under the grill. Brush with lime juice and broil/grill, brushing often with lime sauce. Serve with pan juices mixed with remaining lime sauce, and garnish with lime slices.

Serves 4

Just one more thing... I was shocked to the core to hear from my sister of the skillet, Dr. Caroline Frick in Texas, "Am mortified to say that I still haven't seen ONE episode of *Columbo*, as passed out on your bed from drink during the last tweetathon #notproud." I remember her passing out, but how can it be that she's never seen *Columbo*? Perhaps this book will reveal the splendor of it all to her. Despite her non-Columbo-ness, she was game to try this dish with the assistance of her gentleman caller. She used a bottle of Vermouth found at her parents' house, that she thought, "likely was purchased in 1976." The Frickster's verdict on the dish? "Definitely a winner."

Julie Winfield, self professed garlic lover and seeker of life efficiency, also made William's chicken dish, impressing me by deciding to use a whole, unjointed chicken for her version. I loved her off-piste approach, plus she made a "very delicious gravy," by adding some water, a chicken stock cube, and plain flour to the pan juices. "The skin was deliciously garlicky with a nice limey hint; the Vermouth made very little difference, except in the gravy which I think is actually the star of this recipe. I'm going to try this recipe again sometime (mainly because I have a massive bottle of Vermouth to use up now, haha), but I might try it more as a stew sort of thing, chicken chunks cooked in the sauce, and possibly in a slow cooker." Yes, I think a slow cooked version would be absolutely divine. Finally, Julie did make me laugh with, "I didn't watch the Columbo episode in which Mr. Shatner featured, but I did have *The Transformed Man* playing whilst I cooked. That was traumatizing, to say the least. What WAS he on?!!"

Yinzerella of the awesome Dinner Is Served 1972 website, tested this one too. "It was yummy," was her verdict, and that's all she wrote! It's a busy life recreating 1970s recipes you know!

UNDERCOVER - 1994

This episode is a great stretch of Peter Falk's acting talents. Columbo goes undercover in this episode and calls upon a whole gamut of Italian American movie characters for his pretend personas. Firstly, in an echo of where Falk got his acting start, he assumes the guise of a hoodlum. With hints of Robert de Niro mixed with some Al Pacino, Columbo really throws himself into the role of a wisecracking low-level criminal called Artie Stokes. Later, he comes over all Marlon Brando, playing the role of a member of the Mafia, it's all very *Godfather*.

The plot revolves around the search for several pieces of a photograph, that when assembled will show the location of a large amount of money. The ill-gotten gains of a robbery. Several people have pieces of the picture, and they are gradually being snuffed out, one by one, as others try to gather up pieces of the jigsaw to find the treasure.

The villain of the piece, played by Ed Begley Jr, is an insurance guy called Irving Krutch. He appeals to the police to help him find the pieces of the photograph, and therefore the hidden dough. He gets off on the wrong foot with Columbo right from the get-go, assuming that he is a Detective, rather than a Lieutenant. Irving is very sure of himself. He repeatedly refers to himself in the third person, saying things like "Krutch doesn't welch", and brags about being a Princeton graduate. Columbo doesn't like him, it's easy to tell.

Krutch seems to have airtight alibis. He has a very glamorous girlfriend, and when Columbo asks him where he was at the time a murder was committed, he boasts, "I was in bed with Susan Endicott." Columbo laughs and shakes his head, "Always in bed with Susan Endicott!" "Hey, wouldn't you be?" jokes Krutch. But Susan Endicott isn't as loyal as she appears to be. When she realizes the Lieutenant has some very unusual evidence, she caves in.

When Krutch acknowledges the game is up, he seems almost tearful; he nearly got away with getting rich by gathering the pieces of a photographic jigsaw. At the police station, he holds his hand up, explaining, "I came this close…" To which Columbo responds with the classic line, "Close, but no cigar," as he pops one into his mouth and studies the final piece of the jigsaw, trying to work out where the money is to be found.

The best thing about this episode for me is the glorious Tyne Daly. Alongside Mrs. Peck in *Double Shock*, Dorothea McNally is my favorite minor character. Dorothea opens the door to the Lieutenant with curlers in her hair and wearing a zebra print dressing gown. They have an immediate rapport. She's a hooker with a heart of gold, and Tyne plays the character to the hilt. Tipsy already, she gets even tipsier when Columbo gives her some money for booze. When she offers the Lieutenant a drink, I'm almost certain that she responds, "You want some of this piss?" I'm surprised that would have got past the censors in the UK in 1994, we were a bit prudish here in those days. But, if your guests don't object to swearing you could say this to them when you top up their tipples after watching the episode. You could also memorize this phrase so that you can say it as a toast, "Here's looking up your whole family!"

If you are watching this alone, maybe on a Sunday morning after you have read the papers, why not drink Buck's Fizz (Champagne and orange juice) wearing some elaborate lounging pajamas, makeup, and jewels, like Columbo's early suspect, Gerry Ferguson, played by Sheer Danese, does in this episode.

If not, here's a lovely, vibrant way of serving asparagus, which would be a fresh side dish with whatever else you are having for your dinner. If you are really in the mood for cooking, you could also serve Tyne Daly's Key Lime Pie for dessert!

Ed Begley's Citrus Dressed Asparagus

1 lb / 450g asparagus, tough stem ends removed
4 teaspoons fresh lemon juice
2 teaspoons extra-virgin olive oil
2 teaspoons orange juice
Cayenne pepper, to taste
Salt and pepper

Cut asparagus into three-inch pieces, steam until crisp-tender. Set aside. Meanwhile, in a small bowl, blend lemon juice, olive oil, orange juice, cayenne pepper, plus salt and black pepper to taste. To serve, arrange asparagus on a platter, then drizzle with dressing.

Serves 4

Just one more thing... KSB enjoyed this with her daughter Bethany, and wrote "We both agreed that it was a little tart, but had a great flavor. We even wondered how it would be as a salad dressing. One thing we would suggest trying, is to roast the asparagus instead and see how that would be with the dressing." I'm definitely going to try that, thank you KSB.

Pamela Hutchinson of the wonderful Silent London website made this for herself and her beau. She told me, "We both agreed that Columbo was even better then we remembered and we were glad you gave us a nudge to watch an episode. We hadn't seen one in ages!" Oh, fab! They were both worried that this dish would be too acidic and sharp. As Pamela put it, "Lemon juice and cayenne pepper together made me think of Beyonce's Lemonade Master Cleanse, but we were very pleasantly surprised. We did get the occasional kick at the back of the throat from the cayenne pepper, but overall the flavors worked beautifully. We were also glad to be making a dish with orange juice in it, as Geraldine drinks Bucks Fizz and Susan Endicott drinks fresh OJ in bed with Irving Krutch." I agree with Pamela, "It's more than a coincidence!"

STRANGE BEDFELLOWS - 1995

Can the Lieutenant speak Italian or not? This is one of the great mysteries of *Columbo*. In some episodes, it appears that he can (he launches a tirade at a young Italian waiter in *Murder Under Glass* for example), but in this episode, it seems not. When Rod Steiger's character greets him with a super-enthusiastic and expansive welcome to his home in Italian, Columbo puts his hand to his ear and asks, "Excuse me?" He explains that he doesn't speak Italian, as he "...never got the hang of it."

It's possible of course, that this is one of the Lieutenant's little games (or just some fun for the writers), but it does seem odd that after making such a fuss at the beginning of the episode, about some bad clams he had eaten the night before, he appears to have no idea what Zuppa di Vongole is (Soup With Clams).

If you are of an age to have watched the classic sit-com *Cheers* on TV in the early 1980s-90s, it's hard to forget George Wendt's signature role as chummy, funny, barfly Norm. But here, later in 1995, he plays the villain, Graham McVeigh, who seems to have absolutely no sense of humor (although he does try to make a joke about the Lieutenant's clams). He is a greedy man who wants his brother out of the picture; he will bump him off and then ride away on a teeny-tiny fold-up bicycle to unintentionally comic effect.

Who would have thought that a mouse could hold the secret of a murder? Columbo, that's who. He rattles McVeigh by producing a plastic mouse at the racetrack. McVeigh pretends not to have a clue what the Lieutenant is getting at with his talk of mice tails and ashtrays. But as Columbo hints, "It's these little things; ashes, tiny mice. They lead you to the big things, and all of a sudden, there it is, as clear as day!" A great summation of how seemingly insignificant details never pass him by. It is usually via the little things, that Columbo gets his man.

If your dinner guests have a sense of humor you could serve Zuppa di Vongole after this episode. As an extra in-joke, have a bottle of Pepto-Bismol wrapped in brown paper on the table. Alternatively, Rod offered up this great recipe for Chicken Grand Marnier; French, rather than Italian, but very, very good!

To drink? Scotch and soda, "easy on the soda" as the villain drinks. Or Pellegrino, favored by the Rod Steiger character.

I have been unable to find frozen orange juice in the UK, it just doesn't seem to exist here. I would suggest using an extra tablespoon of Grand Marnier instead of the frozen orange concentrate and an extra ½ teaspoon of grated orange rind. Or you could try replacing it with orange blossom water.

Rod Steiger's Baked Chicken Grand Marnier

2 whole chicken breasts
1 tablespoon vegetable oil
1 cup / 150g minced/finely chopped white onion - divided use
1 teaspoon salt
¼ teaspoon paprika (or white pepper to taste)
½ teaspoon finely grated orange rind
¼ cup / 60ml evaporated milk
1 tablespoon fresh lemon juice
1 tablespoon frozen orange concentrate
1 egg yolk
1 tablespoon Grand Marnier (or Cointreau)

Preheat oven to 350 degrees F / 175 degrees C / gas mark 4.

Cut chicken breasts into halves. Spray vegetable oil lightly on a non-stick frying pan. Brown chicken breasts quickly on both sides, remove from heat.

Lightly grease bottom of oven-proof casserole dish. Cover with half the minced onion, top with chicken breasts. Season breasts with salt and paprika (or white pepper).

Top with remaining onions, cover, cook in the oven for about 40 minutes.

Combine orange rind, milk, lemon juice, orange concentrate, beaten egg yolk and Grand Marnier (or Cointreau). Spread over chicken. Cook uncovered 15 minutes longer (or under broiler/grill with flame set low to brown and crispen).

Rod suggests serving with a crisp green salad dressed with diet Roquefort dressing. He also suggests serving with a good bottle of Beaujolais.

Serves 2-4 depending on size of your chicken breasts.

Just one more thing... My chums Susan Dirks and Kent Stevens in McMinnville, Oregon, tried this dish and loved it. Susan wrote, "This recipe is delicious! We made a few minor changes, but I think the most important change would be to *double the quantity of the sauce.* There is just not enough of it to fully cover the chicken and it is so good we wanted more for each bite of chicken!" I can understand that! Susan and Kent watched *Strange Bedfellows* alongside their meal, and were impressed with Steiger's performance, feeling that he, "seemed to be having a marvelous time portraying the Italian gangster. (We also enjoyed the *Godfather*-esque musical theme on the soundtrack each time he entered a scene.)" It is definitely a fun episode and I loved Susan's comment, "Too bad there isn't a recipe out there for Rod Steiger's Veal Piccata or Clam Soup, but of course, he wasn't really Italian -- and neither was Peter Falk!"

Susan and Kent kindly took the time to create their own version of Rod's dish and you'll find it in the "Columbo's Chili and Other Delights" section.

A TRACE OF MURDER - 1997

The Lieutenant usually catches on really quickly to the identity of the perpetrator of the crime. But in this case, things are a little different. He doesn't seem to work out who has actually done the deed, until about an hour into the episode. This means less sparring with his adversary, so there's not so much time for Columbo's usual fun and games. He tells one of the suspects how very busy he is, "The first day of a homicide investigation... It's murder!"

Patrick Kinsley, played by David Rasche, is working alongside the Lieutenant as a forensic analyst and is over-confident that he can cover up the crime he has committed. He fancies himself pretty good at pulling the wool over the Lieutenant's eyes. When he tells Columbo that a comparison he has made between a cigar butt found at the scene of the crime and one from a suspect's ashtray has come up trumps, the Lieutenant shakes his hand, exclaiming, "You're a good man." Patrick is pretty smug and obviously thinks Columbo is a bit of a fool. When the Lieutenant turns up at the forensics lab with a huge fruit basket, Patrick remarks to Cathleen, his partner in crime, "He's handing out apples! I think the guy is a little goofy!"

Columbo is on a bit of a health kick in this episode. He tells Patrick that he always eats the whole of the apple, skin, seeds everything. They have a little joke about the fact that apple seeds contain cyanide. Patrick is trying to charm him. It's not just apples that Columbo seems to be pushing; when the Lieutenant first arrives at the scene of the crime, he's carrying a large grocery bag. He calls out to one of the cops on the scene, "Hey John, do you want a banana? They are very healthy..." He continues, "They're the best. I don't know about above the lungs," gesturing around his upper chest, "but this whole area here is protected." All the cops on the crime scene accept his kind offer of bananas. They don't seem as interested in the coffee and doughnuts the much flashier Patrick has brought along for them.

It takes a while for Columbo to spot the flaws in the murderer's plan and he seems genuinely shocked when it eventually dawns on him that the man who is the lead forensic analyst on this case, is also the killer. It's at Barney's Beanery, the favorite watering hole of the Lieutenant, where Patrick and Cathleen give themselves away over a simple cup of coffee. We saw in *Columbo Cries Wolf,* that how the way a woman takes her coffee, can really seal a deal, and so it is here. As always, no small detail is lost on the Lieutenant.

Learned from her grandmother, this is a fabulous recipe for stuffed peppers from Shera Danese (who of course was married to Peter Falk for many years). If you want to go to town, why not order (or make yourself) an enormous fruit basket all wrapped up in cellophane for dessert. You can carry it around with you, handing out apples to all your guests. So goofy!

Shera Danese's Italian Stuffed Peppers

8 red bell peppers
6 tablespoons fine-grade olive oil, divided use
¼ cup / 5g chopped parsley
3-4 cloves fresh garlic, crushed
4 Italian tomatoes, chopped
½ cup / 75g dry breadcrumbs, preferably Italian-seasoned
¾ lb / 340g seafood: shrimp, mussels or crab meat (uncooked, chopped or flaked)
1 onion, chopped, or 2 hard-boiled eggs, chopped
½ cup / 90g well-drained capers, mashed
Pinch of oregano
Salt and pepper

Preheat oven to 350 degrees F / 175 degrees C / gas mark 4.

Wash peppers; remove tops with a sharp knife and remove the seeds. Heat half of the olive oil in a frying pan with parsley and garlic; sauté until limp, stirring occasionally. Add tomatoes and cook to reduce volume until thick. Add tomato-garlic sauce to breadcrumbs, seafood, onion, capers, oregano in mixing bowl. Add salt and pepper to taste. Mix well.

Stand peppers upright in a small pan. Fill each pepper with seafood mixture. Bake uncovered in the oven for 45 minutes or until done. Baste tops of peppers with remaining olive oil every 10 minutes.

Shera advises serving with Champagne or a good white Burgundy, and I agree!

Serves 8

Just one more thing... Mandy Wedgwood made these as a starter course for her Columbo Dinner Party, and she was as impressed with them as I was, "We really enjoyed these. I was a bit nervous about using raw seafood in them at first, but figured it would be fine. I used large prawns, white crabmeat, and Queen scallops cut into quarters. I think the breadcrumb amount is just right, any more and it would just turn into a squishy mess inside. The capers added just the right amount of piquancy to the dish."

ASHES TO ASHES - 1998

The wonderful Rue McClanahan plays Hollywood gossip columnist, Verity Chandler, who is about to dish the dirt on a dodgy undertaker, played by Patrick McGoohan, in this great, late episode. Eric Prince is no ordinary undertaker though; he's a tinsel-town undertaker to the stars. This episode is very glossy, starry, and all the more fabulous because of it.

Verity's dog is called Louella, presumably after the legendary gossipmonger of the golden era of Hollywood, Louella Parsons. There are some great comedy moments with Columbo, his own dog, and Louella. He persists in referring to Louella, obviously a female dog, as a "he," and eventually just "the pup." The Lieutenant's understanding of the behavior patterns of dog lovers is key to the plot of this brilliant episode.

This is the fourth episode in which Patrick McGoohan plays the villain, and as always, he is excellent. He is very high and mighty, and certain in his conviction that he's going to get away with his dirty deed. But the haughty mortician hasn't reckoned with the Lieutenant's intellect. "Where's the oven?" Columbo inquires matter-of-factly, as he's being given the tour. He begins a play-of-words with Eric, joking that the "burning question" is why Verity's pager stopped working abruptly; wondering aloud whether she was killed at the funeral home. Eric seems a little smug when he asks if the Lieutenant has any evidence in the form of bodies. When the answer is in the negative, he more or less crows, "No bodies, no case... that's the tricky thing about burning questions, once they're burned they are just ashes... ashes!"

But it is the ashes that contain the evidence, of course.

The ingredient list for Rue's Wonder Women cookies does look dauntingly long, but these are definitely worth the effort. Super-tasty, and you can absolutely tell yourself that they are good for you. I think this is the kind of "health cookie" that Mrs. Peck would have served to Lieutenant Columbo in the *Double Shock* episode. As we know, the Lieutenant is extremely fond of health cookies...

Rue McClanahan's Wonder Women

½ cup / 65g non-fat dry milk/milk powder
¼ teaspoon baking powder
¼ teaspoon baking soda/bicarbonate of soda

½ teaspoon salt
¾ cup / 90g whole wheat/wholemeal flour
⅓ cup / 37g wheat germ
¾ cup / 180g butter or margarine
¼ cup / 56g peanut butter
1 cup / 180g brown sugar, packed
1 large egg, beaten
2 tablespoons honey
1 teaspoon vanilla extract
2 tablespoons milk
1 cup / 90g oats, uncooked
½ cup / 75g chopped pecans
⅓ cup / 46g sunflower seeds (optional)
1 cup / 150g seedless raisins, light or dark
1 cup / 190g dried apricots, chopped

Preheat oven to 375 degrees F / 190 degrees C / gas mark 5.

Mix and sift together dry milk, baking powder, baking soda, and ½ teaspoon of salt. Stir in whole wheat flour and wheat germ. In a separate bowl, cream butter until consistency of mayonnaise then blend in peanut butter. Add brown sugar to the butter mixture and mix until fluffy. Then add egg, honey, and vanilla; mixing well. Add the flour mixture alternately with milk. Stir in oats, nuts and sunflower seeds; then work in fruits. Drop by heaping teaspoons on a greased baking sheet (allow room for cookies to spread). Bake for 10 minutes, or until golden brown.

"These cookies are good for you," claims Rue. "You might try different fruits and nuts - dates, chopped apple or shredded carrots might be good - but to me, it's the apricots that make it happen!"

Makes about 36 cookies

Just one more thing... Expert baker KSB, agreed with me that this recipe makes a very soft dough and suggests adding ½ cup more of both the oatmeal and the flour (even then she felt that the dough was still too soft so chilled it in the fridge for 30 minutes before baking). KSB also suggests cutting back on the sugar by ½ cup too.

Margie Compton liked Rue's cookies, "These taste great! The apricots really do "make" them!" She shared them with co-workers in the archive and reported "Rue's cookies are disappearing from the staff room here. I've had several "Those cookies are good!" comments… there are only two left out of about fifteen I brought in. My boss thought the ingredient list made them sound blech, but she likes them." Thanks Margie, this was the first time I'd ever seen the world blech, but now I use it in conversation all the time! I also loved this comment from Margie, "I used golden raisins as an homage to The Golden Girls!"

MURDER WITH TOO MANY NOTES - 2001

Have you ever passed off someone else's idea as your own? I do hope not. If you have, let's hope that you haven't made a habit of it at work. Sucking up someone else's creativity until you are left with no ideas of your own, and making a success of your career on the back of someone else's talent is totally unethical and you'll get found out in the end. Be sure of it, especially if Columbo is around.

Billy Connolly plays a musician, Finlay Crawford, world-famous in the field of soundtrack composition. He's been taking advantage of a talented composer called Gabriel, and not giving him any credit for his work. But Gabriel has had enough of being in the shadows, he's about to expose his mentor as a fraud; it's time for Finlay to take up the baton, and do something about it.

Columbo is offered a drink and a cigar by Finlay in this episode, both offers are refused. The drink, because Columbo is still on duty and the cigar because as Columbo puts it, he's "kinda used to" the ones he usually smokes. By this stage in his career, Columbo has ceased to accept small invitations to cozy up to his prey. He seems to want to stay focused on solving the crime.

Finlay claims that the murder victim, Gabriel, was like a son to him. It seems slightly strange, therefore, that shortly after his death, he's having a big sing-song with Columbo, leading him in a gutsy rendition of "My Darling Clementine." Later at the film studio, Finlay introduces the Lieutenant to his orchestra, making an assumption, that because of his name, Columbo is surely Italian. Finlay prompts the orchestra to break out with a lusty rendition of "That's Amore," the Lieutenant wags his finger at Finlay and seems to enjoy singing along. He plays along with a *Name that Tune* guessing game. Finlay sets the orchestra playing various movie soundtrack classics, including one that has Columbo clutching his head exclaiming, "The fish, the fish picture." The orchestra help him out by shouting, "JAWS!"

There's no real antagonism between the Lieutenant and Finlay. There is no protest from the maestro when Columbo reveals that he knows exactly how the crime was committed. Finlay obviously realizes that the game is up. Signing autographs for loyal fans until the very last minute, he inquires, "Mr. Columbo, you seem to be a fund of information would you know of a penitentiary with a decent music program?" He then fairly skips off to his sentence.

For those of us who grew up knowing Billy Connolly as the stand-up comedian also known as The Big Yin, it's difficult to think of him as a cold-blooded killer. But anything is possible in *Columbo,* of course.

I would have expected Billy's favorite recipe to have been something more traditionally Scottish. But no haggis, neeps, and tatties here, Billy likes Stuffed Trout, and here's the simple recipe for the way he prepares it. He encourages, "May your taste buds dance a wild jig!"

Billy Connolly's Stuffed Trout

2 fresh trout, preferably brown
2 peeled and chopped tomatoes
1 teaspoon fresh basil
2 teaspoons ground walnuts and almonds
Salt and pepper
2 hard-boiled eggs
1 tablespoon chopped scallions/spring onions

Preheat oven to 350 degrees F /175 degrees C / gas mark 4.

Have the trout cleaned, or do this yourself. Rinse and pat dry. To make the stuffing, combine the tomatoes, basil, and nuts. The consistency is up to you, but Billy likes it to be a thick, stiff-ish paste. Season to taste. Stuff the trout with the mixture and wrap each fish in a piece of lightly greased foil. Bake for 50 minutes.

Just before the fish is ready, mash the hard-boiled eggs with the scallions/spring onions. Serve this with the trout.

Serves 2

Just one more thing... I love the fact that my work colleague, Neil Owens, tested this recipe with a couple of fish he'd caught himself, how cool is that?! Neil found the recipe, "Very tasty, in a delicate way - the light, herby stuffing goes well with the fish. It's an excellent summer supper. Or chilled and taken on a picnic, with a bottle of dry white." Oh, I do like that idea! Neil mentioned that he only cooked his trout for 35 minutes saying, "fish should be 'just' cooked in my opinion." Well, he's an expert angler, so I trust him on this one.

COLUMBO LIKES THE NIGHTLIFE - 2003

I always feel a little sad when I watch *Columbo Likes the Nightlife*, because it is, of course, the final *Columbo*. Knowing that there are no more to come is a sorry state of affairs; but oh how wonderful that there are 69 episodes, and once we have watched all of those, we can go right back to the beginning and watch them all again!

This episode is the glossiest, hippest and trendiest, and the most self-consciously modern. Because the central character is a nightclub promoter, Columbo gets to go clubbing, wear something neon, and wave a glow stick. Well, of course Columbo likes the nightlife, and because he is game for anything, he even starts shopping for colorful Hawaiian shirts to get into the groove.

It's also an unusual *Columbo*, as the initial murder is not pre-meditated, and the perpetrator of the crime very much takes a back seat. It feels a little like a situation that any one of us could get ourselves into. To defend ourselves against someone violent, we might strike out, and then a chain of events begins to unravel that soon gets out of control. The protagonists in this episode are young and striving to succeed in their careers, but they are mixed up with the Mafia, so of course, big trouble will ensue.

Columbo seems to quite like the Matthew Rhys character, Justin Price, in this series finale. He often likes his suspects of course, but in this case, there seems to be no antagonism between them. Perhaps the Lieutenant is picking up on the Ecstasy and MDMA-driven love vibe that was around so much at nightclubs from the mid-1980s onwards. This episode aired in 2003, so the term "raves" that the main character uses for his parties, was probably a little passé by then, but what would Columbo care about that? When the Lieutenant has to wander through a full dance floor, he is all smiles. "What's this, a new look?" he's asked as he turns up at the DJ booth wearing a pink feather boa. Justin seems to be a little amused by the Lieutenant being out of place in his oh, so trendy club, underestimating the intelligence of the shambling sleuth.

The final line of the final Columbo is uttered by the Lieutenant. He is talking to a member of the Mob, who offers to help him out whenever he needs it. "Well that's very nice of you, I really appreciate that," says our man, refusing the proffered business card.

Well, we really appreciate *you*, Lieutenant. Thanks for all the fun Columbo!

I have saved my favorite Peter Falk recipe for last. I love this dish! It's difficult to get vinegar peppers here in the UK, so I make this with Peppadew peppers, which are available in most large supermarkets.

Peter Falk's Pork Chops With Vinegar Peppers

¼ cup / 60ml olive oil
6 tenderloin pork chops
1 onion, finely chopped
¼ cup / 60ml white vinegar
1 teaspoon thyme
Vinegar peppers [Peter doesn't say how many, so to your taste]
½ cup / 120ml liquid from the vinegar peppers jar
Potatoes (optional)
Cornstarch/cornflour to thicken gravy

Preheat oven to 350 degrees F / 175 degrees C / gas mark 4.

Heat oil in large frying pan and brown the pork chops with the onion.

Remove chops and place them in a heavy iron ovenware casserole dish. Add vinegar to frying pan, stir in all brown bits and add to the casserole dish. Add some cracked pepper, very little salt, and the thyme. Now add 1 cup / 240ml water and half a cup / 115ml of liquid from the vinegar peppers.

Bake for one and half hours. Add vinegar peppers.

Bake 15 minutes and serve. Thicken gravy with cornstarch/cornflour.

Potatoes may be added if desired 1 hour before chops are finished. Cut potatoes in quarters for faster cooking.

Serves 3-6 depending on the size of your chops.

Just one more thing... My chums, Susan Dirks and Kent Stevens in Oregon, used ½" thick pork chops for this recipe, and only baked the casserole for 15-20 minutes. As Susan puts it, "Peter's recipe comes from the days when everyone thought they'd get trichinosis from pork unless it was cooked to the consistency of leather. The chops turned out moist and tender at this cooking time." Susan added, "Due to this short baking time, we did not add potatoes to the chops. Instead, we made potatoes on the stove top, and stirred butter and chopped parsley in them before serving. They made a nice contrast to the vinegary sauce." Susan cooked her chops in a little oil first, then cooked the onions until golden brown, She then recommended deglazing the pan with the vinegar, stirring until almost all the liquid is gone and brown bits are incorporated into the onions. After this step she continues, "Then we put the onion on top of the chops in the baking pan, poured the vinegar from the peppers jar around the edges, and added just enough water to come about halfway up the sides of the chops. We then scattered the peppers on top and baked." Susan and Kent, Peter Falk would be proud of you, that sounds utterly delicious!

If anyone has any doubts that Peter Falk could cook a pork chop, I'd like to end with a quote from his wonderful memoirs, *Just One More Thing: Stories From My Life*.

"Men with one eye were not drafted and in the Merchant Marine they were not allowed to work on deck or below deck, but they could work in the kitchen. I sailed out as a third cook. My speciality was pork chops. We left New York, crossed the Atlantic for Marseilles, France, where we picked up two thousand soldiers… My duties on the return trip were to cook each day 400 pork chops for lunch."

COLUMBO'S CHILI AND OTHER DELIGHTS

COLUMBO'S CHILI AND OTHER DELIGHTS

I have over 7000 movie star favorites in my recipe collection and I wanted to share some more *Columbo* related goodies in this book. Be warned though, unlike the episode-specific recipes that have gone before, I have not tested all of the recipes in this extra section. I couldn't bring myself to try the Ricardo Montalban's Mexican Calves Brain Soup for example, could you?

I haven't converted the recipes in this section to metric measurements. If you are a cook that doesn't use American cup measurements, I can recommend a website called convert-me.com which has a special cooking converter. Also, recipes of the past often assumed cooks would know what temperature to cook things for, and for how long. If anything is unclear in these recipes, I would recommend googling for a similar recipe online.

If you do try any of these recipes (especially Ricardo's), please do let me know how they turn out.

Columbo's Chili

Chili is the Lieutenant's favorite dish, no doubt about it. We see him eating it on many occasions, in scuzzy diners, in fancy restaurants, at Barney's Beanery… One night he'll have it with beans, the next night without. This, to the Lieutenant, is variety. He loves crumbling saltines into his chili, "You see, it's the crackers that make the dish."

So, let's kick off this section of extra recipes, with a legendary chili, the Chasen's chili. Much beloved of Hollywood movie stars such as Elizabeth Taylor and Clark Gable, this chili is the subject of an in-joke in *Publish or Perish* where we see the Lieutenant ordering a bowl. He asks for ketchup and crackers, so be sure to have some on hand to serve with this chili, Columbo-style

As the Lieutenant himself puts it, talking about how Mrs. Columbo is on a health kick, "The things she's been buying, I wouldn't eat much of that either. The soya beans, the wheatgerm, not that it's not good for you, I'm sure it's terrific. See, I happen to like a bowl of chili…

Chasen's Chili

½ lb dried pinto beans
1 (28-ounce) can diced tomatoes in juice
1 large green bell pepper, chopped
2 tablespoons vegetable oil
3 cups onions, coarsely chopped
2 cloves garlic, crushed
½ cup parsley, chopped
½ cup butter
2 lbs beef chuck, coarsely chopped
1 lb pork shoulder, coarsely chopped
⅓ cup Gebhardt's chili powder
1 tablespoon salt
1½ teaspoons pepper
1½ teaspoons Farmer Brothers ground cumin

Rinse the beans, picking out debris. Place beans in a Dutch oven with water to cover. Boil for two minutes. Remove from heat. Cover and let stand one hour. Drain off liquid.

Rinse beans again. Add enough fresh water to cover beans. Bring mixture to a boil. Reduce heat and simmer, covered, for one hour or until tender.

Stir in tomatoes and their juice. Simmer five minutes. In a large skillet sauté bell pepper in oil for five minutes. Add onion and cook until tender, stirring frequently. Stir in the garlic and parsley. Add mixture to bean mixture. Using the same skillet, melt the butter and sauté beef and pork chuck until browned. Drain. Add to bean mixture along with the chili powder, salt, pepper, and cumin.

Bring mixture just to a boil. Reduce heat. Simmer, covered, for one hour. Uncover and cook 30 minutes more or to desired consistency. Chili shouldn't be too thick - it should be somewhat liquid but not runny like soup. Skim off excess fat and serve.

William Shatner's Deluxe Hamburgers

As soon as this book is published, I am going to celebrate by making these.

2 lbs lean ground beef
½ cup minced Bermuda onion
¼ teaspoon garlic powder (optional)
Salt, freshly ground pepper to taste
½ cup dry red wine (Use quality domestic vintage either Pinot Noir or Cabernet Sauvignon)
8 cleaned mushroom caps
¼ teaspoon sage
4 slices aged cheddar cheese
English muffins (just muffins if you are a Brit!) - or hamburger buns.

Place meat, onion, garlic, thyme, wine and salt and pepper to taste in a mixing bowl. Mix thoroughly with the fingers. Divide into eight, making 1-inch thick patties. On each of four patties place slice of cheese and two mushroom caps. Cover with remaining patties, sealing edges carefully. Broil over charcoal to desired doneness. (Or pan broil in cast iron frying pan on top of stove by heating pan until red hot, scatter surface with generous sprinkling of salt. Plunk in hamburgers, broil over high heat, turning once.) Serve patties alone with thick slices of beefsteak tomatoes or on toasted split English muffins. Adorn with a choice of condiments (catsup, hot mustard, pickle relish, chutney, chopped onion, bottled Escoffier sauce).

Makes 4 generous servings.

Myrna Loy's Senegalese Soup

I've made this a few times, it is unusual but good!

Slice two onions and two apples. Put into a pan and brown, add two tablespoons of good curry powder and two tablespoons of flour. Mix all well together. Add slowly chicken broth and let come to a boil. Strain, cool off and when ready to serve, add heavy cream, say two tablespoons to a cup. Also place in the bottom of the cup white meat of chicken, chopped fine. Curry powder may be added to taste.

George Hamilton's Candied Fruit Parfait

I've never seen candied fruit cake mix in the UK, better get myself over to the USA to obtain some.

Soak candied fruit cake mix in whiskey or rum for several days. Add extra pineapple and candied cherries. Chop slivered almonds and toast slightly. Do not soak them. Make parfaits by putting small amount of fruit, then ice cream, then fruit until glasses are full. Top with cherry. Take from refrigerator a short time before serving.

Ross Martin's Chocolate Mousse

This is lovely, and a special treat to serve after his Beef in Anchovy Cream. You would definitely be "huffing and puffing on the sofa" after that two-course extravaganza!

Melt 4 oz sweet and 4 oz bitter chocolate in top of double boiler over simmering water. Beat 3 egg whites until stiff and beat in ½ cup sugar. Combine with chocolate and fold in 2 cups whipped heavy cream. Turn into a mold rinsed in cold water and chill mousse for 2 hours. Unmold and decorate with whipped cream.

Serves 6

Martin Landau's Vodka Martini Straight Up

I have Greg Swenson's wonderful *Recipes For Rebels* book to thank for introducing me to this excellent Martini recipe. My squeeze Mr. Rathbone christened this the Martini Landau which I thought was very clever, so that's what they are known as round at Silver Screen Suppers Towers.

2 oz good quality vodka
½ oz or splash of vermouth
2 pimiento stuffed olives or lemon twists

Chill martini glasses in freezer. Pour vodka into cocktail shaker filled with ice, shake until very cold, (at least 10 seconds). Pour vermouth into cocktail glass, swirl and dump out. Strain martini into chilled glass. Serve straight up (no ice in the glass) garnished with 2 olives on a cocktail pick or with a twist of lemon peel.

Donald Pleasence's Sole Bonne Femme

This is a dish I can very much imagine Adrian Carsini enjoying with a very expensive bottle of vintage wine. He'd either order this in a high-end restaurant, or perhaps it's something that Karen would rustle up for him as a romantic dinner à deux. Wherever he's eating it, everyone around him better beware of ruining an exciting meal by the presence of any liquid filth.

1 Sole, filleted
1 cup stock (get head, bones, etc. for the stock or use an extra fillet, chopped)
½ lb button mushrooms
1 dozen medium mushroom caps

Ingredients - Buerre Marnié:

2 tablespoons flour
2 shallots, finely chopped
Lemon Juice
Oil
Bouquet Garni
White wine (enough to cover fish, plus wine to add later but no more than 1 cup altogether)
2 tablespoons butter
Liquid drained from baking Sole

Method

Make the fish stock, using the head and bones, etc., or an extra fillet. Put in a saucepan, add a cup of water and simmer for 10 minutes.

Strain. Season to taste.

Preheat oven to 350 degrees F / 175 degrees C / gas mark 4.

Put fillets in bottom of buttered earthenware baking dish. Sprinkle with finely chopped shallots and button mushrooms. Add enough wine to cover, and add the fish stock. Now add the bouquet garni, bring to the boil, cover with buttered paper, and bake in a moderate oven for 10 minutes.

Drain off the liquid from the baking dish and add some more white wine, making the total used no more than 1 cup. Put this liquid in a saucepan and keep warm.

Make a Beurre Manié by kneading the flour and the butter with fingers as though you were rubbing fine pastry. Form into small balls and add them to the liquid, stirring well. It will thicken.

In another pan, sauté the mushroom caps in oil and lemon juice. Pour sauce over the sole and decorate with the mushroom caps.

Susan Clark's Peach Salad

An alternative to Susan's slightly strange Shrimp Curry for the *Lady in Waiting* episode.

6 tablespoons sour cream (heaping)
2 tablespoons raisins or chopped dates
2 tablespoons chopped nuts
6 peach halves

Mix cream, nuts, raisins and/or dates together. Heap mixture onto peach halves. Place on lettuce and serve cold.

Roddy McDowall's Red Cabbage

I'm a big fan of red cabbage and I like Roddy's way of preparing it.

1 medium head red cabbage
Shred. Wash with running water. Drain

3 tablespoons butter or bacon drippings
2 tablespoons onion, finely chopped
Melt butter in a frying pan or Dutch oven. Add onions. Cook for a short time. Add cabbage.
Cover. Cook for 10 minutes.

¼ teaspoon salt
¼ teaspoon black pepper
2 tablespoons vinegar
1 tablespoon sugar
1 apple, thinly sliced and cored
Add. Cover and cook slowly for 20 minutes, or until cabbage is tender.
Serves 4

Gena Rowlands and John Cassavetes' Cherry Torte

I really like this recipe, and buy sour cherries whenever I spot them so that I can make one of these. This would be lovely after John's Youvarlakia for the *Étude in Black* episode.

1 cup sugar
1 can sour cherries, drained - reserve the syrup
1 egg
2 tablespoons butter
½ cup chopped nuts
1 cup flour
1 teaspoon baking soda/bicarbonate of soda

Work sugar into butter, add beaten egg, add flour mixed with baking soda, nuts, and cherries. Bake in a 9" x 9" square pan in a 300 degrees F / 150 degrees C / gas mark 2 oven for 45 minutes. (Requires no liquid for mixing, cherries provide moisture.)

Hot Sauce to Serve Over Squares of Torte

4 tablespoons sugar
Cherry juice from drained cherries
½ cup orange juice
1 tablespoon of cornstarch/cornflour

Cook until thickened.

Serves 6

Mariette Hartley's - Chicken Wonderful

Here's a nice easy way to cook chicken from the lovely Mariette who appears in two episodes, *Publish or Perish* and *Try and Catch Me*.

Sauté chicken parts (used preferred seasonings) in an iron frying pan in butter, margarine, or oil, depending on whether or not watching weight. Do not brown. Turn frequently, then cover with heavy foil and a tight lid. Bake in a pre-heated 400 degrees F / 200 degrees C / gas mark 6 for 45 minutes. Delicious hot and marvelous cut up cold for salad.

Vincent Price's Quenelles Ambassador

Columbo was after Investigator Brimmer's recipe for Quenelles in *Death Lends a Hand*. He should have asked Vincent Price!

SAUCE AMÉRICAINE

1. Sauté 6 shallots, minced, 1 small onion, minced, and 2 cloves garlic, minced, in 3 tablespoons butter for 5 minutes, without letting the vegetables brown.

2. Add ¼ cup cognac and simmer for 5 minutes.

3. Add 1½ cups white wine (not too dry), 4 tablespoons tomato puree, 2 tablespoons minced parsley, and 1 tablespoon minced fresh tarragon (or 1 teaspoon dry tarragon). Simmer for about 20 minutes, or until sauce is reduced by one-third.

4. Season with ¼ teaspoon salt, or to taste, and ⅛ teaspoon cayenne pepper. Swirl in 2 tablespoons butter. Set aside.

FISH DUMPLINGS (QUENELLES)

1. In saucepan bring to a boil: ½ cup milk, ¼ cup butter, ½ teaspoon salt, and ⅛ teaspoon white pepper.

2. Add all at once: ½ cup flour and cook, stirring rapidly until mixture forms a ball in middle of pan. Empty into mixing bowl or bowl of an electric beater.

3. Beat in: 2 eggs, one at a time, beating well after each addition until paste is smooth and glossy. Chill. Makes 1 cup or ½ lb panada.

4. Dice: ½ lb very cold, raw whiting to make 1½ cups diced fish. Pound in a mortar to a smooth paste, or blend half at a time in an electric blender. Work the ground fish through a food mill into a mixing bowl or the bowl of an electric beater.

5. Beat in: the panada, 1 whole egg, and 2 egg yolks, beating well after each addition. Gradually beat in: ¾ cup cold butter, ¼ teaspoon salt, ⅛ teaspoon white pepper, and 1 tablespoon cream. Chill for at least 2 hours.

6. Shape the fish forcemeat into small croquettes on a floured board, using a good tablespoon of the mixture for each dumpling. Carefully

lower the dumplings into a frying pan containing 1 inch simmering salted water and poach for 10 minutes, without letting the water boil. Remove with slotted spoon onto a towel to drain. Makes 20 quenelles.

PRESENTATION

Heat the sauce Américaine to simmering. Strain it into 1 cup of sauce hollandaise and heat, stirring, over simmering water. Arrange the quenelles on a warm serving platter and pour the sauce over them.

Luckily, I also have Vincent Price's recipe for hollandaise!

Vincent Price's Hollandaise Sauce

Vincent Price made his Hollandaise in a blender, just like Dexter Paris. Here's his method. Pour a little of the sauce over some steamed asparagus. Martin and the Lieutenant don't put a poached egg on top, but I would, and maybe a toasted English Muffin underneath.

1 cup butter
4 egg yolks
2 tablespoons lemon juice
¼ teaspoon salt
¼ teaspoon Tabasco

In a small saucepan, heat the butter until very hot, but not brown. Put the egg yolks, lemon juice, and Tabasco into the container of an electric blender. Cover container and turn motor on low speed. Immediately remove cover and pour in the hot butter in a steady stream. When all butter is added, turn off motor. Serve immediately or keep warm by setting container into a saucepan containing 2 inches of hot water. If the sauce becomes too thick to pour when ready to use, return container to the blender, add 1 tablespoon hot water and blend briefly.

Makes 1 and ¼ cups

Janis Paige's Feijoada

After Mrs. Peck and Dorothea McNally, Goldie is my favorite *Columbo* character. I like to think Janis wore plenty of gold lamé when she was cooking, which she claimed to do every night of her life! Janis was a big fan of Brazilian food, so here's her recipe for Feijoada.

3 cups dried black beans
1 lb jerked (dried) beef (or uncooked corn beef, cut into small pieces)
1 lb smoked sausage
½ lb smoked pork (or 3 smoked pork chops)
Small smoked tongue
½ lb bacon
1½ lbs lean fresh pork, cut in 2-inch pieces
1 pig's foot (optional)
1 tablespoon peanut (or vegetable oil)
Medium yellow onion, peeled and chopped
1 small clove garlic, crushed
½ teaspoon ground red chili pepper

Soak beans overnight. Drain, place in deep saucepan, cover with cold water. Bring to boil, cover, simmer, cook about 2 hours until almost tender. Add more liquid as needed.

Soak jerked beef overnight. Drain, place in a saucepan, bring to boil, simmer about 20 minutes, drain and cool. If corned beef is used, soaking is not necessary. To a large stock pot add beef (or corned beef), sausage (reserve small piece for sauce), smoked pork or chops, tongue, bacon, fresh pork and pig's foot. Cover with water. Bring to boil, simmer about 2 hours.

Combine contents of the two pots. Cook beans and meats together, simmer until meats are fork tender and beans can be easily mashed with a fork. Remove about 1 cup cooked beans, mash or put through blender. Reserve.

Heat oil in frying pan. Add onion, garlic and piece of sausage cut up. Add seasonings. Cook over low heat until onion and sausage are lightly browned. Add 1 cup cooked mashed beans to the onion-sausage mixture with enough liquid from the beans to form a thick sauce. Simmer 5 minutes over low heat, stirring to blend well. Add sauce to beans and meats in the stockpot. Correct seasonings. To serve, separate meats and beans. Slice meat in serving pieces and arrange on a heated platter. Place tongue in center of platter. Moisten meats slightly with liquid from the beans. Serve beans in a deep serving dish or soup tureen. Serve along with boiled rice, sliced orange and pepper and lemon sauce.

Serves 8-10

Pepper and Lemon Sauce

3 small hot dried chili peppers
1 small yellow onion, peeled, cut into large pieces
Salt to taste
1 small clove garlic, crushed
Juice of one lemon, squeezed

Pound peppers, onion, salt and garlic to form a thick paste (or put through a blender). Add lemon juice, let stand 1 hour. Note: Sauce must be used immediately, as it ferments upon standing.

Diane Baker's Scampi

Scampi in a basket is the kind of thing I can imagine Joanna Clay having at the piano bar in *Last Salute to the Commodore*, just to try and sober up a bit. Here's Diane's very own recipe, which is a little different to what we Brits know as Scampi.

24 raw jumbo shrimp in shells
½ cup butter or margarine
1 teaspoon garlic, finely chopped
2 tablespoons parsley, chopped
¼ teaspoon salt
½ cup dry white wine
½ teaspoon prepared mustard
2 teaspoons lemon juice

Shrimp should be deveined, leaving shell and tails on. Melt butter in frying pan; add all other ingredients except shrimp. Cook about 4 minutes. Stand shrimp up in a frame-proof dish or pan and brush well with butter sauce. Reserve some to pour over shrimp when served. Place shrimp under broiler for 5 minutes.

Serves 4 for a main course or 8 for appetisers

Mexican Calves' Brain Soup, House of Ricardo Montalban

Do get in touch if you make this, it's a step too far for me!

For beef stock

1 large marrow bone, cracked
4 lbs short ribs of beef or other beef with bones
1 small clove garlic, peeled and mashed
1 teaspoon peppercorns, crushed

1. Place bones and beef in a large kettle. Cover with 2-3 quarts cold water and bring to boil.
2. Cover and simmer 1 hour, or until meat is half-cooked (for browner stock, first sear meat in small amount of oil).
3. Add garlic, salt to taste and peppercorns. Simmer uncovered over low heat 3-4 hours, skimming surface often to remove scum. Strain and reserve meat.
4. Cool, cover and refrigerate. Remove and discard layer of surface fat. Makes about 2 quarts.

To prepare calves brain soup

2 pair calves' brains
1 tablespoon vinegar
½ medium-size yellow onion, peeled and minced
¼ cup butter
2 large potatoes, peeled and thinly sliced
3 large leeks, thinly sliced
2 quarts beef stock
Monterey Jack cheese, grated

1. Wash brains, remove arteries.
2. Add 1 teaspoon salt and the vinegar to 1 quart boiling water. Add brains.
3. Cover, reduce heat; simmer until tender, about 20-30 minutes.
4. Drain. Cover with ice water. Let stand 20 minutes, drain again.
5. Slice brains into small pieces; set aside.
6. Sauté onion in butter in large frying pan. Add potatoes and leeks.
7. Cook over low heat until vegetables begin to tenderize.
8. Add beef stock. Simmer slowly 30 minutes.
9. Add brains, reheat only until meat is heated through (cooking longer toughens meat).

10. Spoon piping hot into soup plates. Garnish with grated cheese. Serve alone or with crisp green salad, tortillas or burritos, French bread and Mexican beer.

Serves 6

Suzanne Pleshette's Bread Pudding

I love Suzanne in *Dead Weight* and I think her Bread Pudding would make a delicious dessert after Eddie Albert's Butterfly Lamb.

3 cups half-and-half (for Brits, single cream diluted with milk)
2 cups oven-dried bread cubes
½ cup sugar
2 eggs, slightly beaten
1 apple, pared, cored and diced
1 can (3½ oz) crushed pineapple, drained
½ cup golden raisins
1 teaspoon pure vanilla extract
½ teaspoon salt
Dash nutmeg or cinnamon butter

Combine half-and-half and bread cubes. Add sugar and eggs; mix well. Add remaining ingredients. Turn into a well greased 10 x 6-inch baking pan. Sprinkle nutmeg or cinnamon over the top and dot with butter. Bake in a pre-heated 300 degrees F / 150 degrees C / gas mark 2 oven for one hour. Serve with lemon sauce.

Lemon Sauce

½ cup sugar
1 tablespoon cornstarch/cornflour
2 tablespoons fresh lemon juice
2 tablespoons butter
1 tablespoon finely grated lemon rind

In a saucepan mix 1 cup of water with sugar and cornstarch. Cook, stirring constantly until thickened and smooth. Remove from heat. Add remaining ingredients, stir to blend. Cool to room temperature.

Ida Lupino's Hot Pot Casserole

Does a Hot Pot Casserole strike you as an oddly prosaic choice for a hugely successful Hollywood based, trail blazing film director/producer/writer/actress? We shouldn't forget that Ida was originally from London, born into a legendary theatrical dynasty. Perhaps Hot Pot reminded her of good old England?

2 lbs mutton or lamb chops
3 lamb kidneys
4 medium potatoes, sliced
½ lb mushrooms, sliced
½ cup minced, cooked ham
3 onions, sliced
1 cup canned bouillon
2 tablespoons butter

Trim excess fat from chops. Wash kidneys; remove fat and membrane; slice about ¼ inch thick. Place half of the sliced potatoes in the bottom of a large casserole; top with chops. Arrange kidney slices on top of chops; add mushrooms, ham, and onions in layers; finish with remaining potatoes. Sprinkle with 1 teaspoon salt and ¼ teaspoon pepper. Pour in bouillon and dot with butter. Cover closely and bake in a slow oven (300 degrees F / 150 degrees F / gas mark 2) about 3 hours.

Serves 6

Anne Francis' Gazpacho Soup

Anne is in two episodes of Columbo, *A Stitch in Crime* and *Short Fuse*, she's great in both. I think this Gazpacho would be lovely to have on a hot day, flaked out on the sofa, watching *Columbo*.

½ clove garlic
½ small onion, sliced
½ green pepper, seeded and sliced
3 ripe tomatoes, peeled and quartered
1 small cucumber, peeled and sliced
1 teaspoon salt
¼ teaspoon pepper
3 tablespoons red wine vinegar
½ cup ice water

Place all ingredients into a blender and cover. Blend on medium speed for about six seconds, or until all ingredients are thoroughly chopped and blended. Chill for about 10 minutes and serve cold.

Note: Too high a speed on the blender will cause the gazpacho to foam; better to use a slower speed and stir occasionally. Serves 4-6

Honor Blackman's Golden Sponge Pudding

This to me seems like a very British pudding. In some corners there is advice that golden syrup and corn syrup are interchangeable, I could not possibly comment. Honor gives credit to legendary British chef Philip Harben for this recipe, but she's written it out in her own enthusiastic way. I can absolutely imagine Lillian Stanhope of *Dagger of the Mind* projecting the final line of this recipe across a stage in glorious Shakespearian style!

3 oz butter or margarine
6 oz self-raising flour
3 oz caster sugar
1 egg
Little golden syrup
Little milk

1. Grease 1 and ¾ pint pudding basin.
2. Put butter - which must not be hard from the fridge, or runny - into a mixing bowl with sugar. Beat to a light cream.
3. Work in beaten egg, little by little
4. Put a dollop of golden syrup in pudding basin and work it right round sides of basin with flat of a knife. Do not stint on syrup.
5. Give mixture another quick beating, then fold in flour and work in enough milk for a dropping consistency.
6. Scoop mixture into basin, cover and steam for at least 2 hours.
7. Then turn lovely light pudding out on to a serving dish.

And as you lift off the basin see the lovely molten syrup trickle down the sides to anoint it with golden glory!

Edith Head's Chicken Casa Ladera

Casa Ladera was Edith Head's home in Goldwater Canyon, Los Angeles. As you would expect from such a stylish woman, her house was full of beautiful objects. I'd absolutely love to see a photo of her kitchen. Edith has a brief guest spot in *Requiem for a Falling Star* so this would be an appropriate dish to accompany that episode.

2 chickens, jointed
Paprika
¼ lb butter
1 lb chicken livers
1 cup chicken broth
1 cup white wine
1 lb fresh mushrooms
Butter for sautéeing
2 tablespoons flour
Chives

Dust chicken parts with salt and paprika; brown in butter. Place in casserole with chicken broth and white wine. Cook 40 minutes at 300 degrees F / 150 degrees C / gas mark 2 until tender. Cover while cooking. Sauté mushrooms in butter. In another pan, sauté chicken livers. Combine liquid from both pans and add flour. Arrange mushrooms and chicken livers on top of chicken in casserole dish, cover with liquid and sprinkle with chives. Serve with rice and French bread.

Vincent Price's Saffron Rice

I make this a lot. If you are doing a big curry with lots of dishes, this is great as it cooks in the oven rather than on the hob. Plus it is yellow!

½ teaspoon saffron, soaked in 1 cup water for about 2 hours
½ cup butter
1 onion, chopped
1 clove garlic, chopped (optional)
2 cups raw rice
Preheat oven to 400 degrees F / 200 degrees C / gas mark 6.

In a heavy casserole melt the butter. Add onion and garlic and cook for 3 minutes, or until onion is soft. Add rice and stir until rice is well coated with butter.

Add saffron and water it's been soaking in, and bring to the boil. Cover tightly and bake in the oven for 10 minutes. Remove cover and stir to mix thoroughly.

Add 2 cups boiling water, cover and continue to bake for 15 minutes.

Turn off the heat, fluff rice with 2 forks, and keep warm until ready to serve.

Steve Forrest's Honey Cake

If you want something to soak up the hard stuff while you are watching *A Bird in the Hand...*, here's a recipe from Steve Forrest who plays the murder victim in this episode. Steve was a passionate beekeeper, so honey from his very own bees was used in this recipe.

½ lb soft butter
1 cup honey
4 well-beaten eggs
1 tablespoon fresh lemon juice
1 teaspoon grated lemon peel
3 scant cups cake flour
2 teaspoons baking powder
½ teaspoon salt
1 cup chopped citron
¾ cup chopped nuts

Cream together butter and honey. Add eggs, lemon juice, and lemon peel. Sift in 3 cups flour with baking powder and salt. Blend smoothly but do not overmix. Add chopped citron and nuts.

Turn into a loaf pan lined with greased brown paper. Bake in a preheated oven - 350 degrees F / 180 degrees C / gas mark 4 - for about 1 hour or until cake tests done when a toothpick inserted in cake comes out clean.

Cool slightly, turn out on wire rack.

Steven Bochco / Barbara Bosson's Brie en Croute (Brie in Pastry)

This recipe was provided to a newspaper by Steven Bochco's wife Barbara Bosson in 1982. It's an hors-d'oeuvre that she enjoyed making for the big parties they used to throw together in Hollywood, so chances are that Steven would have at least had a spoonful or two of this melty cheese delight at some point.

Please note how many this serves, it's for a big, Hollywood style shindig!

1½ cups all-purpose flour
Pinch salt
1 package (8 oz) cream cheese at room temperature
½ cup sweet/unsalted butter or unsalted margarine
4-inch Brie
Caraway or poppy seeds

Combine all ingredients except Brie and seeds in food processor; process into a ball. Chill 15-20 minutes, cut ball into halves. Wrap ½ for freezing (use another time), roll second half on floured board into an 11-inch circle. Sprinkle seeds generously on ball to within 2 inches of border. Place whole Brie in center of dough and wrap. Bring end to top of Brie and twist like a flower. Refrigerate at least 1 hour. Place on pie plate or cookie sheet. Bake in pre-heated 400 degrees F / 200 degrees C / gas mark 6 oven for 10 minutes. Reduce oven temperature to 350 degrees F / 180 degrees C / gas mark 4 for 20 minutes longer. Cool on cookie sheet 45 minutes before placing on serving plate. Slice to serve. Delicious!

Serves 25 to 30

Julie Harris' Curried Zucchini Soup

If Adrian Carsini had got away with his crime in *Any Old Port in a Storm*, this is the kind of dish I imagine Karen cooking for him after she'd got him down the aisle. Served with very expensive vino of course.

6 small zucchini, trimmed and cut into chunks
1 large onion, thinly sliced, about 1 cup
4 tablespoons butter
3 cups chicken broth or bouillon
1½ teaspoons curry powder
½ teaspoon ground ginger
½ teaspoon dry mustard
3 tablespoons uncooked rice
1½ cups milk or cream
Salt and freshly ground pepper to taste
Minced chives for garnish

Sauté zucchini and onions in butter until soft but not brown. Add to chicken broth in saucepan and add curry powder, ginger, and mustard, and bring to boil - then add rice. Lower heat and cover and simmer about

45 minutes. Puree mixture in blender. Add milk or cream, and salt and pepper to taste. Chill thoroughly or serve hot. Garnish with chives.

Serves 6

Shirley Temple Cocktail

This non-alcoholic cocktail was named after child star Shirley Temple and features in the *Sex and the Married Detective* episode. Shirley wasn't a fan of this beverage herself. Saying in an interview in 1986, "The saccharine sweet, icky drink? Yes, well... those were created in the probably middle 1930s by the Brown Derby Restaurant in Hollywood and I had nothing to do with it. But, all over the world, I am served that. People think it's funny. I hate them. Too sweet!"

If you have a sweet tooth though, or you have folks around the place who don't drink alcohol, here's a Shirley Temple recipe from another restaurant who claimed to have invented the drink, Chasen's. If you wanted to jazz up a little, you could use an alcoholic ginger beer such as Crabbie's. That's usually what usually happens at Silver Screen Suppers Towers. Alternatively, you could add vodka or rum, which turns this into a "Dirty Shirley".

7-Up or ginger ale
grenadine
orange slice
maraschino cherry
toothpick

Fill tall glass with five parts 7-Up or ginger ale to one part grenadine. Garnish with an orange slice and a maraschino cherry on a toothpick.

Peter's Vanilla Pudding

We don't have Vanilla Pudding Mix here in the UK so my lovely friend Peter Fuller sent me a recipe for making some Brit style.

1 cup / 200g granulated sugar
¾ cup / 95g cornstarch/cornflour
¾ cup / 95g non-fat dry milk powder
1 teaspoon salt
2 whole vanilla beans

In a medium bowl, whisk together the sugar, cornstarch, milk powder, and salt; set aside.

Split open the vanilla beans and use the back of a knife to scrape out the seeds. Add the seeds to the sugar mixture, and again whisk well to evenly combine, using a fork or the back of the spoon to break up any chunks of vanilla bean seeds. Cut the empty vanilla bean pods into two or three pieces each.

Place the vanilla bean pieces into an airtight container or jar, and add the sugar mixture. Seal it, and then give it a few good shakes to distribute the vanilla bean pieces evenly. Store what you don't use for Roddy's recipe in a cool, dry place.

To make pudding: Combine 2 cups of milk with ½ cup of the instant pudding mix in a medium saucepan over high heat, whisking constantly. Bring to a boil, and then reduce the heat to a simmer and continue whisking until the mixture thickens and coats the back of a spoon (this took around 5 minutes).

Let sit for at least 5 minutes, and then add in 2 tablespoons of sherry (as per Roddy's recipe).

Helen's Veggie Chili for Johnny Cash

When Helen Coniam asked, "You know the Johnny Cash chili recipe? I am going to try a veggie version because I love Johnny so much. Is that OK? " I said, "Hell yeah!" This is such a good chili recipe, good for vegans too, as long as your veggie burgers are vegan. Over to Helen…

There are a lot of ingredients here but don't let that put you off. Spend 10-15 minutes getting them all ready in advance. After that, it is mainly a case of just adding them to the pan in the correct order. No technical cooking skills are needed.

This makes a lot of chili. It will easily serve 4 people.

It is lovely in a big bowl with salted crackers, or you may wish to serve it with rice. Some cooling yogurt or sour cream may also be beneficial.

Feel free to adjust the spicing to suit your individual taste (or fortitude).

½ lb / 225g vegetarian mince
2 vegetarian burgers
1 small onion, chopped finely
2 cloves of garlic, peeled and crushed
1 tablespoon rapeseed oil
14oz / 400g can of chopped tomatoes
Scant cup / /200ml vegetable stock
½ green bell pepper, chopped
½ red bell pepper, chopped
2 jalapeño peppers, deseeded and chopped very small
1 cayenne pepper, deseeded and chopped
2 teaspoons chili seasoning
1 teaspoon chili powder
1 teaspoon cumin
1 teaspoon sage
1 teaspoon oregano
½ tablespoon cayenne pepper
½ a 14oz / 400g can black beans, drained and rinsed
½ a 14oz /400g can pinto beans, drained and rinsed
½ a 14oz /400g can kidney beans in chili sauce
½ a 14oz /400g can kidney beans, drained and rinsed
¾ cup / 170ml beer (about half a bottle)
3 teaspoons / 12g sugar
Handful of self-raising cornmeal (see Johnny's recipe in the entry for *Swan Song* if you wish to make your own)

If the veggie burgers are frozen, defrost them first (just enough to be able to chop them into chunks). Then, heat the oil in a pan and begin to cook the onion and peppers. Add the veggie burgers and fry until they are browned. Add the garlic and stir until it has started to turn golden. Pour in the tomatoes and add the veggie mince.

Pour over the vegetable stock, mix well and heat to a brisk simmer. Then add the herbs and spices: chili seasoning, salt and pepper to taste, chili powder, cumin, sage, oregano and cayenne pepper (This is apparently, the order according to Johnny.) Taste and adjust spicing if necessary.

Add the beans to the mixture and adjust the spicing again. When it is to your liking, pour in the beer and add the sugar.

Simmer for at least 30 minutes. Uncover, add a handful of the cornmeal and stir it in.

Serves 4

Neil's Slow Cooker Version of Ross Martin's Beef in Anchovy Cream

This is a variation of the Ross Martin recipe that accompanies the *Suitable for Framing* episode, made in a slow cooker/crockpot. Thanks to Neil Owens of the AP for this great variation on a theme. Over to Neil.

I used beef short ribs as I'm a cheapskate but think the marrow adds a richness to the dish in a way the cream doesn't. I used fresh anchovy fillets and not the brown ones that come in bottles of oil. I browned the shallots in a pan. At the same time, I flash browned the ribs in a very hot oven for 20 minutes.

I placed the shallots, ribs and anchovy fillets, paprika and brandy, along with a splash of Worcestershire Sauce and the parsley into a slow cooker along with enough fresh beef stock to cover everything and left for 5 hours on low.

After 5 hours I made a simple roux from some of the dripping from roasting the ribs, some plain flour and added the cream making sure not to create any lumps. I ladled out the stock from the slow cooker into the roux to thicken the mix to the required consistency. I like mine just slightly thicker than runny – just nicely coating the back of a spoon without running off kind of thing. I removed the meat from the beef bones and combined this along with the sauce back into the slow cooker pot.

I served mine with American long grain rice and a sprinkling of parsley. I like a nice Rioja to go with this.

Susan and Kent's Baked Chicken Grand Marnier a la Rod Steiger

4 boneless chicken breast halves, 6–8 ounces each
1 tablespoon butter, divided
1 teaspoon salt
¼ teaspoon paprika (or white pepper to taste)
1½ cups / 150g minced / finely chopped white onion (1 large onion)
1 teaspoon finely grated orange rind, plus more for garnish
¼ cup / 60ml evaporated milk
1 tablespoon fresh lemon juice
1 tablespoon frozen orange concentrate
1 egg yolk
1 tablespoon Grand Marnier (or Cointreau)
¼ cup sliced green onion

Melt half the butter in a frying pan. Sauté the onion until translucent. Place half the onions in a lightly greased oven-proof casserole, reserve the other half.

Season the breasts with salt and brown quickly on both sides in the same frying pan. Place them on top of the onions in the casserole and sprinkle with paprika.

Top with remaining onions, cover, cook in preheated 350 degrees F / 180 degrees C / gas mark 4 oven for about 15 minutes.

Combine orange rind, milk, lemon juice, orange concentrate, beaten egg yolk and Grand Marnier (or Cointreau). Spread over chicken. Cook uncovered 15 minutes longer (or under broiler/grill with flame set low to brown and crispen). Garnish with additional orange rind and sliced green onions.

Serve with crisp green salad with diet Roquefort dressing. Serve with a good bottle of Beaujolais (or Oregon Pinot Noir!). Each serving has about 260 calories.

Serves 2

Battenburgbelle's Pastry and Crumb Crust Recipes

Sweet Pastry

350g plain flour
pinch of salt
125g butter, straight from the fridge
125g sugar
2 eggs plus one yolk
Mix flour and salt.

Use a rolling pin to flatten the butter between two butter wrappers/pieces of baking parchment, cover with a little of the flour, then tear into pieces and rub in until the mixture resembles breadcrumbs.

Add the eggs and yolk and mix using a dough scraper or knife and work the dough to form a neat square. Wrap the pastry in baking parchment and leave to rest in the fridge for an hour. Roll out and line a 20cm tart tin, then rest in the fridge again for half an hour.

Preheat the oven to 180°C. Blind bake the pastry case for 20 minutes.

Crumb Crust

150g digestive biscuits
75g butter, melted

Pre-heat the oven to 350°F/180°C/gas mark 4 /

Process the biscuits until they are like crumbs, or put them in a bowl and bash them with a rolling pin. Stir in the butter and mix well. Line the bottom of a 20cm springform tin, pressing the biscuits in with your hands or the back of a spoon.

Bake for 10 minutes.

RECIPE SOURCES

Gene Barry's Kibbee - *Cookbook of the Stars*, Motion Picture Mothers Inc., 1970

Lee Grant's Chicken Malibu - The Morning Call, 19 Oct 1972

Jack Cassidy's Rainbow Trout in a Pouch - The Honolulu Advertiser, 13 Feb 1969

Ray Milland's Chicken Chow Mein - *What Cooks in Hollywood*, Dorothy and Maxwell Hamilton, 1949

Eddie Albert's Butterfly Lamb - *Cookbook of the Stars*, Motion Picture Mothers Inc., 1970

Ross Martin's Beef in Anchovy Cream - *Cookbook of the Stars*, Motion Picture Mothers Inc., 1970

Susan Clark's Shrimp Curry - *Cookbook of the Stars*, Motion Picture Mothers Inc., 1970

Roddy McDowall's Poached Pears - *Celebrity Chefs*, Campbell Soup Company, date unknown

Patrick O'Neal's Ragout de Boeuf Bourguignon - The Palm Beach Post, 3 Aug 1969

John Cassavetes' Youvarlakia - Asbury Park Press, 17 Jan 1971

Ray Milland's Lobster Salad - *282 Ways of Making a Salad*, Bebe Daniels and Jill Allgood, 1950

Valerie Harper's Summer Squash - *The Celebrity Cookbook*, Maurice J. Klein, 1978

Richard Basehart's Beans and Frankfurters - *Stars in Your Kitchen*, Marta Brookfield Michel, 1953

Anne Baxter's Genuine Swiss Quiche - *Celebrities Culinary Classics*, The Greenville Junior Woman's Club, 1984

Leonard Nimoy's Potatoes La Jolla Chez Jay - *The Classic Celebrity Cookbook*, Ken and Joan Collins, 1986

Laurence Harvey's Chicken Pie - *The White Elephant Cookbook*, Stella Richman, 1973

Martin Landau's Jerk Beef Steak - *Cooking Up An End to Childhood Hunger in America - Celebrity Cookbook*, Unilever Bestfoods, 2001

Vera Miles' Mexican Casserole - Suburbanite Economist, 13 Nov1974

Donald Pleasence's No-name Curry - *Favourite Foods of the Famous,* Freda Riseman, 1974

Jack Cassidy's Quickie Green Bean Casserole - Courier-Post, 5 Feb 1969

Jose Ferrer's Eggs Ferrer with Fried Potatoes - *Favorite Recipes of Famous Men, Roy Ald, 1949*

Johnny Cash's Chili - *House of Cash: The Legacies of my Father, Johnny Cash*, John Carter Cash, 2011

Ben Gazzara's Leg of Lamb, Sicilian Style - The Cincinatti Enquirer, 22 Oct 1967

Robert Conrad's Infamous Hangover Eggs - Pensacola News Journal, 25 Oct 1978

Dick Van Dyke's Breast of Chicken Florentine - The Daily Gleaner, 1 Feb 1968

Peter Falk's Pumpkin Lasagna - *The Cop Cookbook*, Greta Garner, Jim Clark, Ken Beck, 1997

Robert Vaughn's Mushroom Stuffed Zucchini - *Cooking With the Stars – Hollywood's Favourite Recipes,* Jane Sherrod Singer, 1970

Oskar Werner's Weiner Schnitzel - The Cincinnati Enquirer, 25 Aug 1968

George Hamilton's Ginger Snap Dandy - *Cookbook of the Stars*, Motion Picture Mothers Inc., 1970

Janet Leigh's Cheese Soufflé - *Paul Denis' Celebrity Cook Book,* Paul Denis, 1952

Hector Elizondo's Famous Pasta Pomodoro - Journal Gazette, 16 Feb 1989

Peter Falk's Avocado - The Salt Lake Tribune, 10 Sept 1967

Ricardo Montalban's Cream of Asparagus Soup - *David Wade's Kitchen Classics,* David Wade, 1969

Jack Cassidy's City Chicken - Asbury Park Press, 2 Feb 1969

Robert Vaughn's Special Fettuccine Alfredo - *Celebrity Chefs*, Campbell Soup Company, date unknown

William Shatner's Steak Picado - The Ithaca Journal, 28 Dec 1979

Celeste Holm's Celestial Chicken - *Recipes of the Stars,* Western Holly Stoves promo booklet, date unknown

Theodore Bikel's Glorified Meatloaf - *Celebrity Cook Book published by Rosary Hill College Class of 1967*

Ruth Gordon's Zucchini Omelet - *Celebrities Culinary Classics,* The Greenville Junior Woman's Club, 1984

Trish Van Devere's All Day Chili In The Pot - The Cincinnati Enquirer, 19 July 1972

Nicol Williamson's Steak Mince and Stovie Potatoes - Fort Lauderdale News, 14 Oct 1970

Jeanette Nolan's Sizzling Livers and Walnuts - Anderson Daily Bulletin, 27 Feb 1974

Anthony Andrews' Spicy Yogurt Chicken Cooked in a Brick, *The Famous Rainbow Recipe Book*, Tony Head and Sarah Fisher, 1995

Columbo's Black and White Ice-Cream Soda - based on various recipes found on the internet

Bavarian Chocolate Cream Pie - based on a recipe found on the Hershey's website

Peter Falk's Veal Scallopini and White Wine - *Celebrity Cook Book published by Rosary Hill College Class of 1967*

Vincent Price's Cioppino - *Come Into the Kitchen Cook Book*, Mary and Vincent Price, 1969

Playboy's Stewed Pheasant in Champagne with Dumplings, *Playboy's Wine & Spirits Cookbook*, Thomas Mario, 1974

Olympia Dukakis' Greek Meatballs - *Autograph Celebrity Cookbook*, Professor Richard Brown, 1992

Ian McShane's Salmon Steaks with Watercress Sauce - Sainsbury's television advert, 1992

Nancy Walker's Chicken a la Nancy - *Habilitat's Celebrity Cookbook Vol II*, The Habilitat, Inc., 1978

Brenda Vaccaro's T-E-R-R-I-F-I-C Italian Sausages - Detroit Free Press, 2 Aug 1971

Peter Falk's Barbecued Spare Ribs, Chinatown Style - The Salt Lake Tribune, 10 Sept 1967

George Hamilton's Smoky Chicken - *Celebrity Cook Book published by Rosary Hill College Class of 1967*

Rip Torn's Omelet Mexicali - The Cincinnati Enquirer, 28 Dec 1966

Juliet Mills' Chive-Sausage Hoppin' John - *Recipes of the Stars*, Leo Pearlstein, 2004

Tyne Daly's Key Lime Pie - *The Cop Cookbook*, Greta Garner, Jim Clark, Ken Beck, 1997

The Faye Dunaway Cocktail - The Globe and Mail, 9 Dec 2011

William Shatner's Lime-Garlic Broiled Chicken - *Habilitat's Celebrity Cookbook Vol II*, The Habilitat, Inc., 1978

Ed Begley's Citrus Dressed Asparagus - *Cooking Up An End to Childhood Hunger in America - Celebrity Cookbook*, Unilever Bestfoods, 2001

Rod Steiger's Baked Chicken Grand Marnier - *Recipes for Rebels: In the Kitchen with James Dean*, Gregory Swenson, 2015

Shera Danese's Italian Stuffed Peppers - Philadelphia Daily News, 18 Apr 1984

Rue McClanahan's Wonder Women - *Great Performances in the Kitchen*, Johna Blinn, 1988

Billy Connolly's Stuffed Trout - *A Taste of Fame*, David Scott, 1986

Peter Falk's Pork Chops With Vinegar Peppers - *The Celebrity Cookbook*, Dinah Shore, 1966

Chasen's Chili - *Chasen's - Where Hollywood Dined*, Betty Goodwin, 1996

William Shatner's Deluxe Hamburgers - The Evening Independent, Mar 28, 1968

Myrna Loy's Senegalese Soup - *What Actors Eat – When They Eat,* Kenneth Harlan and Rex Lease, 1939

George Hamilton's Candied Fruit Parfait - *Cookbook of the Stars*, Motion Picture Mothers Inc., 1970

Ross Martin's Chocolate Mousse - *Cookbook of the Stars*, Motion Picture Mothers Inc., 1970

Martin Landau Vodka Martini Straight Up - *Recipes for Rebels: In the Kitchen with James Dean*, Gregory Swenson, 2015

Donald Pleasence's Sole Bonne Femme, *Celebrities Cookbook*, Leicestershire Region of the National Deaf Children's Society, date unknown

Susan Clark's Peach Salad - *Cookbook of the Stars*, Motion Picture Mothers Inc., 1970

Roddy McDowall's Red Cabbage - *Cooking With the Stars – Hollywood's Favorite Recipes,* Jane Sherrod Singer, 1970

Gena Rowlands and John Cassavetes' Cherry Torte - *Cookbook of the Stars*, Motion Picture Mothers Inc., 1970

Mariette Hartley's Chicken Wonderful - *Cookbook of the Stars*, Motion Picture Mothers Inc., 1970

Vincent Price's Quenelles Ambassade - *A Treasury of Great Recipes*, Mary and Vincent Price, 1965

Vincent Price's Hollandaise Sauce - *A Treasury of Great Recipes*, Mary and Vincent Price, 1965

Janis Paige's Feijoada with Pepper and Lemon Sauce - The Cincinnati Enquirer, 21 July, 1968

Diane Baker's Scampi - *Look Who's Cooking*, St. Louis Life Seekers, 1974

Mexican Calves' Brain Soup, House of Ricardo Montalban - *Celebrity Cookbook*, Johna Blinn, 1981

Suzanne Pleshette's Bread Pudding - The Ithaca Journal, 24 Aug 1979

Ida Lupino's Hot Pot - *The Celebrities' Cookbook,* Grace Turner, 1948.

Anne Francis' Gazpacho Soup - *Habilitat's Celebrity Cookbook Vol II*, The Habilitat, Inc., 1978

Honor Blackman's Golden Sponge Pudding - *Yours Tastefully*, Jean Nyburg, 1984

Edith Head's Chicken Casa Ladera - *The Celebrity Cookbook*, Maurice J. Klein, 1978

Vincent Price's Saffron Rice - *A Treasury of Great Recipes*, Mary and Vincent Price, 1965

Steve Forrest's Honey Cake - The Pittsburgh Press, 28 May 1977

Steven Bochco / Barbara Bosson's Brie en Croute (Brie in Pastry) - Courier-Post, 3 Jan 1982

Julie Harris' Curried Zucchini Soup - *Celebrities Culinary Classics,* The Greenville Junior Woman's Club, 1984

Shirley Temple Cocktail - *Chasen's - Where Hollywood Dined*, Betty Goodwin, 1996

ACKNOWLEDGMENTS

Food writer and photographer Joan Ransley took my wonderful cover photo featuring Peter Falk's Pumpkin Lasagna. Thank you for spending 98p on that lovely plate Joan! You are always an inspiration.

Greg Swenson of Recipes for Rebels designed my fabulous cover. Thank goodness you contacted me about Sal Mineo's pizza recipe back in 2014 Greg! I know that we are friends forever now.

Early readers J T Rathbone, Greg Swenson, Columbophile and Helen Coniam pointed out many grammatical and factual errors, although any mistakes that remain are definitely my own (I found it impossible to stop fiddling around with the book right up until publication date).

Greg also helped me to translate some very British phrases into American English. Were it not for him, Columbo's legendary raincoat would have been referred to as a Macintosh throughout this book. He let me get away with a few Britishisms though!

Lady Catherine Sloman, aka Battenburgbelle, has been my partner in crime in both our kitchens for many years. I love cooking, eating and drinking with her, she's utterly brilliant.

Mr. and Mrs. Prohibition at Prohibition Wines in Muswell Hill, London N10 always have the perfect "liquid filth" to go with any Columbo recipe.

Alastair Hendy, Sophie Grigson, Carole Ann Rice, Andrea Daly-Dickson, Cynthia Morris and Catherine Ryan Howard helped me with the nuts and bolts of writing and with getting this book out into the world.

Heather Temple dreamed up the "Suppers With the Shambling Sleuth" subtitle.

Nathan Church and Lindy McDonnell provided design advice.

I love all the friendships I have made through the Guild of Food Writers.

Thanks also to Polly Mathewson and Hamish Shaw Stewart for my favorite writing retreats, Harbour Cottage in Whitstable and Nothe Cottage on Mersea Island. Both heavenly, peaceful spots to spend time pondering the wonders of *Columbo*.

TEST COOKS

My everlasting love goes to all the wonderful people who took time out of their busy lives to test cook for me. Some are friends, and some are friends I haven't met in person yet. Through the power of the internet, offers to test cook came from all around the world. From London to Barcelona, Berlin to Melbourne, Baltimore to Seattle, Greece to Hastings and many more hotspots, Columbo related cooking was set upon in many kitchens with gusto. Thank you all so much for your time, effort and excellent feedback.

Sarah Bailey, Jessica Maitland, Jodie Botha, DJ Ms Chameleon, Dylan and Arike, Trix Worrell, Rosie Jones, Gaye Fisher, Sanja Adamovic, Neil Owens, Peter Fuller, DiCooks, Liz Wilson, Lynne Barnsley, Lady Catherine Sloman, Juli Farkas, Margie Compton, Bethany B., Lucy Brookes, Jan Manthey, Mike Nicholson, Kelli Cline, Samantha Ellis, Helen Coniam, Ian Baxter and family, Katya de Grunwald, Penny Armstrong, Mandy Wedgwood, Joan Ransley, Vera Roth, Michelle Kerry, Ben Reed, Laura Groves, Jane Fryers, Judy Gelman, Emily Brungo, Rebecca and Jim, Kiran Kaur, Corinna Reicher, Lucy Smee, Jez Fielder, Orlando Murrin, Kelly Patterson, Clive Smith, Miriam Figueras, Lieutenant Columbo aka Columbophile, Mark Brisenden, Kristen Frederickson, Sarah Akrobettoe, J T Rathbone, Ptolemy Mann, The Burrow Family, Vic Pratt, Sarah Wenban, Chris Scales, Greg Swenson, Sarah Broughton, The Tuesday Club in Hastings, Taryn Fryer, Dr. Caroline Frick, Julie Winfield, KSB, Pamela Hutchinson, Susan Dirks and Kent Stevens, Hilary Butler, Gaby Coello, Lisa Mary London, Louise Pankhurst, Paula Otter, Mary Hess, Tracy Meyers, Jerri Flewell-Smith, Michael Halpern, Annette Hoffman.

If you spot any errors, typos, grammatical faux pas or things that don't make sense in the episode guides or the recipes, please do contact me. I can correct bloopers for future editions, and I would definitely like to. Please get in touch via the contact page on the Silver Screen Suppers website. Also, I'd love to hear from Columbo fans and anyone who tries one of these recipes. I love having pen-pals.

ABOUT THE AUTHOR

Jenny Hammerton learned to cook from the glittering screen stars of yesteryear. Many years ago, in a dusty, stamp and postcard collectables shop, she stumbled upon a vintage celebrity cookbook. This chance find would change her life.

The manic collecting began, and her celebrity recipe archive now numbers over 7000. She probably won't live long enough to try all these dishes, but she's going to give it a good go. Movie star recipe successes (and failures) have been documented on the Silver Screen Suppers website for over a decade.

A graduate of the UEA Masters in Film Archiving course, Jenny has worked in film archives for over twenty years. She adores her job and is currently working with the British Movietone cinema newsreel collection.

Jenny lives in Muswell Hill, North London with her DVD box set of *Columbo*.

Website - silverscreensuppers.com
Facebook - Silver Screen Suppers
Twitter - @silverscreensup
Instagram - @silverscreensuppers

AUTHOR NOTE

If you would like to know more about the recipes in this book (and see photographs of how they turned out for myself and test cooks), please visit the Silver Screen Suppers website. In the sidebar, you can search by actor/actress and find reports on all 69 episode specific recipes. You can sign up for my monthly newsletter there too.

I'm always on the hunt for new recipes to try, so if you find something you think I may not have in my collection, please do get in touch via the website contact page. A Patrick McGoohan recipe is my holy grail, closely followed by a Robert Culp signature dish.

If you cook something from this book, I would love to hear about it. I adore getting photos (especially when they include pets looking lovingly at the fodder)!

For more about *Columbo*, I would heartily recommend *The Columbo Phile: A Casebook* by Mark Dawidziak. It's a highly collectable book and currently costs around $100 (but it's definitely worth saving up for). *Just One More Thing: Stories From My Life* by the great man himself, Peter Falk, is also a wonderful read.

My favorite *Columbo*-related website is the excellent and often hilarious columbophile.wordpress.com and there is also much to explore at home.freeuk.net/columbo-site/. *The Columbo Podcast*, hosted by Gerry and Iain is great fun to tune into, as is the *Just One More Thing* podcast hosted by RJ White and Jon Morris.

The #ColumboTV monthly tweet-along is a hoot. *Columbo* fans all around the world watch the same episode at the same time and make each other laugh with comments about the show. It's a joyful and welcoming experience, do join in! Details are here - livetweeting.org/hashtags/columbotv/#101

The last word goes to the wonderful actress who plays *Columbo*'s first female villain, Lee Grant. In response to my tweeting about her Chicken Malibu recipe, Lee sent, "Thanks so much @silverscreensup! As for the chicken, it's been too long since I made it last. Thanks for keeping the recipe alive."

Well Lee (and all other stars of *Columbo)*, it is my absolute pleasure to keep your recipes alive. Eating like the stars is just so much fun!